The Guide to Understanding China and Its Role in The World's Economy

SB Jeffrey

The role of the book within our culture is changing. The change is brought on by new ways to acquire & use content, the rapid dissemination of information and real-time peer collaboration on a global scale. Despite these changes one thing is clear--"the book" in it's traditional form continues to play an important role in learning and communication. The book you are holding in your hands utilizes the unique characteristics of the Internet -- relying on web infrastructure and collaborative tools to share and use resources in keeping with the characteristics of the medium (user-created, defying control, etc.)--while maintaining all the convenience and utility of a real book.

Contents

Articles

China   1
People's Republic of China   1

The Role of Government in China   34
Government of the People's Republic of China   34

The Six Parts of The China's National Government   40
Constitution of the People's Republic of China   40
National People's Congress   45
President of the People's Republic of China   52
State Council of the People's Republic of China   58
Central Military Commission (People's Republic of China)   66
Supreme People's Court of the People's Republic of China   72

The Economic History of China   77
Economic history of China (pre-1911)   77
Economic history of modern China   114
Economic history of the People's Republic of China   124

The Economy of China   152
Economy of the People's Republic of China   152

Economic Reform in China   199
Great Leap Forward   199
Chinese economic reform   213
Grasping the large, letting go of the small   227

Economic Development Plans — **229**

    China Western Development — 229
    Northeast Area Revitalization Plan — 234
    Rise of Central China Plan — 235
    Third Front (China) — 236
    Go Out policy — 238

The Financial System of China — **241**

    Chinese financial system — 241
    Chinese currency — 252
    Central Financial Work Commission — 262

China's Industry and Labor Conditions — **263**

    Industry of China — 263
    Labor relations in the People's Republic of China — 270

References

    Article Sources and Contributors — 276
    Image Sources, Licenses and Contributors — 277

China

People's Republic of China

中文	**This article contains Chinese text.** Without proper rendering support, you may see question marks, boxes, or other symbols instead of Chinese characters.

People's Republic of China 中华人民共和国[a] *Zhōnghuá Rénmín Gònghéguó*
Anthem: "March of the Volunteers" 《义勇军进行曲》 "Yìyǒngjūn Jìnxíngqǔ"

PRC-administered areas in dark green;
PRC territorial claims in light green

Capital		Beijing 39°55′N 116°23′E
	Largest city	Shanghai
	Official language(s)	Standard Mandarin
Recognised regional languages		*See Languages of China*
	Official scripts	Simplified Chinese
Ethnic groups		92% Han; 55 recognised minorities
	Demonym	Chinese
	Government	People's republic, Communist state, [note b]
-	President	Hu Jintao
-	Premier	Wen Jiabao
-	NPCSC Chairman	Wu Bangguo
-	CPPCC Chairman	Jia Qinglin
	Legislature	National People's Congress
	Establishment	
-	People's Republic of China proclaimed.	1 October 1949
	Area	

-	Total	9,640,821 km² [c] or 9,671,018 km² [c] (3rd/4th) 3704427 sq mi
-	Water (%)	2.8 [d]
Population		
-	2010 estimate	1,338,612,968 (1st)
-	2000 census	1,242,612,226
-	Density	139.6/km² (53rd) 363.3/sq mi
GDP (PPP)		2010 estimate
-	Total	$10.084 trillion (2nd)
-	Per capita	$7,518 (99th)
GDP (nominal)		2010 estimate
-	Total	$5.745 trillion (2nd)
-	Per capita	$4,283 (98th)
Gini (2007)		41.5
HDI (2007)		▲ 0.772 (medium) (92nd)
Currency		Chinese yuan (renminbi) (¥) (CNY)
Time zone		China Standard Time (UTC+8)
Date formats		yyyy-mm-dd *or* yyyy年m月d日 (CE; CE-1949)
Drives on the		right, except for Hong Kong & Macau
ISO 3166 code		CN
Internet TLD		.cn[d] .中國 .中国
Calling code		+86[d]

a. See also Names of China.

b. Simple characterizations of the political structure since the 1980s are no longer possible.

c. 9598086 km² (3705842 sq mi) excludes all disputed territories.
9640821 km² (3722342 sq mi) Includes PRC-administered area (Aksai Chin and Trans-Karakoram Tract, both territories claimed by India), Taiwan is not included.

d. Information for mainland China only. Hong Kong, Macau and territories under the jurisdiction of the Republic of China, commonly known as Taiwan, are excluded.

People's Republic of China	
Simplified Chinese	中华人民共和国
Traditional Chinese	中華人民共和國
Literal meaning	Chinese People's Republic

Transliterations	
Hakka	
- Romanization	dung²⁴ fa¹¹ ngin¹¹ min¹¹ kiung⁵⁵ fo¹¹ gued²
Mandarin	
- Hanyu Pinyin	Zhōnghuá Rénmín Gònghéguó
- Bopomofo	ㄓㄨㄥ ㄏㄨㄚˊ ㄖㄣˊ ㄇㄧㄣˊ ㄍㄨㄥˋ ㄏㄜˊ ㄍㄨㄛˊ
Min	
- Hokkien POJ	Tiong-hôa jîn-bîn kiōng-hô-kok
- Min-dong BUC	Dṳ̌ng-huà Ìng-mìng Gê̤ṳng-huò-guók
Wu	
- Romanization	tson平 gho平 zin平 min平 gon去 ghu平 koh入
Cantonese	
- Jyutping	zung¹ waa⁴ jan⁴ man⁴ gung⁶ wo⁴ gwok³
- Yale Romanization	Jūng Wàh Yàhn Màhn Guhng Wòh Gwok

The **People's Republic of China** (**PRC**), commonly known as **China**, is the most populous state in the world with over 1.3 billion people. Located in East Asia, China is governed by the Communist Party of China (CPC) under a single-party system. The PRC exercises jurisdiction over 22 provinces, five autonomous regions, four directly administered municipalities (Beijing, Tianjin, Shanghai, and Chongqing), and two highly autonomous special administrative regions (SARs) – Hong Kong and

Macau. Its capital city is Beijing.

At about 9.6 million square kilometres (3.7 million square miles), the PRC is the world's third- or fourth-largest country by total area (depending on the definition of what is included in that total) and the second largest by land area. Its landscape is diverse, with forest steppes and deserts (the Gobi and Taklamakan) in the dry north near Mongolia and Russia's Siberia, and subtropical forests in the wet south close to Vietnam, Laos, and Burma. The terrain in the west is rugged and at high altitude, with the Himalayas and the Tian Shan mountain ranges forming China's natural borders with India and Central Asia. In contrast, mainland China's eastern seaboard is low-lying and has a 14500-kilometre (9000 mi) long coastline bounded on the southeast by the South China Sea and on the east by the East China Sea beyond which lies Taiwan, Korea, and Japan.

The ancient Chinese civilization—one of the world's earliest—flourished in the fertile basin of the Yellow River which flows through the North China Plain. For more than 6,000 years, China's political system was based on hereditary monarchies (also known as dynasties). The first of these dynasties was the Xia (approx 2000BC) but it was the later Qin Dynasty that first unified China in 221 BC. The last dynasty, the Qing, ended in 1911 with the founding of the Republic of China (ROC) by the Kuomintang (KMT), the Chinese Nationalist Party. The first half of the 20th century saw China plunged into a period of disunity and civil wars that divided the country into two main political camps – the Kuomintang and the communists. Major hostilities ended in 1949, when the communists won the civil war and established the People's Republic of China in mainland China. The KMT-led Republic of China relocated their capital to Taipei on Taiwan, its jurisdiction is now limited to Taiwan, Kinmen, Matsu and several outlying islands. Since then, the People's Republic of China (PRC) has been involved in political disputes with the Republic of China over issues of sovereignty and the political status of Taiwan.

Since the introduction of market-based economic reforms in 1978, China has become the world's fastest growing major economy, the world's largest exporter and second largest importer of goods. China is the world's second largest economy by both nominal GDP and purchasing power parity (PPP) and a permanent member of the United Nations Security Council. It is also a member of multilateral organizations including the WTO, APEC, BRIC, Shanghai Cooperation Organization, and G-20. China is a recognized nuclear weapons state and has the world's largest standing army with the second-largest defense budget. China has been characterized as a potential superpower by a number of academics, military analysts, and public policy and economics analysts.

History

Main articles: History of China, History of the People's Republic of China, History of Hong Kong, and History of Macau

Chairman Mao Zedong proclaiming the establishment of the People's Republic in 1949.

Major combat in the Chinese Civil War ended in 1949 with the Communist Party of China in control of mainland China, and the Kuomintang (KMT) retreating to Taiwan. On 1 October 1949, Mao Zedong proclaimed the People's Republic of China. "Communist China" or "Red China" were two of the names of the PRC.

The economic and social plan known as the Great Leap Forward resulted in an estimated 30 million deaths. In 1966, Mao and his allies launched the Cultural Revolution, which would last until Mao's death a decade later. The Cultural Revolution, motivated by power struggles within the Party and a fear of the Soviet Union, led to a major upheaval in Chinese society. In 1972, at the peak of the Sino-Soviet split, Mao and Zhou Enlai met Richard Nixon in Beijing to establish relations with the United States. In the same year, the PRC was admitted to the United Nations in place of the Republic of China for China's membership of the United Nations, and permanent membership of the Security Council.

After Mao's death in 1976 and the arrest of the Gang of Four, blamed for the excesses of the Cultural Revolution, Deng Xiaoping quickly wrested power from Mao's anointed successor Hua Guofeng. Although he never became the head of the Party or State himself, Deng was in fact the Paramount Leader of China at that time, his influence within the Party led the country to economic reforms of significant magnitude. The Communist Party subsequently loosened governmental control over citizens' personal lives and the communes were disbanded with many peasants receiving multiple land leases, which greatly increased incentives and agricultural production. This turn of events marked China's transition from a planned economy to a mixed economy with an increasingly open market environment, a system termed by some "market socialism", and officially by the Communist Party of China "Socialism with Chinese characteristics". The PRC adopted its current constitution on 4 December 1982.

In 1989, the death of pro-reform official, Hu Yaobang, helped to spark the Tiananmen Square protests of 1989, during which students and others campaigned for several months for more democratic rights and freedom of speech. However, they were eventually put down on 4 June when PLA troops and vehicles entered and forcibly cleared the square, resulting in numerous casualties. This event was widely reported and brought worldwide condemnation and sanctions against the government. The "Tank Man" incident in particular became famous.

President Jiang Zemin and Premier Zhu Rongji, both former mayors of Shanghai, led post-Tiananmen PRC in the 1990s. Under Jiang and Zhu's ten years of administration, the PRC's economic performance pulled an estimated 150 million peasants out of poverty and sustained an average annual GDP growth rate of 11.2%. The country formally joined the World Trade Organization in 2001.

Although the PRC needs economic growth to spur its development, the government has begun to worry that rapid economic growth has negatively impacted the country's resources and environment. Another concern is that certain sectors of society are not sufficiently benefiting from the PRC's economic development. As a result, under current President Hu Jintao and Premier Wen Jiabao, the PRC has initiated policies to address these issues of equitable distribution of resources, but the outcome remains to be seen. More than 40 million farmers have been displaced from their land, usually for economic development, contributing to the 87,000 demonstrations and riots across China in 2005. For much of the PRC's population in major urban centres, living standards have seen extremely large improvements, and freedom continues to expand, but political controls remain tight and rural areas poor.

Politics

Main article: Politics of the People's Republic of China

See also: Government of the People's Republic of China, Chinese nationalism, Propaganda in the People's Republic of China, Chinese law, Politics of the Republic of China, Neoconservatism in China, Politics of Hong Kong, and Politics of Macau

The PRC is regarded by several political scientists as one of the last five Communist states (along with Vietnam, North Korea, Laos, and Cuba), but simple characterizations of PRC's political structure since the 1980s are no longer possible. The PRC government has been variously described as communist and socialist, but also as authoritarian, with heavy restrictions remaining in many areas, most notably on the Internet, the press, freedom of assembly, reproductive rights, and freedom of religion.[citation needed]

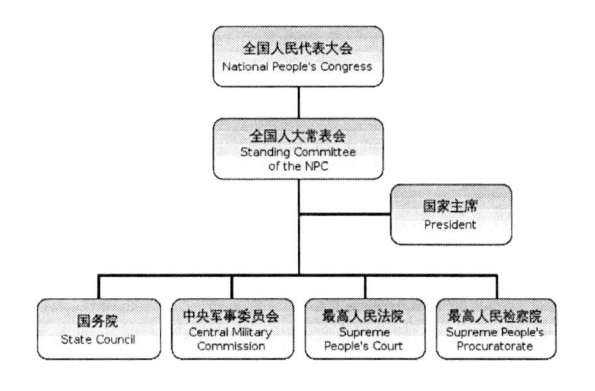

The State organs of the People's Republic of China.

Compared to its closed-door policies until the mid-1970s, the liberalization of the PRC is such that the administrative climate is less restrictive than before, however the PRC is still far from the liberal democracy practiced in most of Europe or North America, and the National People's Congress has been described as a "rubber stamp" body. The PRC's incumbent President is Hu Jintao and its Premier is

Wen Jiabao.

The country is ruled by the Communist Party of China (CPC), whose power is enshrined in China's constitution. The political system is very decentralized with limited democratic processes internal to the party and at local village levels, although these experiments have been marred by corruption. There are other political parties in the PRC, referred to in China as democratic parties, which participate in the People's Political Consultative Conference and the National People's Congress.

The Great Hall of the People in Beijing, where the National People's Congress convenes.

There have been some moves toward political liberalization, in that open contested elections are now held at the village and town levels, and that legislatures have shown some assertiveness from time to time. However, the Party retains effective control over government appointments: in the absence of meaningful opposition, the CPC wins by default most of the time. Political concerns in the PRC include lessening the growing gap between rich and poor and fighting corruption within the government leadership.

The level of support to the government action and the management of the nation is among the highest in the world, with 86% of people who express satisfaction with the way things are going in their country and with their nation's economy according to a 2008 Pew Research Center survey

Foreign relations

Main article: Foreign relations of the People's Republic of China

China maintains diplomatic relations with most major countries in the world. Sweden was the first western country to establish diplomatic relations with the People's Republic on 9 May 1950. In 1971, the PRC replaced the Republic of China as the sole representative of China in the United Nations and as one of the five permanent members of the United Nations Security Council. The PRC was also a former member and leader of the Non-Aligned Movement, and still considers itself an advocate for developing countries.

Hu Jintao with former U.S. President George W. Bush.

Under its interpretation of the One-China policy, the PRC has made it a precondition to establishing diplomatic relations that the other country acknowledges its claim to Taiwan and severs official ties with the Republic of China government; it has acted furiously when any country shows signs of diplomatic overture, or sells armaments to Taiwan. It also opposes publicized foreign travels by separatist ROC officials, such as Lee Teng-hui and Chen Shui-bian, and other separatist figures, such as the 14th Dalai Lama and Rebiya Kadeer.

The PRC has been playing an increasing role in calling for free trade areas and security pacts amongst its Asia-Pacific neighbors. In 2004, the PRC proposed an entirely new East Asia Summit (EAS) framework as a forum for regional security issues that pointedly excluded the United States. The EAS, which includes ASEAN Plus Three, India, Australia and New Zealand, held its inaugural summit in 2005. The PRC is also a founding member of the Shanghai Cooperation Organisation (SCO), with Russia and the Central Asian republics.

Sinophobic attitudes often target Chinese minorities and nationals living outside of China. Sometimes the anti-Chinese attitudes turn violent, such as the 13 May Incident in Malaysia in 1969 and the Jakarta riots of May 1998 in Indonesia, in which more than 2,000 people died. In recent years, a number of anti-Chinese riots and incidents have also occurred in Africa and Oceania. Anti-Chinese sentiment is often rooted in socio-economics.

Much of the current foreign policy is based on the concept of Five Principles of Peaceful Coexistence of Zhou Enlai - non-interference in other states' affairs, non-aggression, peaceful coexistence, and equality and mutual benefits. China's foreign policy is also driven by the concept of "harmony without uniformity" which encourages diplomatic relations between states despite ideological differences. This has led China to support states that are regarded as dangerous by Western nations, such as Zimbabwe, North Korea, or Iran. Conflicts with foreign countries have occurred at times in its recent history, particularly with the United States; for example, the U.S. bombing of the Chinese embassy in Belgrade during the Kosovo conflict in May 1999 and the U.S.-China spy plane incident in April 2001. Its foreign relations with many Western nations suffered for a time following the Tiananmen Square protests of 1989, though they have since recovered.

The relationship between China and Japan has been strained at times by Japan's refusal to acknowledge its wartime past to the satisfaction of the PRC; take for instance revisionist comments made by prominent Japanese officials and in some Japanese history textbooks. Another point of conflict between the two countries is the frequent visits by Japanese government officials to the Yasukuni Shrine. However, Sino-Japanese relations have warmed considerably since Shinzo Abe became the new Japanese Prime Minister in September 2006. A joint historical study conducted by the PRC and Japan released a report in 2010 which pointed toward a new consensus on the issue of WWII atrocities.

Equally bordering the most countries in the world alongside Russia, the PRC was in a number of international territorial disputes. China's territorial disputes have led to localized wars in the last 50 years, including the Sino-Indian War in 1962, the Sino-Soviet border conflict in 1969, and the Sino-Vietnamese War in 1979. In 2001, the PRC and Russia signed the Sino-Russian Treaty of Friendship, which paved the way in 2004 for Russia to transfer Yinlong Island as well as one-half of Heixiazi to China, ending a long-standing Sino-Russian border dispute. Other territorial disputes include islands in the East and South China Seas, and undefined or disputed land borders with India and Bhutan.

While accompanying a rapid economic rise, the PRC since the 1990s seeks to maintain a policy of quiet diplomacy with its neighbors. It does so by keeping economic growth steady and participating in regional organizations and cultivating bi-lateral relations in order to ease suspicion over China's burgeoning military capabilities. The PRC has started a policy of wooing African nations for trade and bilateral co-operation. Xinhua, China's official news agency, states that there are no less than 750,000 Chinese nationals working or living in Africa. There are some discussions about whether China will become a new superpower in the 21st century, with certain commentators pointing out its economic progress, military might, very large population, and increasing international influence but others claiming it is headed for economic collapse.

Human rights

Main article: Human rights in the People's Republic of China

While economic and social controls have been greatly relaxed in China since the 1970s, political freedom is still tightly restricted. The Constitution of the People's Republic of China states that the "fundamental rights" of citizens include freedom of speech, freedom of the press, the right to a fair trial, freedom of religion, universal suffrage, and property rights. However, these provisions do not afford significant protection in practice against criminal prosecution by the State.

With the Chinese economic reform, tens of millions of rural Chinese who have moved to the cities find themselves treated as second-class citizens by China's obsolescent household registration system that controls state benefits, called hukou. The system of property rights is weak, and eminent domain land seizures has abused peasants. In 2003/2004, the average farmer had to pay three times more in taxes even though his income was only one sixth that of the average urban dweller. Since then, a number of rural taxes have been reduced or abolished, and additional social services provided to rural dwellers.

Censorship of political speech and information, including on the Internet, is openly and routinely used to silence criticism of government and the ruling Chinese Communist Party. In 2005, Reporters Without Borders ranked the PRC 159 (out of 167 states) in its Annual World Press Freedom Index. The government has put down demonstrations from organizations and beliefs that it considers a potential threat to "social stability" and control, as was the case with the Tiananmen Square protests of 1989. The Communist Party has had mixed success in controlling information: a very strong media control system faces very strong market forces, an increasingly educated citizenry, and cultural change that are making China more open, especially on environmental issues.

A number of foreign governments and NGOs routinely criticize the PRC, alleging widespread civil rights violations including systematic use of lengthy detention without trial, forced confessions, torture, mistreatment of prisoners, restrictions of freedom of speech, assembly, association, religion, the press, and labor rights. China executes more people than any other country, accounting for 72% of the world's total in 2009, though it is not the largest executioner per capita.

The PRC government has responded by arguing that the notion of human rights should take into account a country's present level of economic development, and focus more on the people's rights to subsistence and development in poorer countries. The rise in the standard of living, literacy, and life expectancy for the average Chinese in the last three decades is seen by the government as tangible progress made in human rights. Efforts in the past decade to combat deadly natural disasters, such as the perennial Yangtze River floods, and work-related accidents are also portrayed in China as progress in human rights for a still largely poor country.

Administrative divisions

Main articles: Administrative divisions of China, Administrative divisions of Hong Kong, and Administrative divisions of Macau

See also: List of cities in the People's Republic of China

The People's Republic of China has administrative control over twenty-two provinces and considers Taiwan to be its 23rd province, despite not having control over Taiwan which is currently administered by the Republic of China. The PRC's claim is disputed by the Republic of China. There are also five autonomous regions, each with a designated minority group; four municipalities; and two Special Administrative Regions that enjoy some degree of autonomy. The twenty-two provinces, five autonomous regions, and four municipalities can be collectively referred to as "mainland China", a term which usually excludes Hong Kong and Macau.

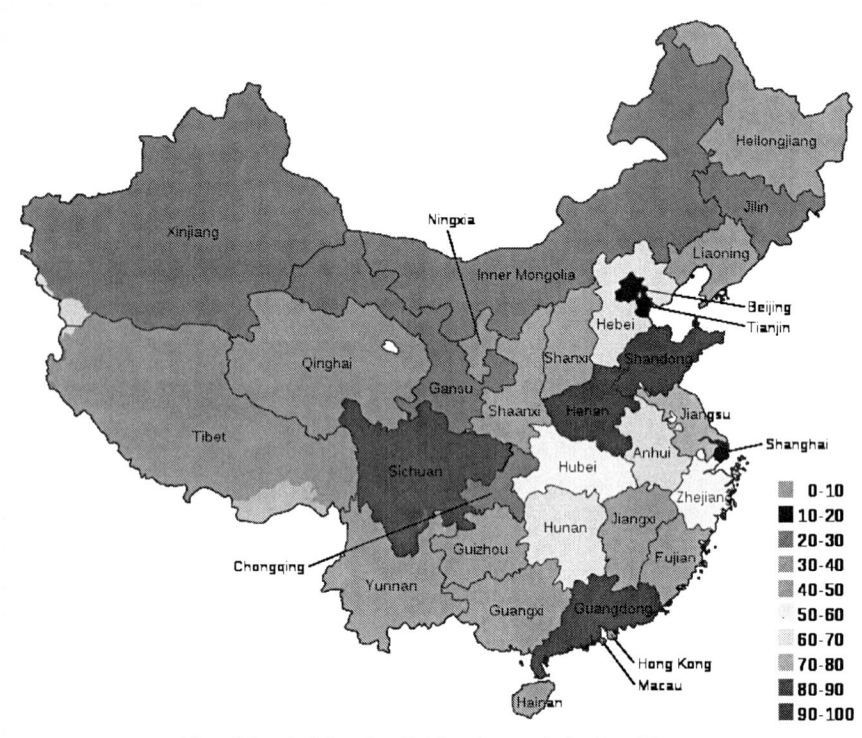

Map of the administrative divisions by population in millions.

Geography and climate

Topography of China

Longsheng Rice Terrace

Li River in Guangxi

Main articles: Geography of China, Geography of the People's Republic of China, Geography of Hong Kong, and Geography of Macau

See also: Environment of China and Water resources of the People's Republic of China

People's Republic of China

Mount Everest in Tibet

South China Sea by Hainan

Jiuzhaigou Valley

The People's Republic of China is the second largest country in the world by land area and is considered the third or fourth largest in respect to total area. The uncertainty over size is related to (a) the validity of claims by China on territories such as Aksai Chin and Trans-Karakoram Tract (both territories also claimed by India), and (b) how the total size of the United States is calculated: *The World Factbook* gives 9826630 km^2 (3794080 sq mi), and the *Encyclopædia Britannica* gives 9522055 km^2 (3676486 sq mi). China borders 14 nations, more than any other country (shared with Russia); counted clockwise from south : Vietnam, Laos, Burma, India, Bhutan, Nepal, Pakistan, Afghanistan, Tajikistan, Kyrgyzstan, Kazakhstan, Russia, Mongolia and North Korea. Additionally the border between PRC and ROC is located in territorial waters. China has a land border of 22117 km (13743 mi), the largest in the world.

The territory of China contains a large variety of landscapes. In the east, along the shores of the Yellow Sea and the East China Sea, there are extensive and densely populated alluvial plains, while on the edges of the Inner Mongolian plateau in the north, grasslands can be seen. Southern China is dominated by hill country and low mountain ranges. In the central-east are the deltas of China's two major rivers, the Yellow River and Yangtze River (Chang Jiang). Other major rivers include the Xi, Mekong, Brahmaputra and Amur. To the west, major mountain ranges, notably the Himalayas, with China's highest point at the eastern half of Mount Everest at 8848 m (29029 ft), and high plateaus feature among the more arid landscapes such as the Taklamakan and the Gobi Desert.

A major issue is the continued expansion of deserts, particularly the Gobi Desert. Although barrier tree lines planted since the 1970s have reduced the frequency of sandstorms, prolonged drought and poor agricultural practices result in dust storms plaguing northern China each spring, which then spread to other parts of East Asia, including Korea and Japan. China is losing a million acres (4,000 km²) per year to desertification. Water, erosion, and pollution control have become important issues in China's relations with other countries. Melting glaciers in the Himalayas could also lead to water shortages for hundreds of millions of people.

China has a climate mainly dominated by dry seasons and wet monsoons, which leads to temperature differences in winter and summer. In winter, northern winds coming from high latitude areas are cold and dry; in summer, southern winds from sea areas at lower latitude are warm and moist. The climate in China differs from region to region because of the country's extensive and complex topography.

Flora and fauna

Main article: Wildlife of China

One of seventeen megadiverse countries, China lies in two of the world's major ecozones, the Palearctic and the Indomalaya. In the Palearctic zone are found such mammals as the horse, camel, tapir, and jerboa. Among the species found in the Indomalaya region are the Leopard Cat, bamboo rat, treeshrew, and various species of monkeys and apes. Some overlap exists between the two regions because of natural dispersal and migration, and deer or antelope, bears, wolves, pigs, and rodents are found in all of the diverse climatic and geological environments. The famous giant panda is found only in a limited area along the Chang Jiang. There is a continuing problem with trade in endangered species, although there are now laws to prohibit such activities.

The Giant Panda

China contains also a variety of forest types. Both northeast and northwest reaches contain mountains and cold coniferous forests, supporting animal species which include moose and Asiatic black bear, along with some 120 types of birds. Moist conifer forests can have thickets of bamboo as an understorey, replaced by rhododendrons in higher montane stands of juniper and yew. Subtropical forests, which dominate central and southern China, support an astounding 146,000 species of flora. Tropical rainforest and seasonal rainforests, though confined to Yunnan and Hainan Island, actually contain a quarter of all the plant and animal species found in China.

Military

Main article: People's Liberation Army

With 2.3 million active troops, the People's Liberation Army (PLA) is the largest military in the world. The PLA consists of an army, navy, air force, and strategic nuclear force. The official announced budget of the PLA for 2009 was $70 billion. However, the United States claims China does not report its real military spending. The Defense Intelligence Agency estimates that the real Chinese military budget for 2008 could be anywhere from US$105 to US$150 billion.

Chengdu J-10 fighter aircraft

China, with possession of nuclear weapons and delivery systems, is considered a major military regional power and an emerging military superpower. China is the only member of the U.N. Security Council to have limited power projection capabilities As a consequence, it has been establishing foreign military relationships that have been compared to a String of Pearls.

Much progress has been made in the last decade and the PRC continues to make efforts to modernize its military. It has purchased state-of-the-art fighter jets from Russia, such as the Sukhoi Su-30s, and has also produced its own modern fighters, specifically the Chinese J-10s and the J-11s. It has also acquired and improved upon the Russian S-300 surface-to-air missile systems, which are considered to be among the best aircraft-intercepting systems in the world, albeit Russia has since produced the new generation S-400 Triumf, with China reportedly already having spent $500 million on a downgraded export version of it. The PRC's armored and rapid-reaction forces have been updated with enhanced electronics and targeting capabilities. In recent years, much attention has been focused on building a navy with blue-water capability.

Little information is available regarding the motivations supporting China's military modernization. A 2007 report by the US Secretary of Defense notes that "China's actions in certain areas increasingly appear inconsistent with its declaratory policies". For its part, China claims it maintains an army purely for defensive purposes.

Some think-tanks such as the Asian European Council have argued that the current tensions between the US and China over Washington's abrupt decision to sell arms to Taipei might trigger a new arms race in Asia fueled essentially by domestic ideological motives, a situation reminiscent in many ways of the McCarthy era when the US hard-right was overtly favorable to the Chiang Kai-shek lobby.

Economy

Main articles: Economy of the People's Republic of China, Economy of Hong Kong, and Economy of Macau

See also: Economic history of China and Foreign exchange reserves of the People's Republic of China

From its founding in 1949 to late 1978, the People's Republic of China was a Soviet-style centrally planned economy. Private businesses and capitalism did not exist. To propel the country towards a modern, industrialized communist society, Mao Zedong instituted the Great Leap Forward. Following Mao's death and the end of the Cultural Revolution, Deng Xiaoping and the new Chinese leadership began to reform the economy and move to a market-oriented mixed economy under one-party rule. In 1978, China & Japan had normalized diplomatic relation & China had decided to borrow money from Japan in soft loans. Since 1978, Japan have been No.1 foreign donor for China. China's economy is mainly characterized as a market economy based on private property ownership. Collectivization of the agriculture was dismantled and farmlands were privatized to increase productivity.

A wide variety of small-scale enterprises were encouraged while the government relaxed price controls and promoted foreign investment. Foreign trade was focused upon as a major vehicle of growth, which led to the creation of Special Economic Zones (SEZs) first in Shenzhen (near Hong Kong) and then in other Chinese cities. Inefficient state-owned enterprises (SOEs) were restructured by introducing western-style management system and the unprofitable ones were closed, resulting in massive job losses.

Since economic liberalization began in 1978, the PRC's investment- and export-led economy has grown 70 times bigger and is the fastest growing major economy in the world. It now has the world's second largest nominal GDP at 34.06 trillion yuan (US$4.99 trillion), although its per capita income of US$3,700 is still low and puts the PRC behind roughly a hundred countries The primary, secondary, and tertiary industries contributed 10.6%, 46.8%, and 42.6% respectively to the total economy in 2009. If PPP is taken into account, the PRC's economy is second only to the US at US$9.05 trillion corresponding to US$6,800 per capita.

Shanghai Stock Exchange building at Shanghai's Pudong financial district

In 1978, Deng Xiaoping initiated the PRC's market-oriented reforms.

The PRC is the fourth most visited country in the world with 50.9 million inbound international visitors in 2009. It is a member of the WTO and is the world's second largest trading power behind the US with a total international trade of US$2.21 trillion – US$1.20 trillion in exports (#1) and US$1.01 trillion in imports (#2). Its foreign exchange reserves have reached US$2.4 trillion, making it by far the world's largest. The PRC owns an estimated $1.6 trillion of U.S. securities. The PRC, holding US$801.5 billion in Treasury bonds, is the largest foreign holder of U.S. public debt. It is the world's third largest recipient of inward FDI by attracting US$92.4 billion in 2008 alone, while the country itself increasingly invests abroad with a total outward FDI of US$52.2 billion in 2008 alone becoming the world's sixth largest outward investor.

The PRC's success has been primarily due to manufacturing as a low-cost producer. This is attributed to a combination of cheap labor, good infrastructure, medium level of technology and skill, relatively high productivity, favorable government policy, and some say, an undervalued exchange rate. The latter has been sometimes blamed for the PRC's bulging trade surplus (US$262.7 billion in 2007) and has become a major source of dispute between the PRC and its major trading partners – the US, EU, and Japan – despite the yuan having been de-pegged and risen in value by 20% against the US$ since 2005.

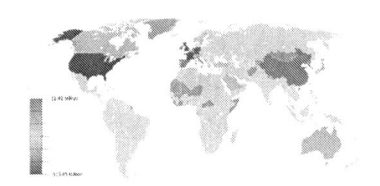

Map of countries by foreign currency reserves and gold minus external debt based on 2009 data from CIA Factbook.

The state still dominates in strategic "pillar" industries (such as energy and heavy industries), but private enterprise (30 million private businesses) now accounts for anywhere between 33% (People's Daily Online 2005) to 70% (BusinessWeek, 2005) of GDP in 2005, while the OECD estimate is over 50% of China's national output, up from 1% in 1978. Its stock market in Shanghai (SSE) is raising record amounts of IPOs and its benchmark Shanghai Composite index has doubled since 2005. SSE's market capitalization reached US$3 trillion in 2007 and is the world's fifth largest exchange.

China now ranks 29th in the Global Competitiveness Index. 46 Chinese companies made the list in the 2010 Fortune Global 500 (Beijing alone with 30). Measured using market capitalization, four of the world's top ten most valuable companies are Chinese. Some of these include first-ranked PetroChina (world's most valuable oil company), third-ranked Industrial and Commercial Bank of China (world's most valuable bank), fifth-ranked China Mobile (world's most valuable telecommunications company) and seventh-ranked China Construction Bank.

Nanjing Road in Shanghai is one of the world's busiest shopping streets.

Although a middle income country by the world's standard, the PRC's rapid growth managed to pull hundreds of millions of its people out of poverty since 1978. Today, about 10% of the Chinese population (down from 64% in 1978) live below the poverty line of US$1 per day (PPP) while life expectancy has dramatically increased to 73 years. More than 93% of the population is literate, compared to 20% in 1950. Urban unemployment declined to 4 percent in China by the end of 2007 (true overall unemployment might be higher at around 10%).

Its middle class population (defined as those with annual income of at least US$17,000) has now reached more than 100 million, while the number of super-rich individuals worth more than 10 million yuan (US$1.5 million) is estimated to be 825,000 according to Hurun Report. China's retail market is worth RMB 8921 billion (US$1302 billion) in 2007 and growing at 16.8% annually. It is also now the world's second biggest consumer of luxury goods behind Japan with 27.5% of the global share.

The PRC's growth has been uneven when comparing different geographic regions and rural and urban areas. The urban-rural income gap is getting wider in the PRC with a Gini coefficient of 46.9%. Development has also been mainly concentrated in the eastern coastal regions while the remainder of the country are left behind. To counter this, the government has promoted development in the western, northeastern, and central regions of China.

The economy is also highly energy-intensive and inefficient – it uses 20%–100% more energy than OECD countries for many industrial processes. It has now become the world's largest energy consumer but relies on coal to supply about 70% of its energy needs. Coupled with a lax environmental regulation, this has led to a massive water and air pollution (China has 20 of the world's 30 most polluted cities). Consequently, the government has promised to use more renewable energy with a target of 10% of total energy use by 2010 and 30% by 2050.

Science and technology

Main articles: Science and technology in the People's Republic of China and List of Chinese inventions

After the Sino-Soviet split, China started to develop its own nuclear weapons and delivery systems, successfully detonating its first surface nuclear test in 1964 at Lop Nur. A natural outgrowth of this was a satellite launching program, which culminated in 1970 with the launching of Dong Fang Hong I, the first Chinese satellite. This made the PRC the fifth nation to independently launch a satellite.

In 1992, the Shenzhou manned spaceflight program was authorized. After four unmanned tests, *Shenzhou 5* was launched on 15 October 2003, using a Long March 2F launch vehicle and carrying Chinese astronaut Yang Liwei, making the PRC the third country to put a human being into space through its own endeavors. China completed its second manned mission with a crew of two, *Shenzhou 6* in October 2005. In 2008, China successfully completed the *Shenzhou 7* mission, making it the third country to have the capability to conduct a spacewalk. In 2007, the PRC successfully sent the Chang'e spacecraft, named after the ancient Chinese moon goddess, to orbit and explore the moon as part of their Chinese Lunar Exploration Program. China has plans to build a space station in the near future and to achieve a lunar landing in the next decade. There are also plans for a manned mission to planet Mars.

The launch of Tianlian, at Xichang Satellite Launch Center.

China has the world's second largest research and development budget, and is expected to invest over $136 billion in 2006 after growing more than 20% in 2005. The Chinese government continues to place heavy emphasis on research and development by creating greater public awareness of innovation, and reforming financial and tax systems to promote growth in cutting-edge industries.

In 2006, President Hu Jintao called for China to make the transition from a manufacturing-based economy to an innovation-based one and the National People's Congress have approved large increases in research funding. Stem cell research and gene therapy, which some in the Western world see as controversial, face minimal regulation in China. China has an estimated 926,000 researchers, second only to the 1.3 million in the United States.

China is also actively developing its software, semiconductor and energy industries, including renewable energies such as hydro, wind and solar power. In an effort to reduce pollution from coal-burning power plants, China has been pioneering the deployment of pebble bed nuclear reactors, which run cooler and safer, and have potential applications for the hydrogen economy.

China currently has the most cell phone users in the world with over 800 million users in July 2010. It also has the largest number of internet and broadband users in the world.

Transportation

Main articles: Transport in the People's Republic of China, Transportation in Hong Kong, and Transportation in Macau

See also: Rail transport in the People's Republic of China

G030 northbound in Hebei. There are 45,000 km (28,000 mi) of expressways in China. This is the second-longest total in the world, and half that of the United States.

Transportation in the mainland of the People's Republic of China has improved significantly since the late 1990s as part of a government effort to link the entire nation through a series of expressways known as the National Trunk Highway System (NTHS). The total length of expressway is 65000 km (40000 mi) at the end of 2009, second only to the United States. China has also the world's longest high-speed rail network with over 6,500 km (4,000 mi) of service routes.

Private car ownership is increasing at an annual rate more than 15%. The sale of automobiles had been increasing rapidly after the financial crisis in 2009, and China surpassed the United States became the largest automobile market in the world with total sales of more than 13.6 million.

Domestic air travel has increased significantly, but remains too expensive for most. Long distance transportation is dominated by railways and charter bus systems. Railways are the vital carrier in China; they are monopolized by the state, divided into various railway bureaus in different regions. At the rates of demand it experiences, the system has historically been subject to overcrowding during travel seasons such as *Chunyun* during the Chinese New Year.

Cities such as Beijing and Shanghai both have a rapidly expanding network of underground or light rail systems, while

A high-speed rail train (CRH). China has the longest high-speed rail system in the world, with over 6,500 km (4,000 miles) of routes in service.

several other cities also have running rapid transit. Numerous cities are also constructing subways. Hong Kong has one of the most developed transport systems in the world. Shanghai has a Maglev rail line connecting Shanghai's urban area to Pudong International Airport.

Demographics

Main articles: Demographics of the People's Republic of China, Demographics of Hong Kong, Demographics of Macau, and List of ethnic groups in China

See also: International rankings of the People's Republic of China

As of July 2010, there are 1,338,612,968 people in the PRC. About 21% (male 145,461,833; female 128,445,739) are 14 years old or younger, 71% (male 482,439,115; female 455,960,489) are between 15 and 64 years old, and 8% (male 48,562,635; female 53,103,902) are over 65 years old. The population growth rate for 2006 was 0.6%.

The PRC officially recognizes 56 distinct ethnic groups, the largest of which are the Han Chinese, who constitute about 91.9% of the total population. Large ethnic minorities include the Zhuang (16 million), Manchu (10 million), Hui (9 million), Miao (8 million), Uyghur (7 million), Yi (7 million), Tujia (5.75 million), Mongols (5 million), Tibetans (5 million), Buyei (3 million), and Koreans (2 million).

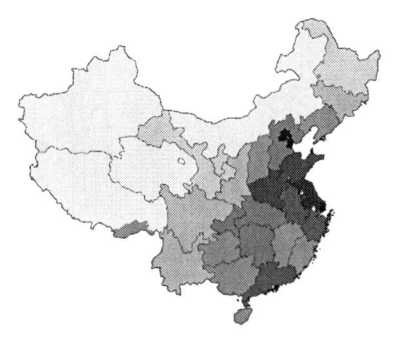

A population density map of the People's Republic of China. The eastern, coastal provinces are much more densely populated than the western interior.

In the past decade, China's cities expanded at an average rate of 10% annually. The country's urbanization rate increased from 17.4% to 46.8% between 1978 and 2009, a scale unprecedented in human history. Between 150 and 200 million migrant workers work part-time in the major cities and return home to the countryside periodically with their earnings.

Today, the People's Republic of China has dozens of major cities with one million or more long-term residents, including the three global cities of Beijing, Hong Kong, and Shanghai.

Major cities in China play key roles in national and regional identity, culture and economics.

Largest cities

See also: List of cities in the People's Republic of China, List of cities in the People's Republic of China by population, and Metropolitan regions of China

The figures below are from the 2008 census, and are only estimates of the population within administrative city limits; a different ranking exists when considering the total municipal populations (which includes suburban and rural populations). The large floating populations of migrant workers make conducting censuses in urban areas difficult; the figures below do not include the floating population, only long-term residents.

Leading Urban Centers of the People's Republic of China

People's Republic of China

Rank	Core City	Division	Urban Population	Municipal Population	Region
1	Shanghai	Shanghai Municipality	9,495,701	18,542,200	East
2	Beijing	Beijing Municipality	7,296,962	17,430,000	North
3	Hong Kong	Hong Kong SAR	7,000,000	7,000,000	South
4	Tianjin	Tianjin Municipality	5,066,129	11,500,000	North
5	Wuhan	Hubei Province	6,660,000	9,100,000	South Central
6	Guangzhou	Guangdong Province	4,154,808	15,000,000	South
7	Shenzhen	Guangdong Province	4,000,000	8,615,500	South
8	Shenyang	Liaoning Province	3,981,023	7,500,000	Northeast
9	Chongqing	Chongqing Municipality	3,934,239	31,442,300	Southwest
10	Nanchang	Jiangxi Province	3,790,000	4,990,184	East
11	Nanjing	Jiangsu Province	2,822,117	7,100,000	East
12	Harbin	Heilongjiang Province	2,672,069	8,499,000	Northeast
13	Xi'an	Shaanxi Province	2,588,987	10,500,000	Northwest
14	Chengdu	Sichuan Province	2,341,203	11,300,000	Southwest
15	Changchun	Jilin Province	2,223,170	7,400,000	Northeast
16	Dalian	Liaoning Province	2,118,087	6,200,000	Northeast
17	Hangzhou	Zhejiang Province	1,932,612	7,000,000	East
18	Jinan	Shandong Province	1,917,204	6,300,000	East
19	Taiyuan	Shanxi Province	1,905,403	3,413,800	North
20	Qingdao	Shandong Province	1,867,365	8,000,000	East

2008 Estimated - suburban and rural area excluded on urban population

Population policy

Main article: One-child policy

With a population of over 1.3 billion, the PRC is very concerned about its population growth and has attempted, with mixed results, to implement a strict family planning policy. The government's goal is one child per family, with exceptions for ethnic minorities and flexibility in rural areas. The government's goal is to stabilize population growth early in the 21st century, though some projections estimate a population of anywhere ranging from 1.4 billion to 1.6 billion by 2025. Hence, the country's family planning minister has indicated that China will maintain its one-child policy until at least the year 2020.

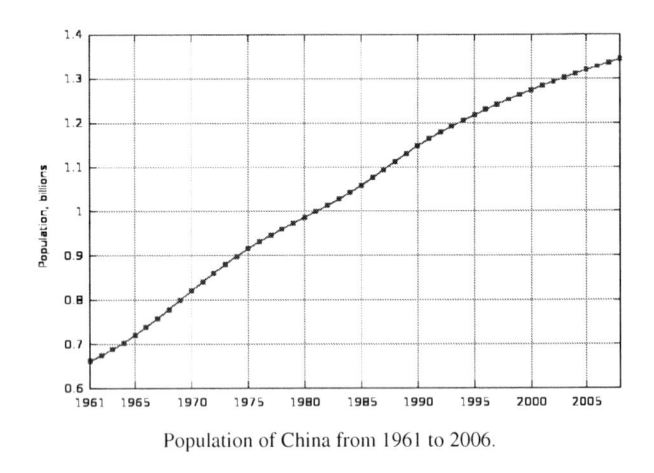

Population of China from 1961 to 2006.

The policy is resisted, particularly in rural areas, because of the need for agricultural labour and a traditional preference for boys (who can later serve as male heirs). Families who breach the policy often lie during the census. Official government policy opposes forced sterilization or abortion, but allegations of coercion continue as local officials, who are faced with penalties for failing to curb population growth, may resort to forced abortion or sterilization, or manipulation of census figures.

The decreasing reliability of PRC population statistics since family planning began in the late 1970s has made evaluating the effectiveness of the policy difficult. Estimates by Chinese demographers of the average number of children for a Chinese woman vary from 1.5 to 2.0. The government is particularly concerned with the large imbalance in the sex ratio at birth, apparently the result of a combination of traditional preference for boys and family planning pressure, which led to the ban of using ultrasound devices for the purpose of preventing sex-selective abortion.

Another factor is the under-reporting of female children to circumvent the law.[citation needed] On the basis of a 2005 report by China's National Population and Family Planning Commission, there were 118.6 boys born for every 100 girls, and in some rural areas the boy/girl ratio could be as high as 130/100.[citation needed] As this trend of gender imbalance is on the increase, experts warn of increased social instability should this trend continue.

Education

Main articles: Education in the People's Republic of China, Education in Hong Kong, and Education in Macau

In 1986, China set the long-term goal of providing compulsory nine-year basic education to every child. As of 2007, there were 396,567 primary schools, 94,116 secondary schools and 2,236 higher education institutions in the PRC. In February 2006, the government advanced its basic education goal by pledging to provide completely free nine-year education, including textbooks and fees. Therefore the current education system in China, introduced compulsory and free education for all Chinese citizens consists of elementary school and middle school, which lasts for 9 years(age 6-15), and almost all children in urban area continue their 3 years high school.

Tsinghua University in Beijing is a well regarded university in mainland China.

As of 2007, 93.3% of the population over age 15 are literate. China's youth (age 15 to 24) literacy rate was 98.9% (99.2% for males and 98.5% for females) in 2000. In March 2007, China announced the decision of making education a national "strategic priority", the central budget of the national scholarships will be tripled in two years and 223.5 billion Yuan (28.65 billion US dollars) of extra funding will be allocated from the central government in the next 5 years to improve the compulsory education in rural areas.

The quality of Chinese colleges and universities varies considerably across the country. The consistently top-ranked universities in mainland China are:

- Beijing: Peking University, Tsinghua University, Renmin University of China, Beijing Normal University
- Shanghai: Fudan University, Shanghai Jiao Tong University, Tongji University, East China Normal University
- Harbin: Harbin Institute of Technology
- Tianjin: Nankai University, Tianjin University
- Xi'an Jiaotong University (Xi'an)
- Nanjing University (Nanjing)
- University of Science and Technology of China (Hefei)
- Zhejiang University (Hangzhou)
- Wuhan University (Wuhan)
- Guangzhou: Sun Yat-sen University (aka Zhongshan University)

Many parents are highly committed to their children's education, often investing large portions of the family's income on education. Private lessons and recreational activities, such as in foreign languages or music, are popular among the middle-class families who can afford them.

Public health and environment

Main articles: Public health in the People's Republic of China and Environment of China

The Ministry of Health, together with its counterparts in the provincial health bureaus, oversees the health needs of the Chinese population. An emphasis on public health and preventative treatment characterized health policy since the early 1950s. At that time, the Communist Party started the Patriotic Health Campaign, which was aimed at improving sanitation and hygiene, as well as attacking several diseases. This has shown major results as diseases like cholera, typhoid, and scarlet fever were nearly eradicated.

Wind turbines in Xinjiang. The Dabancheng project is Asia's largest wind farm.

With economic reform after 1978, the health of the Chinese public improved rapidly because of better nutrition despite the disappearance, along with the People's Communes, of much of the free public health services provided in the countryside. Health care in China became largely private fee-for-service. The country's life expectancy at birth jumped from about 35 years in 1949 to 73.18 years in 2008, and infant mortality went down from 300 per thousand in the 1950s to about 23 per thousand in 2006. Malnutrition as of 2002 stood at 12% of the population according to United Nations FAO sources.

Despite significant improvements in health and the introduction of western style medical facilities, China has several emerging public health problems, which include respiratory problems as a result of widespread air pollution and hundreds of millions of cigarette smokers, a possible future HIV/AIDS epidemic, and an increase in obesity among urban youths. China's large population and close living quarters has led to some serious disease outbreaks in recent years, such as the 2003 outbreak of SARS (a pneumonia-like disease) which has since been largely contained.

Estimates of excess deaths in China from environmental pollution (apart from smoking) are placed at 760,000 people per annum from air and water pollution (including indoor air pollution). In 2007, China has overtaken the United States as the world's biggest producer of Carbon dioxide. Some 90% of

China's cities suffer from some degree of water pollution, and nearly 500 million people lack access to safe drinking water. Reports by the World Bank and the New York Times have claimed industrial pollution, particularly of the air, to be significant health hazards in China.

China has some relevant environmental regulations: the 1979 Environmental Protection Law, which was largely modeled on U.S. legislation. But the environment continues to deteriorate. While the regulations are fairly stringent, they are frequently disregarded by local communities while seeking economic development. Twelve years after the law, only one Chinese city was making an effort to clean up its water discharges.

Part of the price China is paying for increased prosperity is damage to the environment. Leading Chinese environmental campaigner Ma Jun has warned that water pollution is one of the most serious threats facing China. According to the Ministry of Water Resources, roughly 300 million Chinese are drinking unsafe water. This makes the crisis of water shortages more pressing, with 400 out of 600 cities short of water.

With $34.6 billion invested in clean technology in 2009, China is the world's leading investor in renewable energy technologies. China produces more wind turbines and solar panels each year than any other country.

Religion

Confucianism, Taoism, and Buddhism are one, a *litang* style painting portraying three men laughing by a river stream, 12th century, Song Dynasty.

Main articles: Religion in China, Religion in Hong Kong, and Religion in Macau

See also: Feng shui

In mainland China, the government allows a limited degree of religious freedom, however official tolerance is only extended to members of state-approved religious organizations and not to those who worship underground, such as house churches. An accurate number of religious adherents is hard to obtain because of a lack of official data, but there is general consensus that religion has been enjoying a resurgence over the past 20 years. A survey by Phil Zuckerman on Adherents.com found that in 1998, 59% (over 700 million) of the population was irreligious. Meanwhile, another survey in 2007 found that there are 300 million (23% of the population) believers as distinct from an official figure of 100 million.

Despite the surveys' varying results, most agree that the traditional religions – Buddhism, Taoism, and Chinese folk religions – are the dominant faiths. According to a number of sources, Buddhism in China accounts for between 660 million (~50%) and over 1 billion (~80%) while Taoists number 400 million (~30%). However, because of the fact that one person may subscribe to two or more of these traditional beliefs simultaneously and the difficulty in clearly differentiating Buddhism, Taoism, and Chinese folk religions, the number of adherents to these religions can be overlaid. In addition, subscribing to Buddhism and Taoism is not necessarily considered religious by those who follow the philosophies in principle but stop short of subscribing to any kind of divinity.

The Round Mound Altar, the altar proper at the Temple of Heaven in Beijing, where the Emperor communed with Heaven.

Most Chinese Buddhists are nominal adherents because only a small proportion of the population (over 8% or over 100 million) may have taken the formal step of going for refuge. Even then, it is still difficult to estimate accurately the number of Buddhists because they do not have congregational memberships and often do not participate in public ceremonies. Mahayana (大乘, *Dacheng*) and its subsets Pure Land (Amidism), Tiantai and Chán (better known in the west by its Japanese name Zen) are the most widely practiced denominations of Buddhism. Other forms, such as Theravada and Tibetan, are practiced largely by ethnic minorities along the geographic fringes of the Chinese mainland.

Christianity in China was first introduced during the Tang period in the 7th century with the arrival of Nestorian Christianity in 635 CE. This was followed by Franciscan missionaries in the 13th century, Jesuits in the 16th century, and finally Protestants in the 19th century, during which time Christianity began to make significant foothold in China.[citation needed] Of the minority religions, Christianity has been particularly noted as one of the fastest growing (especially since the last 200 years) and today may number between 40 million (3%) and 54 million (4%) according to independent surveys, while official estimates suggested that there are only 16 million Christians. Some sources also reported up to 130 million Christians in China.

Saint Sophia Cathedral in Harbin. In 1921, the city had a population of 300,000, including 100,000 Russians.

Islam in China dates to a mission in 651, eighteen years after Muhammad's death. Muslims came to China for trade, dominating the import/export industry during the Song Dynasty. They became influential in government circles, including Zheng He, Lan Yu and Yeheidie'erding. Nanjing became an important center of Islamic study. The Qing Dynasty waged war and genocide against Muslims in the Dungan revolt and Panthay rebellion. Statistics are hard to find, and most estimates figures that there are 20 to 30 million Muslims (1.5% to 2% of the population).

There are also followers of minority religions including Hinduism, Dongbaism, Bön, and a number of new religions and sects (particularly Xiantianism). In July 1999, the Falun Gong spiritual practice was officially banned by the authorities, and many international organizations have criticized the government's treatment of Falun Gong that has occurred since then. There are no reliable estimates of the number of Falun Gong practitioners in China.

Culture

Main articles: Culture of the People's Republic of China, Culture of Hong Kong, Culture of Macau, and Culture of China

See also: Chinese mythology, Music of China, Chinese literature, Chinese art, Traditional Chinese medicine, Chinese cuisine, Cinema of China, and Media of the People's Republic of China

See also: Society of the People's Republic of China, Zhonghua minzu, Han Chinese clothing, Chinese architecture, and Chinese animation

Chinese meal in Suzhou with rice, shrimp, eggplant, fermented tofu, vegetable stir-fry, vegetarian duck with meat and bamboo.

Beijing opera is a quintessential aspect of traditional Chinese culture and holds an important position in the world treasure of art.

A north corner of Forbidden City, featuring classic construction style.

For centuries, opportunity for economic and social advancement in China could be provided by high performance on Imperial examinations. The literary emphasis of the exams affected the general perception of cultural refinement in China, such as the belief that calligraphy and literati painting were higher forms of art than dancing or drama. China's traditional values were derived from various versions of Confucianism and conservatism.

A number of more authoritarian and rational strains of thought have also been influential, such as Legalism. There was often conflict between the philosophies, such as the individualistic Song Dynasty neo-Confucians, who believed Legalism departed from the original spirit of Confucianism. Examinations and a culture of merit remain greatly valued in China today. In recent years, a number of New Confucians have advocated that democratic ideals and human rights are quite compatible with traditional Confucian "Asian values."

The first leaders of the People's Republic of China were born in the old society but were influenced by the May Fourth Movement and reformist ideals. They sought to change some traditional aspects of Chinese culture, such as rural land tenure, sexism, and a Confucian education, while preserving others, such as the family structure and obedience to the state.

Many observers believe that the period following 1949 is a continuation of traditional Chinese dynastic history, while others say that the CPC's rule has damaged the foundations of Chinese culture, especially through political movements such as the Cultural Revolution, where many aspects of traditional culture were labeled 'regressive and harmful' or 'vestiges of feudalism' by the regime and thus, were destroyed. They further argue that many important aspects of traditional Chinese morals and culture, such as Confucianism, Chinese art, literature, and performing arts like Beijing opera, were altered to conform to government policies and propaganda at the time.

Today, the Chinese government has accepted a great deal of traditional Chinese culture as an integral part of Chinese society, lauding it as an important achievement of the Chinese civilization and emphasizing it as vital to a Chinese national identity. Since the Cultural Revolution ended, various forms of traditional Chinese art, literature, music, film, fashion and architecture have seen a vigorous revival, and folk and variety art in particular have gained a new found respectability, and sparked interest nationally and even worldwide.

Chinese culture and the West were linked by the Silk Route. Artifacts from the history of the silk route, as well as from the natural history of the Gobi desert, are displayed in the Silk Route Museum.

Sports and recreation

Main articles: Sport in the People's Republic of China, Sports in Hong Kong, and Sports in Macau

See also: Public holidays in the People's Republic of China and China at the Olympics

China has one of the oldest sporting cultures in the world, spanning the course of several millennia. There is, in fact, evidence that a form of football was played in China in ancient times. Besides football, some of the most popular sports in the country include martial arts, table tennis, badminton, swimming, basketball and snooker. Board games such as Go (Weiqi), and Xiangqi (Chinese chess) and recently chess are also commonly played and have organized competitions.[citation needed]

Evening pickup basketball game in a Beijing neighborhood.

Physical fitness is widely emphasized in Chinese culture. Morning exercises are a common activity and often one can find the elderly practicing qigong and tai chi chuan in parks or students doing stretches on school campuses.

Young people are also keen on basketball, especially in urban centers with limited space and grass areas. The NBA has a huge following among Chinese youths, with Yao Ming being the idol of many. Major sporting events were also held in Beijing such as the 1990 Asian Games and the 2008 Summer Olympics.

Many traditional sports are also played. The popular Chinese dragon boatracing occurs during the Dragon Boat Festival. In Inner Mongolia, sports such as Mongolian-style wrestling and horse racing are popular. In Tibet, archery and equestrianism are a part of traditional festivals.

China finished first in gold medal count at the most recent Summer Olympic Games which were held in Beijing from 8 August to 24 August 2008.

Other names

Main article: Names of China

See also

- Index of China-related articles
- Outline of China

Further reading

- Chang, Jung (1992). *Wild Swans*. Doubleday. ISBN 0385425473.
- Farah, Paolo, *Five Years of China's WTO Membership. EU and US Perspectives on China's Compliance with Transparency Commitments and the Transitional Review Mechanism*, Legal Issues of Economic Integration, Kluwer Law International, Volume 33, Number 3, pp. 263–304, 2006. Abstract [1].
- Heilig, Gerhard K., *China Bibliography – Online* [2]. 2006, 2007.
- Lynch, Michael (1998). *People's Republic of China 1949–90*. Trafalgar Square Publishing. ISBN 0-340-68853-X.
- Murphey, Rhoads (1996). *East Asia: A New History*. University of Michigan Press. ISBN 0-321-07801-2.
- Sang Ye (2006). *China Candid: The People on the People's Republic*. University of California Press. ISBN 0-520-24514-8.
- Selden, Mark (1979). *The People's Republic of China: Documentary History of Revolutionary Change*. New York: Monthly Review Press. ISBN 0853455325.
- Terrill, Ross (2003). *The New Chinese Empire, And What It Means For The United States*. New York: Basic Books. ISBN 0-465-08412-5.
- Thurston, Anne F. (1994). *China Bound: A Guide to Academic Life and Work in the PRC*. Washington: National Academies Press. ISBN 0-309-04932-6.

External links

Overviews

- People's Daily: China at a Glance [3]
- BBC News — *Country Profile: China* [4]
- China [5] entry at *The World Factbook*
- "Rethinking 'Capitalist Restoration' in China" [6] by Yiching Wu

Documentaries

- "China on the Rise" [7] PBS Online NewsHour. October 2005.
- *China Rises* [8] a documentary co-produced by *The New York Times*, *Discovery Times*, CBC, ZDF, France 5 and S4C. 9 April 2006.
- *China in the Red* [9], 1998–2001. PBS Frontline.
- *China From the Inside* [10] A documentary series co-produced by KQED Public Television and Granada Television.

Government

- The Central People's Government of People's Republic of China [11] (English)
- China Internet Information Center (China.org.cn) [12] (English) - Authorized government portal site to China

Studies

- Assertive Pragmatism: China's Economic Rise and Its Impact on Chinese Foreign Policy [13] – analysis by Minxin Pei, IFRI Proliferation Papers n°15, 2006
- The Dragon's Dawn: China as a Rising Imperial Power [14] 11 February 2005.
- History of The People's Republic of China [15] Timeline of Key Events since 1949.
- Media, advertising, and urban life in China. [16]

Travel

- China travel guide from Wikitravel

Maps

- Google Maps – China [17]
- Google Maps – China [18] Interesting locations
- Wikimedia Atlas of the People's Republic of China

[edit [19]]

1. REDIRECT Template:Navboxes

1. REDIRECT Template:Navboxes

Geographical coordinates: 35°00′N 105°00′E

ace:Rèpublik Rakyat Cina krc:Къытай Халкъ Республика mwl:República Popular de la China frr:China pnb:چین pcd:République populoère d' Chine

The Role of Government in China

Government of the People's Republic of China

> **People's Republic of China**
>
> This article is part of the series:
> **Politics and government of the People's Republic of China**
>
> Other countries · Atlas
> **Politics portal**

All power within the **government of the People's Republic of China** is divided among three bodies: the Communist Party of China, the state, and the People's Liberation Army (PLA). This article is concerned with the formal structure of the state, its departments and their responsibilities. Most, but not all, positions of significant power in the state structure and in the army are occupied by members of the Communist Party of China which is controlled by the Politburo Standing Committee of the Communist Party of China, a group of 4 to 9 people, usually all older men, who make all decisions of national significance. As the role of the Army is to enforce these decisions in times of crisis, support of the PLA is important.

The legal power of the Communist Party is guaranteed by the PRC constitution and its position as the supreme political authority in the PRC is realised through its comprehensive control of the state, military, and media. According to a prominent government spokesman:

> We will never simply copy the system of Western countries or introduce a system of multiple parties holding office in rotation, although China's state organs have different responsibilities, they all adhere to the line, principles and policies of the party.

The primary organs of state power are the National People's Congress (NPC), the President, and the State Council. Members of the State Council include the Premier, a variable number of vice premiers (now four), five state councilors (protocol equal of vice premiers but with narrower portfolios), and 29 ministers and heads of State Council commissions. During the 1980s there was an attempt made to separate party and state functions, with the party deciding general policy and the state carrying it out. The attempt was abandoned in the 1990s with the result that the political leadership within the state are also the leaders of the party, thereby creating a single centralized focus of power.

At the same time there has been a move for having party and state offices be separated at levels other than the central government. It is unheard of for a sub-national executive to also be party secretary. This frequently causes conflict between the chief executive and the party secretary, and this conflict is widely seen as intentional to prevent either from becoming too powerful. Some special cases are the Special Administrative Regions of Hong Kong and Macau where the Mainland Chinese national laws do not apply at all and the autonomous regions where, following Soviet practice, the chief executive is typically a member of the local ethnic group while the party general secretary is non-local and usually Han Chinese.

Under the Constitution of the People's Republic of China, the NPC is the highest organ of state power in China. It meets annually for about two weeks to review and approve major new policy directions, laws, the budget, and major personnel changes. Most national legislation in the PRC is adopted by the Standing Committee of the National People's Congress. Most initiatives are presented to the NPCSC for consideration by the State Council after previous endorsement by the Communist Party's Politburo Standing Committee. Although the NPC generally approves State Council policy and personnel recommendations, the NPC and its standing committee has increasingly asserted its role as the national legislature and has been able to force revisions in some laws. For example, the State Council and the Party have been unable to secure passage of a fuel tax to finance the construction of freeways.

Constitution

Main article: Constitution of the People's Republic of China

The ACR Constitution was first created on September 20, 1954. Before that, an interim Constitution-like document created by the Chinese People's Political Consultative Conference was in force.

The 2nd and 3rd promulgations of the PRC Constitution took place against the backdrop of the Cultural Revolution. The 2nd promulgation in 1975 shortened the Constitution to just about 30 articles, and contained Communist slogans and revolutionary language throughout. The role of courts was slashed, and the Presidency was gone. The 3rd promulgation in 1978 expanded the number of articles, but was still under the influence of the just-gone-by Cultural Revolution.

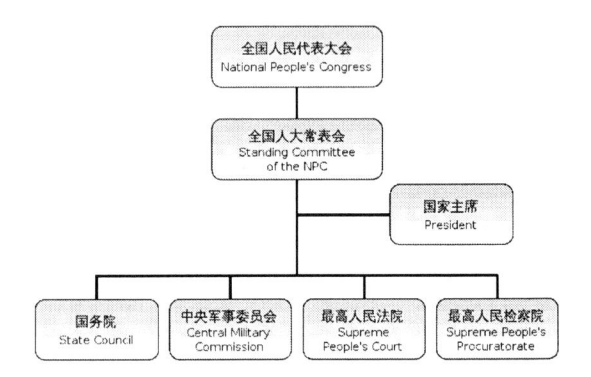

The State organs of the People's Republic of China.

The current Constitution is the PRC's 4th promulgation. On December 4, 1982, it was promulgated and has served as a stable Constitution for over 20 years. The role of the Presidency and the courts were normalized, and under the Constitution, all citizens were equal. Amendments were made in 1988, 1993, 1999, and most recently, in 2004, which recognised private property, safeguarded human rights, and further promoted the non-public sector of the economy.

National People's Congress

Main article: National People's Congress

The National People's Congress is the highest state body and the only legislative house in the People's Republic of China. Although the membership of the NPC is still largely determined by the Communist Party of China, since the early 1990s it has moved away from its previous role as a symbolic but powerless rubber-stamp legislature, and has become a forum for mediating policy differences between different parts of the Party and the government. For the NPC to formally defeat a proposal put before them is a rare, but not non-existent event, and the NPC has been quite active in being the forum in which legislation is debated before being put to a vote.

President

Main article: President of the People's Republic of China

The President (literally, Chairman) and Vice President are elected by the National People's Congress for five-year terms. The President is the head of state. The office was created by the 1982 Constitution. Formally, the President is elected by the National People's Congress in accordance with Article 62 of the Constitution. In practice, this election falls into the category of 'single-candidate' elections. The candidate is recommended by the Presidium of the National People's Congress.

Currently the President of China is Hu Jintao and the Vice President is Xi Jinping.

State Council

Main article: State Council of the People's Republic of China

The State Council is the chief authority of the People's Republic of China. It is appointed by the National People's Congress and is chaired by the Premier and includes the heads of each governmental department and agency. There are about 50 members in the Council. In the politics of the People's Republic of China, the Central People's Government forms one of three interlocking branches of power, the others being the Communist Party of China and the People's Liberation Army. The State Council directly oversees the various subordinate People's Governments in the provinces, and in practice maintains an interlocking membership with the top levels of the Communist Party of China creating a fused center of power.

Currently the Premier of State Council is Wen Jiabao.

Central Military Commission

Main article: Central Military Commission (People's Republic of China)

The Central Military Commission exercises the command and control of the People's Liberation Army and is supervised by the Standing Committee of the National People's Congress. The state CMC is nominally considered the supreme military policy-making body and its chairman, elected by the National People's Congress, is the commander-in-chief of the armed forces. In reality, command and control of the PLA, however, still resides with the Central Military Commission of the Chinese Communist Party Central Committee—the 'party CMC'.

Supreme People's Court and Supreme People's Procuratorate

Main articles: Supreme People's Court of the People's Republic of China and Supreme People's Procuratorate

The Supreme People's Court is the highest court in the judicial system of the People's Republic of China. Hong Kong and Macau, as special administrative regions, have their own separate judicial systems based on British common law traditions and Portuguese civil-law traditions respectively, and are out of the jurisdiction of the Supreme People's Court. The judges of the Supreme People's Court are appointed by the National People's Congress.

The Supreme People's Procuratorate is the highest agency at the national level responsible for prosecution in the People's Republic of China. Hong Kong and Macau, as special administrative region, have their own separate judicial systems, based on common law traditions and Portuguese legal traditions respectively, and are out of the jurisdiction of the SPP.

Provincial and local government

Main article: Administrative divisions of China

The governors of China's provinces and autonomous regions and mayors of its centrally controlled municipalities are appointed by the central government in Beijing after receiving the nominal consent of the National People's Congress (NPC). The Hong Kong and Macau special administrative regions (SARs) have some local autonomy since they have separate governments, legal systems, and basic constitutional laws, but they come under Beijing's control in matters of foreign affairs and national security, and their chief executives are handpicked by the central government. Below the provincial level in 2004 there were 50 rural prefectures, 283 prefecture-level cities, 374 county-level cities, 852 county-level districts under the jurisdiction of nearby cities, and 1,636 counties. There also were 662 cities (including those incorporated into the four centrally controlled municipalities), 808 urban districts, and 43,258 township-level regions. Counties are divided into townships and villages. While most have appointed officials running them, some lower-level jurisdictions have direct popular elections. The organs of self-governing ethnic autonomous areas (regions, prefectures, and counties)—people's congresses and people's governments—exercise the same powers as their provincial-level counterparts but are guided additionally by the Law on Regional Ethnic Autonomy and require NPC Standing Committee approval for regulations they enact "in the exercise of autonomy" and "in light of the political, economic, and cultural characteristics of the ethnic group or ethnic groups in the areas."

Civil service

Main article: Civil service of the People's Republic of China

See also

- Chinese government
- List of Chinese (People's Republic of China) government entities
- Politics of the People's Republic of China
- Chinese Political Parties

External links

- www.gov.cn [1] (English version [11])
- China e-Government Network [2]
- China Government Innovation Network [3]
- China Government Procurement Information Network [4]
- Chinese Government Public Information Online Service Platform [5]
- Guide to Chinese Government Agencies [6]
- Links to information regarding branches and departments of the PRC [7]
- US-China Business Council's PRC Central Government Structure Report [8]

The Six Parts of The China's National Government

Constitution of the People's Republic of China

People's Republic of China

This article is part of the series:
Politics and government of the People's Republic of China

Other countries · Atlas
Politics portal

The **Constitution of the People's Republic of China** (simplified Chinese: 中华人民共和国宪法; traditional Chinese: 中華人民共和國憲法; pinyin: *Zhōnghuá Rénmín Gònghéguó Xiànfǎ*) is the highest law within the People's Republic of China. The current version was adopted by the 5th National People's Congress on December 4, 1982 with further revisions in 1988, 1993, 1999, and 2004. Three previous state constitutions—those of 1954, 1975, and 1978—were superseded in turn. The Constitution has five sections which are the preamble, general principles, fundamental rights and duties of citizens, structure of the state (which includes such state organs as the National People's Congress, the State Council, the Local People's Congress and Local People's Governments and the People's Courts and the People's Procuratorates), the national flag and the emblems of the state.

History

Main article: Constitutional history of the People's Republic of China

The first Constitution of the People's Republic of China was promulgated in 1954. After two intervening versions enacted in 1975 and 1978, the current Constitution was promulgated in 1982. There were significant differences between each of these versions, and the 1982 Constitution has subsequently been amended several times. In addition, changing Constitutional conventions have led to significant changes in the structure of Chinese government in the absence of changes in the text of the Constitution.

1982 document

The 1982 document reflects Deng Xiaoping's determination to lay a lasting institutional foundation for domestic stability and modernization. The new State Constitution provides a legal basis for the broad changes in China's social and economic institutions and significantly revises government structure

There have been four major revisions by the National People's Congress (NPC) to the 1982 Constitution.

Much of the PRC Constitution is modeled after the 1936 Constitution of the Soviet Union, but there are some significant differences. For example, while the Soviet constitution contains an explicit right of secession, the Chinese constitution explicitly forbids secession. While the Soviet constitution formally creates a federal system, the Chinese constitution formally creates a unitary multi-national state.

The 1982 State Constitution is a lengthy, hybrid document with 138 articles. Large sections were adapted directly from the 1978 constitution, but many of its changes derive from the 1954 constitution. Specifically, the new Constitution de-emphasizes class struggle and places top priority on development and on incorporating the contributions and interests of non-party groups that can play a central role in modernization.

Article 1 of the State Constitution describes China as "a socialist state under the people's democratic dictatorship" meaning that the system is based on an alliance of the working classes—in communist terminology, the workers and peasants—and is led by the Communist Party, the vanguard of the working class. Elsewhere, the Constitution provides for a renewed and vital role for the groups that make up that basic alliance—the CPPCC, democratic parties, and mass organizations. The 1982 Constitution expunges almost all of the rhetoric associated with the Cultural Revolution incorporated in the 1978 version. In fact, the Constitution omits all references to the Cultural Revolution and restates Mao Zedong's contributions in accordance with a major historical reassessment produced in June 1981 at the Sixth Plenum of the Eleventh Central Committee, the "Resolution on Some Historical Issues of the Party since the Founding of the People's Republic."

There also is emphasis throughout the 1982 State Constitution on socialist law as a regulator of political behavior. Unlike the Constitution of the Soviet Union, the text of the Constitution itself doesn't explicitly mention the Communist Party of China and there is an explicit statement in Article 5 that states that the Constitution and law are supreme over all organizations and individuals.

Thus, the rights and obligations of citizens are set out in detail far exceeding that provided in the 1978 constitution. Probably because of the excesses that filled the years of the Cultural Revolution, the 1982 Constitution gives even greater attention to clarifying citizens' "fundamental rights and duties" than the 1954 constitution did, like the right to vote and to run for election begins at the age of eighteen except for those disenfranchised by law. The Constitution also guarantees the freedom of religious worship as well as the "freedom not to believe in any religion" and affirms that "religious bodies and religious affairs are not subject to any foreign domination."

Article 35 of the 1982 State Constitution proclaims that "citizens of the People's Republic of China enjoy freedom of speech, of the press, of assembly, of association, of procession, and of demonstration." In the 1978 constitution, these rights were guaranteed, but so were the right to strike and the "four big rights," often called the "four bigs": to speak out freely, air views fully, hold great debates, and write big-character posters. In February 1980, following the Democracy Wall period, the four bigs were abolished in response to a party decision ratified by the National People's Congress. The right to strike was also dropped from the 1982 Constitution. The widespread expression of the four big rights during the student protests of late 1986 elicited the regime's strong censure because of their illegality. The official response cited Article 53 of the 1982 Constitution, which states that citizens must abide by the law and observe labor discipline and public order. Besides being illegal, practicing the four big rights offered the possibility of straying into criticism of the Communist Party of China, which was in fact what appeared in student wall posters. In a new era that strove for political stability and economic development, party leaders considered the four big rights politically destabilizing. Except for the ostentatious six democratic parties, Chinese citizens are prohibited from forming parties.

Among the political rights granted by the constitution, all Chinese citizens have rights to elect and be elected. According to the later promulgated election law, rural residents have only 1/4 vote power of townsmen. As Chinese citizens are categorized into rural resident and town resident, and the constitution has no stipulation of freedom of transference, those rural residents are restricted by the Hukou (registered permanent residence) and have less rights on politics, economy and education. This problem has largely been addressed with various and ongoing reforms of hukou in 2007.

The 1982 State Constitution is also more specific about the responsibilities and functions of offices and organs in the state structure. There are clear admonitions against familiar Chinese practices that the reformers have labeled abuses, such as concentrating power in the hands of a few leaders and permitting lifelong tenure in leadership positions. On the other hand, the constitution strongly oppose the western system of separation of powers by executive, legislature and judicial. It stipulates the NPC as the highest organ of state authority power, under which the State Council, the Supreme People's Court, and the Supreme People's Procuratorate shall be elected and responsible for the NPC.

In addition, the 1982 Constitution provides an extensive legal framework for the liberalizing economic policies of the 1980s. It allows the collective economic sector not owned by the state a broader role and provides for limited private economic activity. Members of the expanded rural collectives have the right "to farm private plots, engage in household sideline production, and raise privately owned livestock." The primary emphasis is given to expanding the national economy, which is to be accomplished by balancing centralized economic planning with supplementary regulation by the market.

Another key difference between the 1978 and 1982 state constitutions is the latter's approach to outside help for the modernization program. Whereas the 1978 constitution stressed "self-reliance" in modernization efforts, the 1982 document provides the constitutional basis for the considerable body of laws passed by the NPC in subsequent years permitting and encouraging extensive foreign participation in all aspects of the economy. In addition, the 1982 document reflects the more flexible and less ideological orientation of foreign policy since 1978. Such phrases as "proletarian internationalism" and "social imperialism" have been dropped..

2004 Amendments

The Constitution was amended on March 14, 2004 to include guarantees regarding private property (*"legally obtained private property of the citizens shall not be violated,"*) and human rights (*"the State respects and protects human rights."*) This was argued by the government to be progress for Chinese democracy and a sign from CCP that they recognised the need for change, because the booming Chinese economy had created a new class of rich and middle class, who wanted protection of their own property.

Wen Jiabao was quoted by the Washington Post as saying, "These amendments of the Chinese constitution are of great importance to the development of China." "We will make serious efforts to carry them out in practice." [1] Some question that there is no clear indication that the changes were leading to increased protection for Chinese citizens in terms of human rights or property rights. Chinese people continue to be arrested for trying to challenge government decisions (whether they are legal or not), even when using the law itself. The censure of the media is still in place, as can be seen by the closure of out-spoken publications, or re-staffing to remove editors and journalists who have annoyed officials, such as was the case with the Freezing Point magazine.

Constitutional enforcement

There is no special organization established for the enforcement of the Chinese constitution. Although in the constitution it stipulates that the National People's Congress and its Standing Committee have the power to review whether laws or activities violate the constitution.

Furthermore, under the legal system of the People's Republic of China, courts do not have the general power of judicial review and cannot invalidate a statute on the grounds that it violates the constitution. Nonetheless, since 2002, there has been a special committee of the Standing Committee of the National People's Congress which has reviewed laws and regulations for constitutionality. Although this committee has not yet explicitly ruled that a law or regulation is unconstitutional, in one case, after the subsequent media outcry over the death of Sun Zhigang, the State Council was forced to rescind regulations allowing police to detain persons without residency permits after the Standing Committee of the National People's Congress (NPCSC) made it clear that it would rule such regulations unconstitutional if they were not rescinded.

The Open Constitution Initiative was an organization consisting of lawyers and academics in the People's Republic of China that advocated the rule of law and greater constitutional protections. It was shut down by the government on July 14, 2009.

See also

- Constitutional history of the People's Republic of China
- Law of the People's Republic of China
- Constitution
- Constitutional law
- Constitutional economics
- Constitutionalism

External links

- English version of the Constitution of People's Republic of China (Adopted in 1982) [2]
- Government of China website in English: The Constitution [3]

References

- ⓔ *This article incorporates public domain material from websites or documents* [4] *of the Library of Congress Country Studies. - China* [5]

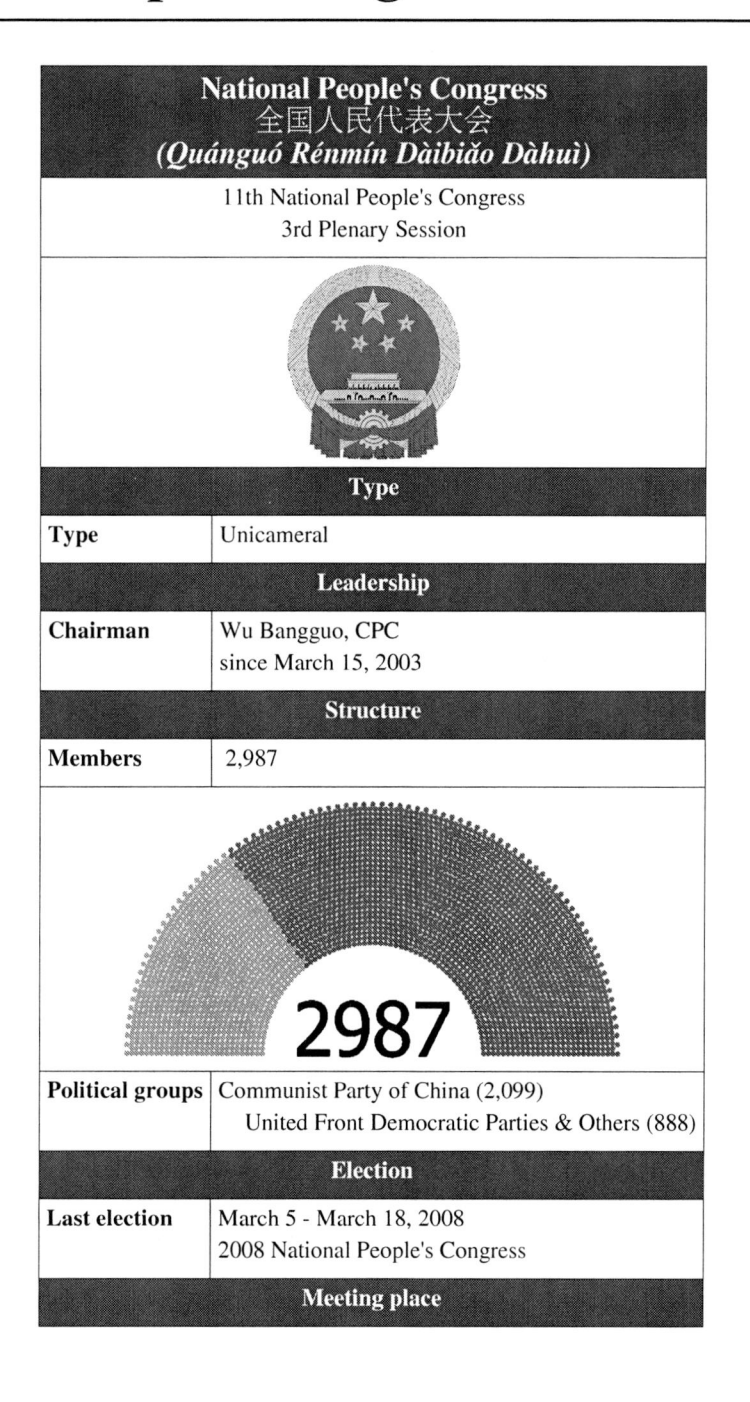

National People's Congress

National People's Congress 全国人民代表大会 (Quánguó Rénmín Dàibiǎo Dàhuì)	
11th National People's Congress 3rd Plenary Session	
Type	
Type	Unicameral
Leadership	
Chairman	Wu Bangguo, CPC since March 15, 2003
Structure	
Members	2,987
2987	
Political groups	Communist Party of China (2,099) United Front Democratic Parties & Others (888)
Election	
Last election	March 5 - March 18, 2008 2008 National People's Congress
Meeting place	

Great Hall of the People, Beijing

Website

npc.gov.cn/englishnpc/ [1]

People's Republic of China

This article is part of the series:
Politics and government of the People's Republic of China

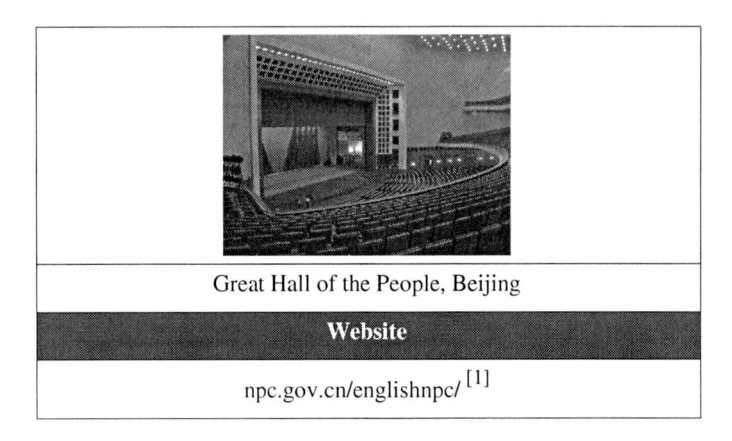

Other countries · Atlas
Politics portal

A similar term is "National Congress", which is a less common translation of People's Political Consultative Conference.

The **National People's Congress** (simplified Chinese: 全国人民代表大会; traditional Chinese: 全國人民代表大會; pinyin: *Quánguó Rénmín Dàibiǎo Dàhuì*; literally "National People's Representatives Congress"), abbreviated **NPC** (Chinese: 人大; pinyin: *Rén-Dà*), is the highest state body and the only legislative house in the People's Republic of China. The National People's Congress is held in the Great Hall of the People, Beijing, capital of the People's Republic of China. The NPC gathers each year along with the People's Political Consultative Conference (CPPCC) whose members represent various defined groups of society. NPC and CPPCC together are often called the Lianghui (Two Meetings), making important national level political decisions.

Although the membership of the NPC is still largely determined by the Communist Party of China, since the early 1990s it has moved away from its previous role as a symbolic but powerless rubber-stamp legislature, and has become a forum for mediating policy differences between different parts of the Party, the government, and groups of society. For the NPC to formally defeat a proposal put before it is a rare, but not non-existent event, and the NPC has been quite active in being the forum in which legislation is debated before being put to a vote.[citation needed] However, the BBC still describes the NPC as a rubber-stamp for party decisions, and has testimony from a member of the NPC, Hu Xiaoyan, that she has no power to help her constituents. She was quoted as saying, "As a parliamentary representative, I don't have any real power."

Powers and functions

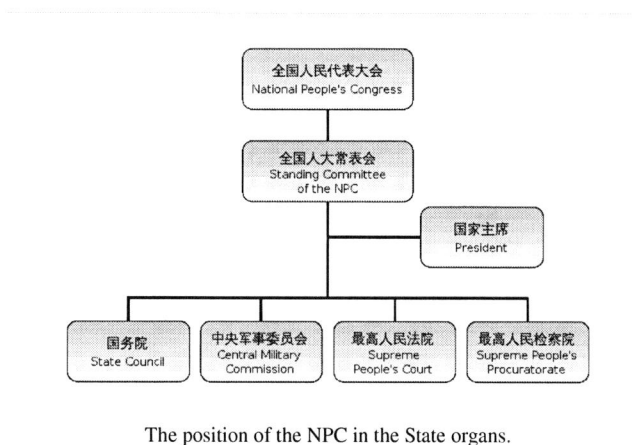

The NPC has a collection of functions and powers, including electing the President of the People's Republic of China and approving the appointment of the Premier of the State Council as well as approving the work reports of top officials. The constitution of the National People's Congress provides for most of its power to be exercised on a day-to-day basis by its Standing Committee.

The position of the NPC in the State organs.

The drafting process of NPC legislation is governed by the *Organic Law of the NPC* (1982) and the *NPC Procedural Rules* (1989). It begins with a small group, often of outside experts, who begin a draft. Over time, this draft is considered by larger and larger groups, with an attempt made to maintain consensus at each step of the process. By the time the full NPC or NPCSC meets to consider the legislation, the major substantive elements of the draft legislation have largely been agreed to. However, minor wording changes to the draft are often made at this stage. The process ends with a formal vote by the Standing Committee of the NPC or by the NPC in a plenary session.

In addition, the NPC now functions as a forum in which legislative proposals are drafted and debated with input from different parts of the government and outside technical experts. However, there are a wide range of issues for which there is no consensus within the Party and over which different parts of the party or government have different opinions. Over these issues the NPC has often become a forum for debating ideas and for achieving consensus.

In practice, although the final votes on laws of the NPC often return a high affirmative vote, a great deal of legislative activity occurs in determining the content of the legislation to be voted on. A major bill often takes years to draft, and a bill sometimes will not be put before a final vote if there is significant opposition to the measure. With respect to proposals by the State Council of the People's

Republic of China, the NPC has rejected a bill on maritime safety, and it is no longer uncommon for the State Council to amend or withdraw a bill on account of NPC opposition.

One important constitutional principle which is stated in Article 8 of the Legislation Law of the People's Republic of China is that an action can become a crime only as a consequence of a law passed by the full NPC and that other organs of the Chinese government do not have the power to criminalize activity. This principle was used to overturn police regulations on custody and repatriation and has been used to call into question the legality of re-education through labor.

Proceedings

The Great Hall of the People, where the NPC convenes

The NPC meets for about two weeks each year at the same time as the Chinese People's Political Consultative Conference, usually in the Spring. The combined sessions have been known as the *two meetings*. Between these sessions, power is exercised by the Standing Committee of the National People's Congress which contains about 150 members.

The sessions have become media events because it is at the plenary sessions that the Chinese leadership produces work reports. Although the NPC has thus far never failed to approve a work report or candidate nominated by the Party, these votes are no longer unanimous. It is considered extremely embarrassing for the approval vote to fall below 70%, which occurred several times in the mid-1990s. More recently, work reports have been vetted with NPC delegates beforehand to avoid this embarrassment.

In addition, during NPC sessions the Chinese leadership holds press conferences with foreign reporters, and this is one of the few opportunities Western reporters have of asking unscripted questions of the Chinese leadership.

A major bill often takes years to draft, and a bill sometimes will not be put before a final vote if there is significant opposition to the measure. An example of this is the Property Law of the People's Republic of China which was withdrawn from the 2006 legislative agenda after objections that the law did not do enough to protect state property. China's laws are usually submitted for approval after at most three reviews at the NPC Standing Committee. However, the debate of the Property Law has spanned nine years, receiving a record seven reviews at the NPC Standing Committee and stirring hot debates across the country. The long-awaited and highly contested Property Law was finally approved at the Fifth Session of the Tenth National People's Congress (NPC) on March 16. Among the 2,889 deputies attending the closing session, 2,799 voted for it, 52 against it, 37 abstained and one didn't vote.

Membership

The NPC consists of about 3,000 delegates. Delegates to the National People's Congress are elected for five-year terms via a multi-tiered representative electoral system. Delegates are elected by the provincial people's assemblies, who in turn are elected by lower level assemblies, and so on through a series of tiers to the local people's assemblies which are directly elected by the electorate.

There is a limit on the number of candidates in proportion to the number of seats available. At the national level, for example, a maximum of 110 candidates are allowed per 100 seats; at the provincial level, this ratio is 120 candidates per 100 seats. This ratio increases for each lower level of people's assemblies, until the lowest level, the village level, has no limit on the number of candidates for each seat. However, the Congress website says "In an indirect election, the number of candidates should exceed the number to be elected by 20% to 50%."

About 70% of current NPC delegates are members of the Communist Party of China.

Membership of Previous National People's Congresses

Congress	Year	Total Number of Deputies	Female Deputies	Minority Deputies	As Percentage to Total Deputies (%) Female Deputies	% Minority Deputies
First Congress	1954	1226	147	178	12.0	14.5
Second Congress	1959	1226	150	179	12.2	14.6
Third Congress	1964	3040	542	372	17.8	12.2
Fourth Congress	1975	2885	653	270	22.6	9.4
Fifth Congress	1978	3497	742	381	21.2	10.9
Sixth Congress	1983	2978	632	403	21.2	13.5
Seventh Congress	1988	2978	634	445	21.3	14.9
Eighth Congress	1993	2978	626	439	21.0	14.8
Ninth Congress	1998	2979	650	428	21.8	14.4
Tenth Congress	2002	2985	604	414	20.2	13.9

Hong Kong, Macau and Taiwan

A number of delegates to the NPC represent Hong Kong, Macau and Taiwan. The delegates from Hong Kong and Macau are elected via an electoral college rather than by popular vote, but do include significant political figures who are residing in the regions. The electoral colleges which elect Hong Kong and Macau NPC members are largely similar in composition to the bodies which elect the chief executives of those regions. The current method of electing SAR delegations began after the handovers of sovereignty to the PRC. Between 1975 and the handovers, both Hong Kong and Macau were represented by delegations elected by the Guangdong Provincial Congress.

The Taiwan delegation is intended to be symbolic of the PRC's claim over the island, but does not include anyone currently residing in Taiwan, but rather includes only people living on the mainland with some connection with Taiwan, such as previous residency or ancestry. The Taiwan delegates are increasingly composed of Taiwanese merchants residing on the mainland and overseas Taiwanese who returned to the mainland. Delegates representing Taiwan are elected by a constituency composed of PRC residents who are or were previously domiciled in Taiwan, or who have ancestry in Taiwan.

PLA and Overseas Chinese

In addition to these delegations, there are delegations from the People's Liberation Army, who under Chinese law are not considered residents of any region, and a delegation which represents returned overseas Chinese.

Relationship with the Communist Party

The ruling Communist Party of China maintains effective control over the composition of people's congresses at various levels, especially the National People's Congress, through this system. At the local level, there is a considerable amount of decentralisation in the candidate preselection process, with room for local in-party politics and for participation by non-Communist Party candidates. The structure of the tiered electoral system makes it difficult for a candidate to become a member of the higher level people's assemblies without the support from politicians in the lower tier, while at the same time making it impossible for the party bureaucracy to completely control the election process.

One such mechanism is the limit on the number of candidates in proportion to the number of seats available. At the national level, for example, a maximum of 110 candidates are allowed per 100 seats; at the provincial level, this ratio is 120 candidates per 100 seats. This ratio increases for each lower level of people's congresses, until the lowest level, the village level, has no limit on the number of candidates for each seat. However, the Congress website says "In an indirect election, the number of candidates should exceed the number to be elected by 20% to 50%." The practice of having more candidates than seats for NPC delegate positions has become standard, and it is different from Soviet practice in which all delegates positions were selected by the Party center. Although the limits on member selection allows the Party leadership to block unacceptable candidates, it also causes unpopular candidates to be removed in the electoral process. Direct and explicit challenges to the rule of the Communist Party of China are not tolerated, but are unlikely due to the control the party center has on delegate selection.

Furthermore, the constitution of the National People's Congress provides for most of its power to be exercised on a day-to-day basis by its Standing Committee. Due to its overwhelming majority in the Congress, the Communist Party has total control over the composition of the Standing Committee, thereby controlling the actions of the National People's Congress.

Although Party approval is in effect essential for membership in the NPC, approximately a third of the seats are by convention reserved for non-Communist Party members. This includes technical experts and members of the smaller allied parties. While these members do provide technical expertise and a somewhat greater diversity of views, they do not function as a political opposition.

Although it has been frequently stated that the NPC has never overturned a resolution proposed by the Chinese Communist Party, this is **incorrect**. In 1993, the NPC refused to consider constitutional amendments proposed by the Chinese Communist Party on the grounds that non-governmental organizations such as the CCP do not have authority to propose legislation. Also in 1994, the Eighth National People's Congress Standing Committee included "Income and Property Law," in the official legislative plan, but was not able to bring it to a vote due to opposition."

See also

- Chinese People's Political Consultative Conference (CPPCC)
- Standing Committee of the National People's Congress (NPCSC)
- Elections in the People's Republic of China

External links

English

- English version of the Official website of the NPC [1]
- NY Times article on the secret government detainment of would-be appeals to the NPC [2]

Chinese

- The official website of the NPC [3]
- News on NPC [4], People's Daily Online

President of the People's Republic of China

President of the People's Republic of China		
	Emblem of the People's Republic of China		
	Incumbent **Hu Jintao** since March 15, 2003		
Residence	Zhongnanhai
Appointer	the National People's Congress
Term length	five years, renewable once consecutively
Inaugural holder	Mao Zedong (1954) Li Xiannian (1983)
Formation	1954-1975 December, 1982
Website	Presidency [1]

The **President of the People's Republic of China** (simplified Chinese: 中华人民共和国主席; traditional Chinese: 中華人民共和國主席; pinyin: *Zhōnghuá Rénmín Gònghéguó Zhǔxí*), literally **Chairman of the People's Republic of China**, or abbreviated *Guójiā Zhǔxí* 国家主席, literally Chairman of State) is an office under the National People's Congress and it is the head of state of the People's Republic of China. The office was created by the 1982 Constitution. Formally, the President is elected by the National People's Congress in accordance with Article 62 of the Constitution. In practice, this election falls into the category of 'single-candidate' elections, which the candidate is recommended by the Politburo of the Communist Party of China.

The term *Zhuxi* refers to the *chairman* in a committee, and was translated as such prior to the 1982 constitution (as in Chairman Mao, although Mao's title refers primarily to the position of Chairman of Party which he held from 1945 until death). The official translation switched to *President* after 1982 in conformity with Western terminology. However, *Zhuxi* stayed in Chinese, and in other contexts still corresponds to *chairman* in English. Meanwhile, the translation of English term *President* as the head of other states remained *Zongtong* (simplified Chinese: 总统; traditional Chinese: 總統; pinyin: *zǒngtǒng*), causing a bit of confusion with regard to usage.Wikipedia:Avoid weasel words

Selection, succession, and requirements

According to the Constitution of the People's Republic of China since 1982, the National People's Congress (NPC), in theory China's top law-making body, has the power to elect and force the resignation of the President. By law, the President must be a Chinese citizen of 45 years of age or older. The President cannot serve for over two successive terms, a term being the equivalent of one session of the NPC, which is five years. Also, all the authorities and works of the President must be done under the NPC and its Standing Committee's order. The President does not have any administrative power; the position is that of a powerless figurehead.

The President promulgates statutes adopted by the NPC and NPCSC without veto. The functions of the President are ceremonial that the President appoints the Premier upon the decision of NPC, Vice-Premiers, State Council members and Ministers of all departments upon the nomination of the Premier, all ambassadors to foreign countries, and all legislative committee chairs, treasurers and secretaries. The President has the responsibility to give Special Presidential Decrees, and declare State of Emergency, and declare War ritually upon the decision of NPC. The President is assisted by the Vice-President.

In the event that the President dies or leaves office, the Vice-President automatically assumes presidential powers. In the event that they both are unable to perform normal duties, the Chairman of the National People's Congress will perform the duties of the President as Acting President until the

NPC can elect a new one.

Relation to the state

As the President is legally China's head of state, he is responsible for China's foreign affairs. Since 1993, the President has also been the General Secretary of CPC who has generally responsible for establishing general policy and direction for the state and leaves responsibility for the implementation details to the Premier of the People's Republic of China, the head of government. The Chinese Presidency has grown to be quite a powerful post since it combines with the General Secretary, the head of the Party.

The position of the President in the State organs.

Relation with the Party

Although President is a powerless figurehead, since the 1990s, it has been general practice for the President to also serve as the General Secretary of the Communist Party of China.

It is key for the general secretary to seal his diplomatic power by adding the presidency to his powerful collection of titles. This effectively shows the Communist leader's national representation.

Relation with the military

The relationship between the President and the military is more difficult to discern. The potential for conflict is lessened when, as during the Jiang era, the President is also chairman of the state Central Military Commission. However, there is a source of potential conflict when this is not the case, shown by the situation in 2003 when top Communist leader Hu Jintao was elected President without being elected the CMC Chair. In addition, most of the members of both the Party and the State Central Military Commission are uniformed senior generals, giving the People's Liberation Army a degree of autonomy. This autonomy, however, is limited by the existence of political officer.

In principle, when the President is also party general secretary, he could order the Party Central Military Commission to order the state Central Military Commission to do something,[citation needed] however how this would work in a crisis is unclear.

There have been proposals to constitutionally change the system of command to form a National Security Council, modelled after the National Security Council of the United States, which would give the President undisputed command of the military which would then be just another ministry. These proposals were not actively discussed because of opposition from senior generals. In September 2004, Jiang stepped down as Chairman of the commission, and President Hu Jintao became the Commander-in-Chief of the People's Liberation Army.

History

After the implementation of the Constitution of People's Republic of China in 1954, Mao Zedong, who had served as the Chairman of the Central People's Government since 1949, was selected Chairman of the People's Republic of China. Mao, who was also Chairman of the Communist Party of China and Chairman of the Central Military Commission, was clearly the most powerful person in China. In the Constitution of 1954, the President (officially translated as "Chairman") of the PRC was intended to be very powerful, serving both as the Head of State, and the Commander-in-Chief of the armed forces. The president had special powers to call upon emergency meetings during a crisis or concerns of national security.

After his failures in the Great Leap Forward, Mao decided to give up the State presidency in 1959. He was succeeded to this post by Liu Shaoqi, who along with Zhou Enlai and Deng Xiaoping, took on a more active role in government to curb the excesses of the Great Leap Forward and restore Soviet-based centrally planned economy. However, in 1966, Mao launched the Cultural Revolution to re-assert his personal power and overthrow the Liu government. The state and party apparatus broke down and in 1968, Chairman Liu Shaoqi was arrested and humiliated by the Red Guards.

Chairman Liu died in prison and he was not replaced. Mao concentrated powers centrally into the hands of the Party Chairman, and the CMC Chairman, which were further exercised by various Revolutionary Committees. The ceremonial duties associated with the Head of State were subsequently passed to the Chairman of the National People's Congress, the national legislature. The exact reason why Mao Zedong refused to reinstate the presidency was unclear, however it is now known that Mao did not want his political struggle with Liu Shaoqi to be remembered as his attempt to claim the title of the presidency for himself. Lin Biao, then China's number-two figure, advocated for the reinstatement of the position of President, with Mao taking the position and himself becoming Vice-President. Mao later considered this to be a threat to his power, as the Vice-President can legally succeed the President in the event of the latter's death. But during the early 1980s, it became clearer that China needed a person to serve as the Head of State, albeit completely ceremonial. Soong Ching-ling, the widow of Sun Yat-sen and former vice-chairwoman of PRC, was named to be the Honorary President of the PRC before the passage of the Constitution of 1982.

In the Constitution of 1982, the President was conceived of as a figurehead head of state with actual state power resting in the hands of the Premier of the People's Republic of China and the General

Secretary of the Communist Party of China, both of which were conceived of as being separate people; the President will only hold the office of the President, and not intervene directly in matters of the State Council or the Party. The President therefore held minor responsibilities such as greeting foreign dignitaries, and signing the appointment of embassy staff. In the original 1982 Constitution plan, the Party would develop policy, the state would execute it, and the power would be divided to prevent a cult of personality from forming as it did with the case of Mao Zedong. Thus in 1982, China perceivably had four main leaders: Hu Yaobang, the Party General Secretary; Zhao Ziyang, the Premier; Li Xiannian, the President; and Deng Xiaoping, the "Paramount Leader", holding title of the Chairman of the CMC.

Subsequent events, although, caused the office to have much larger powers than was originally intended. In 1989, then President Yang Shangkun, in cooperation with the then Chairman of the Central Military Commission Deng Xiaoping, was able to use the office of the President to declare martial law in Beijing and order the military crackdown of the Tiananmen Square protests of 1989. This was in direct opposition to the wishes of Party General Secretary Zhao Ziyang and probably a majority of the Politburo Standing Committee.

In the 1990s, the experiment of separating party and state posts, which led to bitter division, was terminated, and in 1992, the post of President was taken by Jiang Zemin, who as General Secretary and chief of the Central Military Commission continued to make the office of the President a powerful position. When Jiang Zemin stepped down in 2003, the offices of General Secretary and President were once again both given to one man, then Vice-President Hu Jintao.

First Lady

The wives of high ranking Chinese political leaders are encouraged to say little or nothing to the public as one wrong word can ruin their husband's career in this highly competitive and complicated arena of political power plays.[citation needed] For this reason, China's First Lady (Informal title) plays more the gracious host than the independent political figure as is customary, for instance, in the United States. Since the first president, every president has been a married man.

- Hu Jintao
  - Liu Yongqing 2003-(incumbent)
- Jiang Zemin
  - Wang Yeping 1993–2003
- Yang Shangkun
  - Li Bozhao 1988–1993
- Li Xiannian
  - Lin Jiamei 1983–1988
- Liu Shaoqi

- Wang Guangmei 1959–1968
- Mao Zedong
  - Jiang Qing 1954–1958

See also

- List of Presidents of the People's Republic of China
- Vice President of the People's Republic of China
- Political position ranking of the People's Republic of China
- Paramount Leader
- List of Chinese leaders

External links

- The President's Official Website [2] (English)

State Council of the People's Republic of China

State Council of the People's Republic of China	
中华人民共和国国务院	
Zhōnghuá Rénmín Gònghéguó Guówùyuàn	
Emblem of the People's Republic of China	
Agency overview	
Formed	27 September 1954
Preceding agency	Government Administration Council of the Central People's Government
Jurisdiction	Government of the People's Republic of China
Headquarters	Zhongnanhai, Beijing
Agency executives	Wen Jiabao, Premier Li Keqiang Hui Liangyu Zhang Dejiang Wang Qishan, Vice-Premiers
Website	
http://english.gov.cn	

The **State Council** (simplified Chinese: 国务院; traditional Chinese: 國務院; pinyin: *Guówùyuàn*), which is largely synonymous with the **Central People's Government** (Chinese: 中央人民政府) after 1954, is the chief administrative authority (**Cabinet**) of the People's Republic of China. It is chaired by the Premier and includes the heads of each governmental department and agency. There are about 50 members in the Council. In the politics of the People's Republic of China, the Central People's Government forms one of three interlocking branches of power, the others being the Communist Party of China and the People's Liberation Army. The State Council directly oversees the various subordinate People's Governments in the provinces, and in practice maintains an interlocking membership with the top levels of the Communist Party of China creating a fused center of power.

Organization

Standing Committee members of the State Council include the premier, four vice-premiers, five state councilors, and the secretary-general. The State Council meets once a month. Its standing committee meets twice a week.

The vice-premiers and state councilors are nominated by the premier, and appointed by the president with National People's Congress' (NPC) approval. The premier is nominated and appointed by the president with NPC approval. Incumbents may serve two successive five-year terms.

Each vice premier oversees certain areas of administration. Each State Councilor performs duties as designated by the Premier. The secretary-general heads the General Office which handles the day-to-day work of the State Council. The secretary-general has relatively little power and should not be confused with the General Secretary of the Communist Party of China.

Each ministry supervises one sector. Commissions outrank ministries and set policies for and coordinate the related activities of different administrative organs. Offices deal with matters of ongoing concern. Bureaus and administrations rank below ministries.

Although formally responsible to the NPC and its Standing Committee in conducting a wide range of government functions both at the national and at the local levels, in practice the NPC's actual authority is rather limited, although it is not completely non-existent. The State Council acts according by virtue of the authority of the NPC, and there have been at least one case where the NPC has outright rejected an initiative of the State Council and a few cases where the State Council has withdrawn or greatly modified a proposal in response to NPC opposition.

The State Council and the Communist Party of China are also tightly interlocked. Most of the members of the State Council are high level party members. Although, as party members, they are supposed to follow party instructions, because they tend to be senior members of the party they also have large amounts of influence over what those instructions are. This results in a system which is unlike the Soviet practice in which the Party effectively controlled the state. Rather the party and state are fused at this level of government. The members of the State Council derive their authority from being members of the state, while as members of the Party they coordinate their activities and determine key decisions such as the naming of personnel.

Although there were attempts to separate the party and state in the late 1980s under Zhao Ziyang and have the Party in charge of formulating policy and the State Council executing policy, these efforts were largely abandoned in the early 1990s.

As the chief administrative organ of government, its main functions are to formulate administrative measures, issue decisions and orders, and monitor their implementation; draft legislative bills for submission to the NPC or its Standing Committee; and prepare the economic plan and the state budget for deliberation and approval by the NPC. The State Council is the functional center of state power and clearinghouse for government initiatives at all levels. With the government's emphasis on economic modernization, the State Council clearly acquired additional importance and influence.

Despite the inclusion of the Ministry for National Defense in the State Council, it does not control the People's Liberation Army which functions independently of the state council.

Principal officers

State Council of the People's Republic of China

Position	Name	Term
Premier	Wen Jiabao	2003–
Executive Vice Premier (Financial Affairs)	Huang Ju Li Keqiang	2003–2007 2008–
Vice Premier (Foreign Affairs and Commerce)	Wu Yi Wang Qishan	2003–2008 2008–
Vice Premier (Economy)	Zeng Peiyan Zhang Dejiang	2002–2008 2008–
Vice Premier (Agriculture)	Hui Liangyu	2003–
Secretary General	Hua Jianmin Ma Kai	2003–2008 2008–
Finance Minister	Jin Renqing Xie Xuren	2003–2007 2007–
Foreign Minister	Li Zhaoxing Yang Jiechi	2003–2007 2007–
Defense Minister	Cao Gangchuan Liang Guanglie	2003–2007 2007–
Minister of Education	Zhou Ji	2003–
Minister of Commerce	Bo Xilai Chen Deming	2004–2007 2007–
Health Minister	Zhang Wenkang Wu Yi Gao Qiang Chen Zhu	1998–2003 2003–2005 2005–2007 2007-
Minister of National Development and Reform Commission	Ma Kai Zhang Ping	2003–2008 2008–
Minister of Railways	Liu Zhijun	2003–
Minister of Civil Affairs	Li Xueju	2003–
Minister of Labour	Tian Chengping	2005–
Governor of the People's Bank of China	Zhou Xiaochuan	2005–

Organizational structure

General Office of the State Council

- General Office of the State Council

Ministries and Commissions under the State Council

1. Ministry of Foreign Affairs
2. Ministry of National Defense
3. National Development and Reform Commission
4. Ministry of Education
5. Ministry of Science and Technology
6. State Ethnic Affairs Commission
7. Ministry of Public Security
8. Ministry of State Security
9. Ministry of Supervision
10. Ministry of Civil Affairs
11. Ministry of Justice
12. Ministry of Finance
13. Ministry of Human Resources and Social Security
14. Ministry of Land and Resources
15. Ministry of Environmental Protection
16. Ministry of Housing and Urban-Rural Construction
17. Ministry of Railways
18. Ministry of Transport
19. Ministry of Industry and Information Technology
20. Ministry of Water Resources
21. Ministry of Agriculture
22. Ministry of Commerce (MOFCOM)
23. Ministry of Culture
24. Ministry of Health
25. National Population and Family Planning Commission
26. People's Bank of China
27. National Audit Office

Special Organization directly under the State Council

- State-owned Assets Supervision and Administration Commission (SASAC)

Organizations directly under the State Council

1. General Administration of Customs
2. State Administration of Taxation
3. State Administration for Industry and Commerce
4. General Administration of Quality Supervision, Inspection and Quarantine
5. State Administration of Radio, Film and Television
6. General Administration of Press and Publication (National Copyright Administration)
7. State General Administration of Sports
8. National Bureau of Statistics
9. State Forestry Administration
10. State Administration of Work Safety
11. State Intellectual Property Office (SIPO)
12. National Tourism Administration
13. State Administration for Religious Affairs
14. Counselor's Office of the State Council
15. Government Offices Administration of the State Council
16. National Bureau of Corruption Prevention

Administrative Offices under the State Council

1. Overseas Chinese Affairs Office
2. Hong Kong and Macao Affairs Office
3. Legislative Affairs Office
4. State Council Research Office

Institutions directly under the State Council

1. Xinhua News Agency
2. Chinese Academy of Sciences
3. Chinese Academy of Social Sciences
4. Chinese Academy of Engineering
5. Development Research Center
6. National School of Administration
7. China Earthquake Administration
8. China Meteorological Administration
9. China Banking Regulatory Commission (CBRC)

10. China Securities Regulatory Commission
11. China Insurance Regulatory Commission
12. State Electricity Regulatory Commission
13. National Council for Social Security Fund
14. National Natural Science Foundation
15. Taiwan Affairs Office (CPC institution)
16. State Council Information Office (CPC institution)
17. State Archives Administration (CPC institution)

State Administrations and Bureaus under the Ministries and Commissions

1. State Bureau for Letters and Calls
2. State Administration of Grain
3. National Energy Administration
4. State Administration of Science, Technology and Industry for National Defence
5. State Tobacco Monopoly Administration (China National Tobacco Corporation)
6. State Administration of Foreign Experts Affairs
7. State Bureau of Civil Servants
8. State Oceanic Administration
9. Civil Aviation Administration of China (CAAC)
10. State Bureau of Surveying and Mapping
11. State Post Bureau
12. State Administration of Cultural Heritage
13. State Food and Drug Administration (SFDA)
14. State Administration of Traditional Chinese Medicine
15. State Administration of Foreign Exchange
16. State Administration of Coal Mine Safety
17. National Administration for the Protection of State Secrets (CPC institution)
18. State Cryptography Administration (CPC institution)
19. China National Space Administration
20. China Atomic Energy Authority
21. State Language Commission
22. National Nuclear Safety Administration

External links

- Official website [1]
- Organizational structure [2]

Central Military Commission (People's Republic of China)

Central Military Commission of the People's Republic of China	
中华人民共和国中央军事委员会	
Zhōnghuá Rénmín Gònghéguó Zhōngyāng Jūnshì Wěiyuánhuì	
The CMC is housed in the Ministry of National Defense compound ("August 1st Building")	
Agency overview	
Formed	4 December 1982
Preceding agency	National Defense Commission
Jurisdiction	People's Liberation Army
Headquarters	August 1st Building, Beijing
Agency executives	Hu Jintao, Chairman Guo Boxiong Xu Caihou, Vice-Chairmans
Website	
http://english.gov.cn	

The **Central Military Commission** (**CMC**) (simplified Chinese: 中央军事委员会; traditional Chinese: 中央軍事委員會; pinyin: *Zhōngyāng Jūnshì Wěiyuánhuì*) is the national defense organization of the People's Republic of China.

It refers to one of two organizations of the People's Republic of China: either the "Central Military Commission of the People's Republic of China" (a state organ) or the "Central Military Commission of the Communist Party of China" (a party organ).

The command and control of the People's Liberation Army (Chinese armed forces) is exercised in name by the 'state CMC', supervised by the Standing Committee of the National People's Congress. The state CMC is nominally considered the supreme military policy-making body and its chairman, elected by the National People's Congress, is the commander-in-chief of the armed forces. In reality, command and control of the PLA, however, still resides with the Central Military Commission of the Chinese Communist Party Central Committee—the 'party CMC'.

Both commissions are identical in membership, thus actually forming one identical institution under two different names (called simplified Chinese: 一套机构两块牌子; traditional Chinese:

一套機構兩塊牌子; pinyin: *yítào jīgòu liǎngkuài páizi*), in order to fit in both state government and party systems. Both commissions are currently chaired by Chairman Hu Jintao. The 11-man commission issues directives relating to the PLA, including senior appointments, troop deployments and arms spending. Almost all the members are senior generals, but the most important posts have always been held by the party's most senior leaders to ensure absolute loyalty of the armed forces and to ensure the survival of the regime.

The CMC is housed in the Ministry of National Defense compound ("August 1st Building") in western Beijing.

Origin

The party military committee dates back to October 1925, and while operating under various degrees of authority and responsibility, was consistently named the *Zhongyang Junshi Weiyuanhui* (Central Military Affairs Commission). Among Western commentators, "Affairs" is frequently dropped from the title. As a commission, it ranks higher in the party hierarchy than departments such as the Organization or United Front Departments. In the September 1949 reorganization, a government counterpart, the *Zhongyang Zhengfu Geming Junshi Weiyuanhui* (Central Revolutionary Government Military Affairs Commission) was established. This evolved into the September 1954 *Guofang Weiyuanhui* (National Defense Commission) and later into today's State CMC, which was created in 1982 by the Constitution of the People's Republic of China in order to formalize the role of the military within the government structure. Both the National Defense Commission and State CMC have been described as 'consultative' bodies.

Command structure

People's Republic of China

This article is part of the series:
Politics and government of the People's Republic of China

Other countries · Atlas
Politics portal

Unlike in most countries, the Central Military Commission is not considered as just another ministry. Although China does have a Ministry of National Defense, headed by a Minister of National Defense, it exists solely for liaison with foreign militaries and does not have command authority.

The most important chain of command runs from the CMC to the four General Headquarters (General Staff Department, General Political Department, General Logistic Department, General Armament Department) and, in turn, to each of the service branches (ground, navy and air forces) and military regions. In addition, the CMC also has direct control over the Second Artillery Corps (strategic missile force), the National Defense University, and the Academy of Military Science. As stipulated in the 1997 National Defense Law, the CMC also controls the paramilitary People's Armed Police (PAP), who have the politically sensitive role of guarding key government buildings, including the main leadership compound of Zhongnanhai in Beijing. The CMC shares command authority with the Ministry of Public Security of the State Council.

Although in theory the CMC has the highest military command authority, in reality the ultimate decision making power concerning war, armed forces, and national defense resides with the Communist Party's Politburo. The CMC is usually chaired by the General Secretary of CPC, who is supported by two to three Vice Chairmen, including the Minister of National Defense. Members of the CMC normally includes the Directors of the PLA's Four General Headquarters and the Commander of the Air Force, Navy, and Second Artillery.

Political structure

The armed forces of China are commanded by General Staff Headquarters, the General Political Department, the General Logistics Department and the General Armaments Department of the PLA, which implements the directives of the Central Military Commission. Along with the General Secretary of the Communist Party and President, the Chairman of the Central Military Commission is one of the most powerful leaders in Chinese politics.

The Chairman of the CMC was twice in its history held by a senior official who had given up his other posts, as in the case of Deng Xiaoping and Jiang Zemin. In the case of Deng Xiaoping, because of his prestige, he was able to exercise considerable power after his retirement, in part from his position as CMC Chairman. There was speculation that Jiang Zemin would have been able to retain similar authority after his retirement from the positions of General Secretary and President, but this did not turn out to be so. One major factor is that in contrast to Deng Xiaoping, who always had close relations with the People's Liberation Army, Jiang had no military background. In addition, with the promotion of the fourth generation of Chinese leaders to lead the civilian party, there was also a corresponding promotion of military leaders. All the military members of the CMC come from Hu Jintao's generation rather than from Jiang's, and at the time of the leadership transition, there appeared some very sharp editorials from military officers suggesting that the military would have strong objections to Jiang attempting to exercise power behind the scenes. Jiang Zemin retired from his post as Chairman of the party's Central Military Commission in September 2004 to Hu Jintao, and from the state's in March 2005, solidifying Hu's position as paramount leader.

In China's state-party-military tripartite political system, the CMC itself is a decision-making body whose day-to-day affairs are not nearly as transparent as that of the Central Committee or the State Council. As one of China's three main decision making bodies the relative influence of the CMC can vary depending on the time period and the leaders. In the event of war or political crisis, for example, the CMC may well function as a *de facto* executive for the country's daily affairs.

The Tiananmen Protests of 1989 illustrates how the Central Military Commission functions. CMC Chairman Deng Xiaoping proposed the imposition martial law and the use of armed soldiers to suppress unarmed demonstrations in Beijing. Under the constitution of the Chinese Communist Party, the CMC is subordinate to the Politburo.

Election of members

Theoretically, the CCP (party) CMC is elected by the Central Committee of the Communist Party of China and is subordinate to the Politburo and the Politburo Standing Committee (PBSC). In practice, membership is very closely controlled by the PBSC.

Similarly, the State CMC is nominally elected by the National People's Congress and theoretically reports to the Congress, but is in practice indistinguishable from the CCP CMC. This difference in elections also results in the only difference in membership between the two bodies, as party organs, such as the party congress and the Central Committee assemble at different times than the National People's Congress. For example, some were elected into the party CMC in the Sixteenth National Congress of the Communist Party of China in November 2002, but they entered the state CMC in March 2003, when the 10th National People's Congress convened.

The members are generally uniformed military commanders, except for the chairman and first vice-chairman, who have both been drawn from the Politburo in recent years. The military members are generally members of neither the Politburo Standing Committee nor the State Council outside of the Minister of National Defense, although they all tend to be members of the Communist Party and are members of the Central Committee. The military members are apparently chosen with regular promotion procedures from within the PLA.

Membership

According to the Constitution of the People's Republic of China, the CMC is composed of the following: the Chairman; the Vice-Chairmen; and Members. The Chairman of the Central Military Commission has overall responsibility for the commission.

As of May 2009 (dates refer to tenure on the CCP MAC):

Chairman:

- Chairman of the Central Military Commission — Hu Jintao (also General Secretary of the Chinese Communist Party, President of the People's Republic of China) (since September 2004)

Vice Chairmen:

- Vice Chairman of the Central Military Commission — General Guo Boxiong (since November 2002)
- Vice Chairman of the Central Military Commission — General Xu Caihou (since September 2004)

Members:

- Minister of National Defense - General Liang Guanglie (since November 2002)
- Chief of General Staff of the People's Liberation Army — General Chen Bingde (since September 2004)
- Director of the General Political Department — General Li Jinai (since November 2002)
- Director of the General Logistics Department — General Liao Xilong (since November 2002)
- Director of the General Armament Department — General Chang Wanquan (since October 2007)
- Commander of the PLA Navy — Navy General Wu Shengli (since October 2007)
- Commander of the PLA Air Force and PLA Deputy Chief-of-Staff— Air Force General Xu Qiliang (since October 2007)
- Commander of the Second Artillery Corps — General Jing Zhiyuan (since September 2004)

Organization

The exact internal organisation of the CMC is highly secretive. However, it is known that the CMC contains at least five key organs.

- General Staff Department
- Legal Affairs Bureau
- Arms Trading Office
- Discipline Inspection Commission
- Audit Bureau

The General Staff Department is the nerve center of the entire Chinese military command and control system, responsible for daily administrative duties of the CMC. The General Office processes all CMC communications and documents, coordinate meetings, and convey orders and directives to other subordinate organs.

Proposed reorganization

There has been an effort to establish a national security council-type body that would presumably assume greater control over government bodies vital to national security, including the People's Liberation Army. It is not clear what role the CMC would play in such a reorganization.[citation needed]

See also

- List of leaders of the Communist Party of China
- Central Guard Unit

References

- "Central Military Commission" [1]. *SinoDefence.com*. Retrieved 2007-11-21.
- "Chinese parliament approves premier, CMC vice-chairmen" [2]. *news.xinhuanet.com/english*. Retrieved 2008-03-16.

Supreme People's Court of the People's Republic of China

Supreme People's Court of the People's Republic of China 中华人民共和国最高人民法院 *Zhōnghuá Rénmín Gònghéguó* *Zuìgāo Rénmín Fǎyuàn*	
	The main gate of the Supreme People's Court in Beijing.
Established	September 1954
Jurisdiction	People's Republic of China
Location	Beijing
Composition method	Presidential selection with National People's Congress approval
Authorized by	Constitution of the People's Republic of China
Judge term length	5 years
Website	http://www.court.gov.cn/
	**Chief Justice**
Currently	Wang Shengjun
Since	March 2008

People's Republic of China

This article is part of the series:
Politics and government of the People's Republic of China

Other countries · Atlas
Politics portal

The **Supreme People's Court** (最高人民法院; pinyin: Zuìgāo Rénmín Fǎyuàn) is the highest court in the mainland area of the People's Republic of China. Hong Kong and Macau, as special administrative regions, have their own separate judicial systems based on British common law traditions and Portuguese civil-law traditions respectively, and are out of the jurisdiction of the Supreme People's Court.

The court includes over 340 judges which meet in smaller tribunals to decide cases.

Since March 2008, the President of the Supreme People's Court and Chief Grand Justice has been Wang Shengjun (王胜俊).

The SPC trial process consists of a four level, two-hearing system.

History

Procedure

In 2005, the Supreme People's Court announced its intent to "[take] back authority for death penalty approval" over concerns about "sentencing quality", and the National People's Congress officially changed the Organic Law on the People's Courts requiring all death sentences to be approved by the Supreme People's Court on 31 October, 2006. It has been reported that since the new review process, the court has rejected 15 percent of the death sentences decided by lower courts.

Organization

Courts of the SPC:

- criminal
- civil
- economic
- administrative trials
- other courts set up according to actual needs

There are also National Courts with ties to the SPC:

- Military Court
- Maritime Court
- Railway Transportation Court
- Forestry Court

Departments within the SPC:

- research office
- general affairs office
- personnel department
- judicial affairs department
- administrative affairs department
- office affairs bureau
- foreign affairs bureau
- education department

Presidents and Vice Presidents of the Court

1. 1949 - 1954
   - President: Shen Junru
2. 1954 - 1959: 1st National People's Congress
   - President: Dong Biwu
   - Vice Presidents: Gao Kelin, Ma Xiwu, Zhang Zhirang
3. 1959 -1965: 2nd National People's Congress
   - President: Xie Juezai
   - Vice Presidents: Wu Defeng, Wang Weigang, Zhang Zhirang
4. 1965 - 1975: 3rd National People's Congress
   - President: Yang Xiufeng
   - Vice Presidents: Tan Guansan, Wang Weigang, Zeng Hanzhou, He Lanjie, Xing Yimin, Wang Demao, Zhang Zhirang

5. 1975 - 1978: 4th National People's Congress
   - President: Jiang Hua
   - Vice Presidents: Wang Weigang, Zeng Hanzhou, He Lanjie, Zheng Shaowen
6. 1978 - 1983: 5th National People's Congress
   - President: Jiang Hua
   - Vice Presidents: Zeng Hanzhou, He Lanjie, Zheng Shaowen, Song Guang, Wang Huaian, Wang Zhanping
7. 1983 - 1988: 6th National People's Congress
   - President: Zheng Tianxiang
   - Vice Presidents: Ren Jianxin, Song Guang, Wang Huaian, Wang Zhanping, Lin Huai, Zhu Mingshan, Ma Yuan
8. 1988 - 1993: 7th National People's Congress
   - President: Ren Jianxin
   - Vice Presidents: Hua Liankui, Lin Huai, Zhu Mingshan, Ma Yuan, Duan Muzheng
9. 1993 - 1998: 8th National People's Congress
   - President: Ren Jianxin
   - Vice Presidents: Zhu Mingshan, Xie Anshan, Gao Changli, Tang Dehua, Liu Jiachen, Luo Haocai, Li Guoguang, Lin Huai, Hua Liankui, Duan Muzheng, Wang Jingrong, Ma Yuan
10. 1998 - 2003: 9th National People's Congress
    - President: Xiao Yang
    - Vice Presidents: Zhu Mingshan, Li Guoguang, Jiang Xingchang, Shen Deyong, Wan Exiang, Cao Jianming, Zhang Jun, Huang Songyou, Jiang Bixin
11. 2003 - 2007: 10th National People's Congress
    - President: Xiao Yang
    - Vice Presidents: Cao Jianming, Jiang Xingchang, Shen Deyong, Wan Exiang, Huang Songyou, Su Zelin, Xi Xiaoming, Zhang Jun, Xiong Xuanguo
12. 2008 - current: 11th National People's Congress
    - President: Wang Shengjun
    - Vice Presidents:

See also
- Court system of the People's Republic of China
- Supreme People's Procuratorate - the highest legal supervisory body, charged with safeguarding the constitution, laws and people's rights.
- Three Supremes

External links
- The Supreme People's Court of the People's Republic of China [1] Official site.
- Chinacourt [2] English website sponsored by the Supreme People's Court, with court news and legal information including biographical information for the Grand Justices.
- PRC Laws [3] Links to English versions of the Constitution, General Principles of Civil Law, Administrative Procedure Law, Civil and Criminal Procedure Laws, and the Judges Law.
- The Supreme People's Court [4] Court information in English, maintained at People's Daily Online.

The Economic History of China

Economic history of China (pre-1911)

The **economic history of China** stretches over thousands of years and has undergone alternating cycles of prosperity and decline. According to the book 'China and the Knowledege Economy: Seizing the 21st Century', China was for a large part of the last two millennia the world's largest economy, even though its wealth remained average. China's history is usually divided into three periods: The pre-imperial era, consisting of the era of before the unification of Qin, the early imperial era from Qin to Song, and the late imperial era, marked by the economic revolution that occurred during the Song Dynasty.

A Chinese dragon seen floating among clouds, engraved on a golden canteen dated to the 15th century, during the Ming Dynasty (1368–1644 CE)

By roughly 10,000 BCE, in the Neolithic Era, agriculture was practiced in China. Stratified bronze-age cultures, such as Erlitou, emerged by the third millennium BCE. Under the Shang (ca. 1600–1045 BCE) and Zhou (1045–771 BCE), a dependent labor force worked in large-scale foundries and workshops to produce bronzes and silk for the elite. The agricultural surpluses produced by the manorial economy supported these early handicraft industries as well as urban centers and considerable armies. This system began to disintegrate after the collapse of the Western Zhou Dynasty in 771 BCE, preceding the Spring and Autumn and Warring states eras.

As the feudal system collapsed, much legislative power was transferred from the nobility to local kings. A merchant class emerged during the Warring States Period, resulting in increased trade. The new kings established an elaborate bureaucracy, using it to wage wars, build large temples, and perform public works projects. This new system rewarded talent over birthright; important positions were no longer occupied solely by nobility. The adoption of new iron tools revolutionized agriculture and led to a large population increase during this period. By 221 BCE, the state of Qin, which embraced reform more than other states, unified China, built the Great Wall, and set consistent standards of government. Although its draconian laws led to its overthrow in 206 BCE, the Qin institutions survived. During the Han Dynasty, China became a strong, unified, and centralized empire of self-sufficient farmers and artisans, though limited local autonomy remained.

The Song Dynasty (960–1279 CE) brought additional economic reforms. Paper money, the compass, and other technological advances facilitated communication on a large scale and the widespread circulation of books. The state's control of the economy diminished, allowing private merchants to prosper and a large increase in investment and profit. Despite disruptions during the Mongol conquest of 1279, the population much increased under the Ming Dynasty and Qing Dynasty, but its GDP per capita remained static since then. In the later Qing period, China's economic development began to slow and Europe's rapid development since the Late Middle Ages and Renaissance enabled it to surpass again China—an event known as the great divergence.

Pre-Imperial Era (ca. 10,000 – 221 BCE)

By Neolithic times, the tribes living in what is now the Yellow River valley were practicing agriculture. By the third millennium BCE, stratified bronze-age societies had emerged, most notably the Erlitou culture. The Erlitou dominated northern China and is identified with the Xia Dynasty, the first dynasty in traditional Chinese histiography. Erlitou was followed by the Shang and Western Zhou Dynasties, which developed a manorial economy similar to that of medieval Western Europe. By the end of the Spring and Autumn period, this system began to collapse and was replaced by a prosperous economy of self-sufficient farmers and artisans by the Warring States Era. This transformation was completed when the State of Qin unified China in 221 BCE, initiating the imperial era of Chinese history.

The Neolithic and the early Bronze Age

Agriculture began almost 10,000 years ago in several regions of modern-day China. The earliest domesticated crops were millet in the north and rice in the south. Some Neolithic cultures produced textiles with hand-operated spindle-whorls as early as 5000 BCE. The earliest silk remains date to the early third millennium BCE. By the Longshan period (north China, ca. 3000-2000 BCE), a large number of communities with stratified social structures had emerged.

The Erlitou culture (ca. 1900-1350 BCE, named after a representative site in modern Henan) dominated northern China in the early second millennium BCE, when urban societies and bronze casting first appeared in the area. The cowries, tin, jade, and turquoise that were buried in Erlitou suggest that the Erlitou polity traded with many neighbors. A considerable labor force would be required to build the rammed-earth foundations of Erlitou buildings. Although the "highly stratified" Erlitou society has left no writing, some historians have identified Erlitou as a site from the possibly mythical Xia dynasty mentioned in traditional Chinese sources as preceding the Shang.

Only a strong centralized state led by rich elites could have produced the bronzes of the Erligang culture (ca. 1600–1400 BCE or 1500–1300 BCE). The Erligang state, which archaeologist Robert Bagley has called "... the first great civilization of East Asia," interacted with neighboring states, which imported bronzes or the artisans who could cast them. These exchanges allowed the technique of bronze metallurgy to spread to surrounding polities. Some historians have identified Erligang as a Shang site because it corresponds with the area where traditional sources say the Shang were active, but no written source from the time exists to confirm this identification.

The Shang dynasty (ca. 1600 – ca. 1045 BCE)

The first site unequivocally identified with the Shang dynasty by contemporaneous inscriptions is Anyang, a Shang capital that became a major settlement around 1200 BCE. The staple crop of the Shang, a predominantly agricultural society, was millet, but rice and wheat were also cultivated in fields owned by the royal aristocracy. Agricultural surpluses produced by royal fields supported the Shang royal family and ruling elite, advanced handicraft industries (bronze, silk, etc.) and large armies. Large royal pastures provided animals for sacrifices and meat consumption. Other agricultural produce supported the population of Shang, estimated to be about 5.5 to 8 million people.

Since land was only cultivated for a few years before being left fallow, new lands constantly needed to be opened by drainage of low-lying fields or by clearing scrubland or forests. These tasks were performed by corvée labor under state supervision, often in the context of hunting expeditions.

Like their Neolithic predecessors, the Shang used spindle-wheels to make textiles, but the Shang labor force was more formally organized. By Shang times, controlled workers produced silk in workshops for the aristocracy. Fields and workshops were manned by labor of varying degrees of servitude. Some historians have called these dependent workers "slaves" and labelled the Shang a "slave society," but others reject such labels as too vague because we know too little about the nature of this labor force.

The Western Zhou (ca. 1045 – 771 BCE)

By traditional dating, the Zhou Dynasty defeated the Shang around 1045 BCE and took control of the Wei and Yellow River valleys that the Shang had dominated. Land continued to belong to the royal family, which re-distributed it among its dependents in a system that many historians have likened to the feudal organization of medieval Europe. Epigraphic evidence shows that, as early as the late 10th century BCE, land was being traded, though it was not yet considered private property. Edward Shaughnessy hypothesizes that this increase in the land exchanges resulted from the division of elite lineages into branches, increasing demand for land while its supply was diminishing.

The fourth-century book *Mencius* claims that the early Zhou developed the well-field system, a pattern of land occupation in which eight peasant families cultivated fields around a central plot that they farmed for the landlord. The system was named after the Chinese character for "well" (*jing* 井), which resembles the grid-like pattern in which these nine fields were supposedly arranged. Historians have generally doubted the existence of this idealized system, but some maintain that it may have existed informally in the early Zhou, when dependent tenants working on manorial estates paid corvée to their landlords instead of rent, as they would later.

Handicraft industries developed during the Shang, such as textiles, bronze and the production of weapons, were continued during the Zhou, but they were completely state-controlled. The Zhou government also controlled most commerce and exchange through appointing officials whose titles were "Jia", which later came to mean "merchant".

Spring and Autumn period (771–475 BCE)

The collapse of the Zhou initiated the Spring and Autumn Period, named after Confucius' Spring and Autumn Annals. It was a time of war between states, when the Chinese feudal system fell into decline and trade began to flourish. Competition between states led to rapid technological advancement. Iron tools became available, producing agricultural surpluses that led to the collapse of the well-field system. Towards the end of this era, the introduction of iron technology caused the complete collapse of the feudal system and ushered in a new era of development.

During the Spring and Autumn Period, many cities grew in size and population. The prosperous capital of Qi, Linzi had a population estimated at over 200,000 in 650 BCE, becoming one of the largest cities in the world.[citation needed] Alongside other large cities, Qi served as a center of administration, trade, and economic activity. Most of the cities' populations engaged in husbandry and were thus self-sufficient. The growth of these cities was an important development for the ancient Chinese economy.

Large-scale trade began in the Spring and Autumn Period as merchants transported goods between states. Currency was issued en masse to accommodate the new trade. Although some states restricted trade, others encouraged it. Zheng in Central China, promised not to regulate merchants. Zheng merchants became powerful throughout China as they carried goods from Yan in the north to Chu in the south.

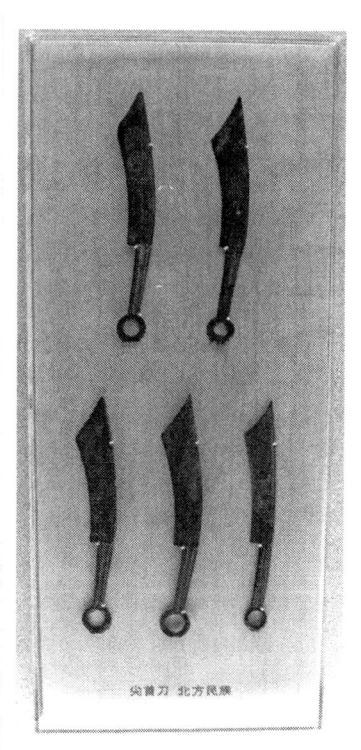

As lords expanded their quantity of plots, the well-field system began to collapse, and this was hastened when the State of Lu changed its taxation system in 594 BCE. Under the new laws, grain producers were taxed upon each mou (A Chinese unit of land measurement about 666 meters squared) cultivated, rather than an equal amount being collected from each noble. As other states followed this example, large estates began to disintegrate, ending the well-field system. Free peasants became the majority of the population and provided a tax base for the emerging centralized state.

Warring States (475–221 BCE)

Bronze knife money from the ancient State of Yan, which was conquered by Qin in 222 BCE

Main article: Warring States Period

The Warring States Period saw rapid technological and philosophical advances. As rulers competed with each other to take control of China's states, they implemented various reforms, greatly changing China's economic system. Iron tools were produced on a massive scale, leading to the disintegration of the feudal system. Common-born landowners and merchants prospered and the aristocracy lost influence. Some merchants, such as Lü Buwei, may have become as wealthy as some states.

Cast iron was invented in China during the 4th century BCE.[citation needed] Although iron tools were manufactured during the Spring and Autumn Period, they became ubiquitous during the Warring States Era after large states began producing iron under government control.[citation needed] Governments, which controlled the large iron smelting works, had a monopoly on military equipment, which strengthened the state at the expense of the feudal lords. Iron agricultural tools allowed a massive increase in surplus farm goods, making the well-field system redundant.

After Shang Yang's reforms in the 3rd Century BCE, land could be bought and sold, stimulating economic progress in agriculture and an increase in productivity. The newly powerful states undertook large-scale irrigation projects, such as the Zhengguo Canal and the Dujiangyan Irrigation System. Thousands of mou of previously desolate land were cultivated and integrated into the Qin economy.

The agricultural boom allowed larger armies. New agricultural techniques were introduced that formed the basis of Chinese agriculture for centuries to come.[citation needed] In the 6th century BCE, among other innovations, the iron plow, row cultivation, and intensive hoeing were introduced. The introduction of oxen in cultivation also began during this period.

In this era, the growing power of the state strengthened the monarchy, allowing it to undertake reforms to strengthen the monarch's authority. The most extensive of these reforms was carried out in Qin by Shang Yang, including the abolition of the feudal nobility, redistribution of nobles' land based on military merit, and allowing private ownership of land by discontinuing the Jintian system. Shang Yang encouraged the cultivation of unsettled lands, gave noble ranks to soldiers who performed well in battle, and established an efficient and strict legal code. Absolute monarchy persisted in China until its gradual weakening under the Song and Ming dynasties.

Early Imperial Era (221 BCE – 960 CE)

The Early imperial era was marked by a strong, unified and centralized monarchy, though local officials still maintained limited autonomy. During the early imperial era, self-sufficient peasant farmers and artisans dominated the economy and largely operated independently of the overall market. Commerce was relatively frequent, increasing after the Han Dynasty with the development of the silk road. Sinologist Joseph Needham has claimed that China's GDP per capita exceeded Europe from the 5th century BCE onwards by a substantial margin,[citation needed] while economic historian Angus Maddison estimates that China's GDP per capita remained below that of Western Europe until the fall of the Roman Empire. The Wu Hu uprising crippled the economy, which did not recover until the Tang, under which it transformed into the mercantile economy of the Song and Ming Dynasties.

Qin Dynasty (221–206 BCE)

In 221 BCE, the State of Qin conquered the remaining states in China, becoming what scholars consider the first unified Chinese state. It quickly expanded, extending the Southern frontier from the Yangtze to modern Vietnam, and the northern frontier to modern Mongolia. While the early Xia, Shang, and Zhou Dynasties had nominal authority over all of China, the feudal system gave most regions a large degree of autonomy. Under the Qin, however, a centralized state was established, and the entire empire had uniform standards and currency to facilitate trade. In addition, the Qin government undertook many public works projects, like the Great Wall of China. The Qin initiated what is considered the "first Chinese empire", which lasted until the Wu Hu uprising.

The Qin emperor unified standards of writing, weight measurement, and wheel length, while abolishing the old currencies, which varied between states. He also issued a uniform code of laws throughout the empire, which made trade easier. Defensive walls between states were demolished because of their disruptive influence upon trade. The Qin Empire did not return to the old feudal system, but set up a system of 36 commandries, each governing a number of counties. Other Qin policies including heavy taxation of salt and iron manufactures, and forced migration of many Chinese towards new territories in the south and west.

The Qin government undertook many public works projects, the workers often being conscripted by the state in order to repay a tax debt. The most famous of these projects is the Great Wall of China, built to defend the state against Xiongnu incursions. Other Qin projects include the Lingqu Canal, which linked subsidiaries of the Yangtze and Pearl rivers and made possible the Qin's southern conquests, as well as an extensive road system estimated at 4250 mi (6840 km).

However, Qin's legalist laws and the heavy burden of its taxes and corvee were not easily accepted by the rest of the empire. Unlike the other states, Qin specifically enacted laws to exile merchants and expropriate their wealth, as well as imposing monopolies on salt, iron, forests and other natural resources. Scholars note that the list of prominent merchants during the Warring States compiled in Sima Qian's Shiji (Grand History) during the Han dynasty does not include a single merchant from Qin. Rebellions occurred soon after the death of the first Qin emperor, and by 206 BCE, the Qin had collapsed.

Han Dynasty (206 BCE – 220 CE)

Main article: Economy of the Han Dynasty

The Han Dynasty is remembered as the first of China's Golden Ages. Emerging from the devastation of the Chu-Han contention, the Han Dynasty rapidly recovered to become one of the most powerful and populous nations on Earth. The Han reached its peak size under Emperor Wu, who subdued the Xiongnu and took control of the Hexi Corridor, opening up the Silk Road. The economy boomed during the Han, who had a registered population of 58 million. Large-scale enterprises emerged, some which were later temporarily nationalized during the Western Han. Technological innovations, such as the wheelbarrow, paper and a seismograph, were invented during this period.

Woven silk textile from Tomb No. 1 at Mawangdui, Changsha, Hunan province, China, dated to the Western Han Dynasty, 2nd century BCE

Government policy under Western Han

The reigns of the Emperors Wen and Jing were a period of peace and prosperity. During their reigns, state control of the economy was minimal, following the Taoist principle of Wu wei (無為), literally meaning "do nothing". As part of their laissez-faire policy, agricultural taxes were reduced from 1/15 of agricultural output to 1/30 and for a brief period, abolished entirely. In addition, the labor corvée required of peasants was reduced from 1 month every year to one month every three years. The minting of coins was privatized.

Both the private and public sectors flourished during this period. Under Emperor Jing,

> ... the ropes used to hang the bags of coins were breaking apart due to the weight, and bags of grain which had been stored for several years were rotting because they had been neglected and not eaten.

Severe criminal punishments, such as cutting off the nose of an offender, were abolished.

The Han taxation system was based on two taxes; a land property tax and a poll tax. The average individual's tax burden consisted of one-thirtieth of the output on land, and a poll tax of 20 coins paid for every person between 7 and 14, with another poll tax for those above 14. Late in the Han Dynasty, the taxation rate for agriculture was reduced to one-hundredth, the lost revenue being made up with increased poll taxes. Merchants were charged at double the individual's rate. Another important component of the taxation system was Corvee labor. Every able-bodied man, defined as a man in good health above 20, was eligible for two years of military service or one month of military service and one year of corvee labor (later those above 56 were exempt from any military or corvee labor service).

Emperor Wu, on the other hand, sparked debate when he intervened into the economy to pay for his wars. His interventions were hotly debated between the Reformists, who were composed mainly of Confucian scholars favoring laissez-faire policies, and the Modernists, a group of government officials who supported the state monopolies on salt and iron and high taxation policies that Emperor Wu had pioneered. These debates were recorded in the book *Discourses on Salt and iron*, an important document showing ancient Chinese economic thought. Although the Modernist policies were followed through most of the Western Han after Emperor Wu, the Reformists repealed these policies in Eastern Han, save for the government monopoly on minting coins.

Developments in industry

In the early Western Han, the wealthiest men in the empire were merchants who produced and distributed salt and iron and gained wealth that rivalled the annual tax revenues collected by the imperial court. These merchants invested in land, becoming great landowners and employing large numbers of peasants. A salt or iron industrialist could employ over one thousand peasants to extract either liquid brine, sea salt, rock salt, or iron ore. Advanced drilling techniques that allowed drilling up to 4800 feet were developed, allowing Chinese to extract salt and even natural gas for use in fuel and lighting.[citation needed]

Emperor Wu of Han (r. 141–87 BCE) viewed such large-scale private industries as a threat to the state, as they drew the peasants' loyalties away from farming and towards the industrialists. Nationalizing the salt and iron trades eliminated this threat and produced large profits for the state. This policy was in line with Emperor Wu's expansionary goals of challenging the nomadic Xiongnu Confederation while colonizing the Hexi Corridor and what is now Xinjiang of Central Asia, Northern Vietnam, Yunnan, and North Korea. Historian Donald Wagner estimates that the production of the Han iron monopoly was roughly around 5,000 tons (assuming 100 tons per iron office), though the true figure was much higher due to illegal private production and growth after the privatization under Later Han.[citation needed]

A pottery dog found in a Han tomb wearing a decorative dog collar; production of ceramic figurines represented a significant part of the funerary industry, which produced goods such as this for a tomb occupant's afterlife.

Although many industrialists were bankrupted by this action, the government drafted former merchants like Sang Hongyang (d. 80 BCE) to administer the national monopolies. Although a political faction in the court succeeded in having the central government monopolies abolished from 44 to 41 BCE, the monopolies resumed until the end of Wang Mang's (r. 9–23 CE) regime. After his overthrow, the central government relinquished control of these industries to private businessmen.

Liquor, another profitable commodity, was also nationalized by the government for a brief period between 98 and 81 BCE. After its return to private ownership, the government imposed heavy taxes on alcohol merchants.

In addition to the state's short-lived monopolies, the government operated a separate sector of handicraft industries intended to supply the needs of the court and army, a practice that was continued throughout Chinese history, though the importance of this sector decreased after the Tang Dynasty.

Light industries such as textiles and pottery also developed substantially during this period. In particular, hand-made pottery was made in large quantities; its price dropped substantially, allowing it to replace the bronze vessels that had been used during the Zhou. Porcelain also emerged during this period.

Developments in Agriculture

Widespread use of iron tools that had begun under the Warring States period allowed Chinese agriculture to increase its efficiency. These include the "two-teeth" plow and an early sickle. The use of cattle-pulled plows improved with the introduction of three-cattle plow which required two operators and the two-cattle plow requiring one. Another important invention was the invention of the horse collar harness, in contrast with the earlier throat harness. This innovation, along with the wheelbarrow, integrated the Chinese economy by drastically decreasing transportation costs and allowing long-distance trade.

The seed drill was also developed during this period, allowing farmers to drill seeds in precise rows, instead of casting them out randomly. During the reign of Emperor Wu of Han, The 'Dai Tian Fa', an early form of crop rotation was introduced. Farmers divided their land into two portions, one of which would be planted, the other being left fallow.

Trade and currency

Sources of revenue used to fund Emperor Wu's military campaigns and colonization efforts included seizures of lands from nobles, the sale of offices and titles, increased commercial taxes, and the issuing of government minting of coins. The central government had previously attempted—and failed—to monopolize coin minting, taking power from the private commandery-level and kingdom-level mints. In 119 BCE the central government introduced the *wushu* (五銖) coin weighing 3.2 g (0.11 oz), and by 113 BCE this became the only legally accepted coin in the empire, the government

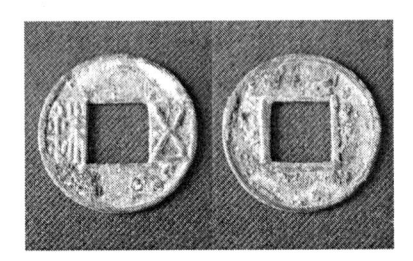

A *wushu* (五銖) coin issued during the reign of Emperor Wu (r. 141–87 BCE), 25.5 mm in diameter

having outlawed private mints. Wang Mang's regime introduced a variety of new, lightweight currencies, including archaic knife money, which devalued coinage. The *wushu* coin was reinstated in 40 CE by the founder of Eastern Han, Emperor Guangwu, and remained the standard coin of China until the Tang Dynasty (618–907 CE).

Trade with foreign nations on a large scale began during the reign of Emperor Wu, when he sent the explorer Zhang Yi to contact nations west of China in search of allies to fight the Xiongnu. After the defeat of the Xiongnu, however, Chinese armies established themselves in Central Asia, starting the famed Silk Road, which became a major avenue of international trade.

Wang Mang and the Later Han

In 8 CE, the Han chancellor Wang Mang usurped the throne of the Han emperors and established his own dynasty, the Xin. Wang Mang wanted to restore the Han to what he believed to be the "idyllic" condition of the early Zhou. He outlawed the trading of land and slaves, and instituted numerous state monopolies. These ultra-modernist policies proved highly unpopular with the population, who overthrew and executed him in 25 CE and restored the Han dynasty.

Under the Later-or Eastern-Han Dynasty, which followed Wang Mang's overthrow, earlier laissez-faire policies were reinstated, and the government abolished conscription and withdrew from managing the economy. A new period of prosperity and intellectual thought, called the Rule of Ming and Zhang, began. This period saw the birth of the great scientist, Zhang Heng, and the invention of paper. However, by the end of the 2nd Century CE, Han society began to disintegrate. In 184 CE, a peasant preacher started a rebellion called the Yellow Turban Rebellion, which ended the Han Dynasty in all but name.

Wei & Jin (220–304 CE)

Also known as the Three kingdoms period, the Wei and Jin eras, which followed the collapse of the Han Dynasty, saw large-scale warfare envelope China for the first time in more than 150 years. The death toll and subsequent economic damage were significant. Powerful aristocratic landowners offered shelter to displaced peasants, using their increased authority to reclaim privileges abolished during the Qin and Han. These refugees were no longer taxable by the state. During the Jin, the taxable population was 20 million; during the Han it had been 57 million. Most of North China was unified by Cao Cao, who founded the Wei Dynasty (220–265 CE), and the Jin reunified the remainder of China in 280 CE. The centralized state weakened after losing the tax revenue of those under the protection of large landowners. Nevertheless, the economy recovered slightly under the policies of Cao Cao, who nationalized abandoned land and ordered peasants to encourage peasants to work on them, as well as re-instituting the hated iron monopoly, which would continue under Jin and the Southern Dynasties. Later, the War of the Eight Princes, which, coupled with the a Jin policy of moving the barbarian Wu Hu into China to alleviate labor shortages caused the eventual fall of China.

Wu Hu (304–420 CE)

See also: Wu Hu uprising

In 304 CE, there was a massive uprising of barbarian clans that were under Chinese control. Following several years of civil war between the various princes of the Jin dynasty, the Xiongnu, led by Liu Yuan, revolted and declared their independence from China. Several other groups under Chinese control subsequently revolted, including the Jie, Qiang, Di, and Xianbei. These groups became collectively known as the Wu Hu, committing genocide against Han Chinese in the Yellow River valley. The collapse of the Jin Empire quickly followed these revolts. The Wu Hu invasion caused large-scale depopulation and the market economy that developed during the Qin, Han, Wei and Jin to declined rapidly, allowing the feudal manorial economy returned to prominence. Large manorial estates were self-sufficient and isolated from the wider market. These estates were self-contained economies that practiced agriculture, herding, forestry, fishing, and the production of handicraft goods. Exchange was no longer carried out through money, but barter. Following the economic revival after the unification of the Sui, the manorial economy again declined.

A brief economic recovery occurred in the North under Fú Jiān, the Di ruler of Former Qin, who reunified North China. Fu Jian repaired irrigation projects constructed under Han and Jin, and set up hotels and stations for traders every 20 kilometers. Under Fu Jian's rule, trade and agriculture were significantly revived, and many nations again sent tribute to Fu Jian's court. This recovery ended when Fu Jian was defeated at the battle of Fei by Jin forces, causing his empire to collapse into a series of small states. This battle is considered one of the most important in Chinese history because it preserved Chinese civilization from the danger of destruction.

Meanwhile, the legitimate Jin dynasty had fled to the south, then an undeveloped periphery of the Chinese Empire. Jin rulers attempted to develop this region as a center of rule and as a base for the reconquest of their homeland. Jin rulers granted large tracts of land in the south to Chinese immigrants and landowners fleeing barbarian rule, who preserved the system of government that was in place before the uprising. The migration of northern people stimulated the southern economy, allowing it to rival the northern economy. Improved agricultural techniques introduced to the south increased production and a market economy survived as Jin rulers enforced laws. The improvement of the southern economy can be seen later when it financed Liu Yu's expeditions to recover Sichuan and most of the Chinese heartland from the barbarian states of the north.

Southern and Northern Dynasties (420–581 CE)

The Southern and Northern Dynasties, despite constant war, largely recovered from the Wu Hu uprising. The early part of the era saw the greater part of China reunified by the native Liu Song Dynasty, whose northern border extended to the Yellow River. The Liu Song founder and general, Liu Yu, reclaimed much of China's heartland, conquering most of the states that the Wu Hu had established in the 4th century CE, excluding the Xianbei state of Northern Wei. Under his son, China witnessed a brief period of prosperity during the Yuanjia era. However, a later Xianbei invasion once more confined the Chinese dynasties to the territories south of the Huai River. Henceforth, China was divided into the Northern and Southern dynasties, which developed separately; the north prospering under a new equal-field system, while the southern economy continued to develop in the fashion of Wei and Jin. In 589 CE, the Sui Dynasty restored native rule to northern China and reunified the country.

The Yuanjia era and development in the South

The Yuanjia era, inaugurated by Liu Yu and his son, Wen Ti, was a period of prosperous rule and economic growth, despite ongoing war. Emperor Wen Ti was known for his frugal administration and his concern with the welfare of the people. Although he lacked the martial power of his father, he was an excellent economic manager. He reduced taxes and levies on peasants and encouraged them to settle in areas that had been reconquered by his father. He reduced the power of wealthy landowners and increased the taxable population. He also enacted a system of reviewing the performance of civil servants. As a result of his policies, China experienced an era of prosperity and economic recovery.

A limestone statue of the Bodhisattva, from the Northern Qi Dynasty, 570 AD, made in what is now modern Henan province.

During the Yuanjia era, the Chinese developed the co-fusion process of steel manufacturing, which involved melting cast iron and wrought iron together to create steel, increasing the quality and production volume of Chinese iron.[citation needed]

Towards the end of Wen Ti's reign, the Xianbei state of Northern Wei began to strengthen, and decisively defeated an attempt by Wen Ti to destroy it. Following this victory, Wei launched repeated incursions into the northern provinces, finally capturing them in 468 CE.

The economic prosperity of southern China continued after Liu Song's fall and was greatest during the succeeding Liang Dynasty, which briefly reconquered the North with 7,000 troops under the command of general Chen Qingzhi. The Liang emperor, Wu Ti, gave a grant of 400 million coins to Buddhist monasteries, indicating the amount of wealth present in the south. It was recorded that during his reign, the city of Nanjing had a population of up to 1.4 million, exceeding that of Han-era Luoyang. The Southern Dynasties' economy eventually declined after the disastrous sacking of Nanjing by the barbarian general Hou Jin.

Sinification and division in the North

After the Xianbei conquest of Northern China, it experienced an economic recovery under the Northern Wei that was even greater than the prosperous era of Yuanjia. This came mostly under the rule of Emperor Xiaowen of Northern Wei, who introduced several reforms designed to further sinify Northern Wei, which included banning the Xianbei language and customs and promoting Chinese law, language and surnames. A new agricultural system was introduced; in the equal-field system, the state rented land to the peasant laborers for life, reclaiming it after the tenant's death. Peasants also received smaller, private plots that could be inherited. Cattle and farm tools were also rented or sold to peasants.

The state also introduced the Fubing system, where soldiers would farm as well as undergoing military training. This military system was used until the Tang Dynasty, and empowered Han Chinese, who comprised the majority of the army. In addition, Xiaowen strengthened the state's control over the provinces by appointing local officials rather than relying on local landowners, and paying officials with regular salaries. The capital was moved to Luoyang, in the center of the North China Plain, which revitalized the city and the surrounding provinces. Xiaowen's reforms were very successful and lead to prosperity for north China. Under Emperor Xiaowen, the taxable population was an estimated 30 million, which surpassed that under the Jin.

After Xiaowen's rule, Northern Wei's economy began to deteriorate, and famines and droughts undermined Wei rule. From 523 CE onwards, conservative Xianbei noblemen dominated the north and reversed much of Xiaowen's reforms, setting up their own regimes and warring against each other. It was not until 577 that North China was again reunited by Northern Zhou, which was soon usurped by Han Chinese Yang Jian, who restored native rule over North China.

Sui Dynasty (581–618 CE)

The Sui Dynasty was established over the Northern Zhou, whose throne was usurped by Yang Jian in 581 CE. Yang Jian quickly enacted a series of policies to restore China's economy. His reunification of China marked the creation of what some historians call the 'Second Chinese Empire', spanning the Sui, T'ang and Northern Song dynasties. Despite its brevity, the Sui reunified China, and its laws and administration formed the basis of the later Tang, Song and Ming dynasties. The Sui Dynasty had a population of about 45 million at its peak.

One of Yang Jian (or Sui Wen Ti)'s first priorities was the reunification of China. Chen, which ruled the south, was weak compared to Sui and its ruler was incompetent and pleasure-loving. South China also had a smaller population than the north. After eight years of preparation, Sui armies marched on and defeated Chen in 589 CE, reunifying China and prompting a recovery in the Chinese economy. The registered population increased by fifty percent from 30 to 46 million in twenty years. To encourage economic growth, the Sui government issued a new currency to replace those issued by its predecessors, Northern Zhou and Chen. They also encouraged foreign merchants to travel to China and import goods, and built numerous hotels to house them.

The Sui continued to use the equal-field system introduced by Northern Wei. Every able-bodied male received 40 mou of freehold land and a lifetime lease of 80 mou of land, which was returned to the state when the recipient died. Even women could received a lifetime lease of 40 mou of land which was returned to the state upon her death. The Sui government charged three "Shi" of grain each year. Peasants were required to perform 20 days of labor for the state per year, but those over 50 could instead pay a small fee.

In 604 CE, Wen Ti was assassinated by his son Yang Guang, who became Yang Ti of Sui. Yang Ti was an ambitious ruler who immediately undertook many projects, including the building of the Grand Canal and the reconstruction of the Great Wall. Thousands of forced laborers died while building the projects, and eventually women were required to labor in the absence of men. Sui Yang Ti also launched a series of unsuccessful campaigns against Goguryeo. These campaigns negatively impacted the image of the dynasty, while his policies drove the people to revolt. Agrarian uprisings and raids by the Gokturks became common. In 618 CE, Yang Ti was assassinated and the Sui Dynasty ended.

Tang dynasty (618–907 CE)

The Tang Dynasty was another golden age, beginning in the ruins of the Sui. By 630, the Tang had conquered the powerful Gokturk Khagnate, preventing threats to China's borders for more than a century. A series of strong and efficient rulers, beginning with the founder and including a woman, expanded the Tang Empire to the point that it rivaled the later Yuan, Ming and Qing. The Tang was a period of rapid economic growth and prosperity, seeing the beginnings of woodblock printing. Tang rulers issued large amounts of currency to facilitate trade and distributed land under the equal-field system. The population recovered to and then surpassed Han levels, reaching an estimated 80 million.[citation needed] Although the state weakened after the disastrous An Shi Rebellion, and withdrew from managing the economy in the 9th century, this withdrawal encouraged economic growth and helped China's economy to develop into the mercantile economy of the Song and Ming Dynasties.

A Tang-era Chinese *sancai*-glazed Bactrian Camel ridden by a bearded merchant from Persia; camels were the key pack animals used in the Silk Road trade.

Economic development before the An Shi Rebellion

Emperor Taizong of Tang, the second ruler of the Tang Dynasty, is regarded as one of the greatest rulers in Chinese history. Under his rule, China progressed rapidly from the ruins of a civil war to a prosperous and powerful nation. His reign is called the Zhenkuan era. Taizong reduced conscript labor requirements and lowered taxes; in addition, he was careful to avoid undertaking projects that might deplete the treasury and exhaust the strength of the population. Under his reign, a legal code called the Code of Tang was introduced, moderating the laws of the Sui.

During Taizong's reign and until the An Shi Rebellion, the Chinese Empire went through a relatively peaceful period of economic development. Taizong and his son's conquest of the Gokturk, Xueyantue, Gorguryeo and other enemy empires ensured relative peace for China. Control over the western provinces of China reopened the Silk Road, allowing trade between China and the regions to its west to flourish. Tang armies repeatedly intervened in the western regions to preserve this state of peace and prosperity.

The equal-field system did not allow large land transactions and thus during the early Tang estates remained small. The Tang government managed the economy through the bureaucratic regulation of markets, limiting the times where they could exchange goods, setting standards for product quality, and regulating prices of produce.

During the Tang, the taxation system was based on the equal-field system, which equalized wealth among the farmers. The tax burden of peasants was based on population per household, rather than the value of property. The standard tax amounted to 2 tan (about 100 litres) of grain, as well as 2 Zhang (around 3 1/3 meters) and 5 Chi (about 1/3 of a meter) of cloth. The peasant was eligible for 20 days' conscripted labor; if he defaulted he was obliged to pay 3 Chi of cloth per day missed. Assuming each farmer had 30 mou of land which produced 1 tan of grain a year, the tax rate amounted to 25% of the farmer's income. Commercial taxes were lighter, at 3.3% of income.

The Tang government operated a huge handicraft industry, separate from the private handicraft industry that served the majority of the population. The public handicraft industry provided the Tang government, army and nobility with various products. The government's handicraft industries retarded the growth of the private sector which did not develop rapidly until after the Anshi Rebellion, when the Tang government's interference in the economy (and the size of its government handicraft industries) drastically decreased. Despite this, a large number of households worked in private industry; scholars have estimated that 10% of Tang China's population lived in cities.

The height of Tang prosperity came during the Kaiyuan Era of Emperor Xuanzong of Tang, who expanded Tang influence westward to the Aral Sea. Emperor Xuan was a capable administrator, and his Kaiyuan Era is often compared with the earlier Zhenkuan era in efficiency of administration. After this era, the Tang Dynasty started to decline.

Economic development after the An Shi Rebellion

Emperor Xuanzong's reign ended with the Arab victory at Talas and the An Shi Rebellion, the first war inside China in over 120 years, lead by a barbarian general named An Lushan who used a large number of barbarian troops. The Tang economy was devastated as the northern regions, the mainstay of economic activity, were destroyed. The cities of Luoyang and Chang'an were reduced to ruins. After the war, the Tang central government never recovered its former power, and local generals became independent of Tang rule. These generals wielded enormous power, passed on their titles by heredity,

Beauties Wearing Flowers, by Zhou Fang, 8th century

collected taxes, and raised their own armies. Although most of these jiedushi were quelled by the early 9th century, the jiedushi of Hebei, many of them former officers of An Lushan, retained their independence.

The weakened Tang government was forced to abolish many of its regulations and interventions after the rebellion; this unintentionally stimulated trade and commerce in Tang China, which reached an apogee in the early 9th century. The economic center of China shifted southwards because the north had been devastated.

The equal-field system, which had formed the basis of agriculture for the past two and a half centuries, began to collapse after the An Shi Rebellion. The equal-field system had relied on the state having large amounts of land, but state landholdings had decreased as they were privatized or granted to peasants. Landowners perpetually enlarging their estates exacerbated the collapse. The Fubing system, in which soldiers served the army and farmed on equal-field land was abolished and replaced with the Mubing system, which relied on a volunteer and standing army. In 780 CE, the Tang government discontinued the equal field system and reorganized the tax system, collecting taxes based on property value twice a year, in spring and autumn.

Woodblock printing began to develop during the 8th and 9th centuries. This grew out of the huge paper industry that had emerged since the Han. Woodblock printing allowed the rapid production of many books, and increased the speed at which knowledge spread. The first book to be printed in this manner, with a production date, was the *Jin Gang Jin*, a Buddhist text printed in 868 CE, but the hand-copying of manuscripts still remained much more important for centuries to come. ntil During the latter era of the Tang Dynasty, overseas trade also began with East Africa, India, and the Middle East.[citation needed]

Although the economy recovered during the 9th century, the central government was weakened. The most pressing issue was government's salt monopoly, which raised revenue after the equal-field system collapsed and the government could no longer collect land tax effectively. After the An Shi Rebellion, the Tang government monopolized salt to raise revenue; it soon accounted for over half the central government's revenues. During the reign of emperors Shi and Yi, private salt traders were executed, and the price of salt was so high that many people could not afford it. Eventually, private salt traders allied and rebelled against the Tang army. This rebellion, known as the Huang Chao Rebellion, lasted ten years and destroyed the countryside from Guangzhou to Chang'an. Following the rebellion, two generals, the Shatuo Li Keqiang and the former rebel Zhu Wen, dominated the Tang court. Civil war broke out again in the early 10th century, ending with Zhu Wen's victory. Following his victory, Zhu Wen forced the Tang emperor to abdicate, and the Tang empire disintegrated into a group of states known as the Five Dynasties and Ten Kingdoms.

Five Dynasties & Ten kingdoms (907–960 CE)

The Five Dynasties and Ten Kingdoms was a period of warfare and disruption. After 907 CE, the Tang government effectively disintegrated into several small states in the south, while the north saw a series of short-lived dynasties and barbarian invasions. A key event of the era was the conquest of North China by the Shatuo Turks. During their rule, the Shatuo gave the vital Sixteen Prefectures area, containing the natural geographical defenses of North China and the eastern section of the Great Wall, to the Khitan, another barbarian people. This effectively left Northern China defenseless against incursions from the north, a major factor in the later fall of the Song Dynasty. The Shatuo and Khitan invasions severely disrupted economic activity in the north and displaced economic activity southwards, and native Chinese rule was not restored until the Later Zhou dynasty, the Song's precursor.

The southern provinces remained relatively unaffected by the collapse. The Five Dynasties and Ten Kingdoms period was largely one of continued prosperity in these regions.

Late Imperial Era (960–1911 CE)

In 960 CE, Zhao Kuangyi led a coup which established the sixth dynasty in fifty years. The Song Dynasty saw a steep economic rise of China. The Late Imperial Era, encouraged by technological advancement, saw the beginnings of large-scale enterprise, waged labor and the issuing of paper money. The economy underwent large increases in manufacturing output. Overseas trade flourished under the Ming Dynasty. Investment, capital, and commerce were liberalized as technology advanced and the central state weakened. Government manufacturing industries were privatized. The emergence of rural and urban markets, where production was geared towards consumption, was a key development in this era. China's growing wealth in this era lead to the loss of martial vigor; the era involved two periods of native rule, each followed by periods of alien rule. By the end of the isolationist Manchu Qing Dynasty (1662–1911 CE), China's development slowed, falling behind that of the west.

Chinese coins from the Tang to the Qing dynasties

Song Dynasty (960–1279 CE)

Main article: Economy of the Song Dynasty

In 960 CE, the Later Zhou general Zhao Kuanyi overthrew his imperial master and established a the Song Dynasty, the sixth in fifty-three years. Nineteen years later, he had reunified most of China. This was one of the most prosperous periods in Chinese history. Unlike its predecessors, the monarchy and aristocracy weakened under the Song, allowing a class of non-aristocratic gentry to gain power. The central government withdrew from managing the economy (except during Wang Anshi's chancellorship and the Southern Song), provoking drastic economic changes. Technological advances encouraged growth; the so-called Four Great Inventions: gunpowder, woodblock printing, and the compass, were invented or perfected during this era. The population rose to more than 100 million during the Song period. However, the Song eventually became the first unified Chinese dynasty to be completely conquered by invaders.

Developments in industry

During the 11th century, China developed sophisticated technologies to extract and use coal for energy, leading to soaring iron production. Iron production rose fivefold from 800 to 1078, to about 125,000 English tons (114,000 metric tons), not counting unregistered iron production. Initially, the government restricted the iron industry, but the restrictions on private smelting was lifted after the prominent official Bao Qingtian's petition to the government Production of other metals also soared; officially registered Song production of silver, bronze, tin, and lead increased to 3, 23, 54, and 49 times that of

Tang levels. Officially registered Salt production also rose at least 57%.

The government regulated several other industries. Sulfur, an ingredient in gunpowder - a crucial new weapon introduced during the Tang - became a growth industry, and in 1076 was placed under government control. In Sichuan province, revenue from the Song government's monopoly on tea was used to purchase horses for the Song's cavalry forces. Chancellor Wang Anshi instated monopolies in several industries, sparking controversy.

In order to supply the boom in the iron and other industries, the output of mines increased massively. Near Bianjing, the Song capital, according to one estimate over one million households were using coal for heating, an indication of the magnitude of coal use. Light industries also began to prosper during the Song, including porcelain – which replaced pottery – shipbuilding and textiles. Compared with the Tang, textile production increased 55%. The historian Xie Qia estimates that over 100,000 households were working in textile production by Song times, an indicator of the magnitude of the Song textile industry. The urbanization rate of the Song increased to 12%, compared with 10% during the Tang.

Developments in agriculture

Agriculture advanced greatly under the Song. The Song government started a series of irrigation projects that increased cultivatable land, and encouraged peasants to cultivate more land. The total area of cultivated land was greatly increased to 720 million mou, a figure unsurpassed by later dynasties. A variety of crops were cultivated, unlike the monocultures of previous dynasties. Specialized crops like oranges and sugar cane were regularly planted alongside rice. Unlike the earlier self-sufficient peasantry of the Han and Tang eras, rural families produced a surplus which could be sold. The income allowed families to afford not only food, but charcoal, tea, oil, and wine. Many Song peasants supplemented their incomes with handicraft work.

New tools, like the Water Wheel, greatly enhanced productivity. Although most peasants in China were still primarily rice farmers, some farmers specialized in certain crops. For example, Luoyang was known for its flower cultivation; flower prices reached such exorbitant prices that one bulb reached the price of 10,000 coins. An important new crop introduced during the Song was Champa rice, a new breed which had superior yields to earlier forms of rice and greatly increased rice production. The practice of multiple cropping, which increased yields by allowed farmers to harvest rice twice a year, was a key innovation of the Song era. Per-mou agricultural output doubled for South China, while increasing only slightly in the north. Scholars offer "conservative estimates" which suggest that agricultural yields rose at least 20% during the Song. Other scholars note that although taxable land rose only 5% during the Song, the actual amount of grain revenues taken in increased by 46%.

Agricultural organization also changed. Unlike the Han and Tang, in which agriculture was dominated by self-sufficient farmers, or the pre-Warring states era and era of division (period between Han and Tang), which was dominated by aristocratic landowners, during the Song agriculture was dominated by non-aristocratic landowners. The majority of farmers no longer owned their land; they became tenants of these landowners, who developed the rural economy through investment. This system of agriculture was to continue until the establishment of the People's Republic of China under Mao.

Developments in Commerce

During the Song Dynasty, the merchant class became more sophisticated, well-respected, and organized. The accumulated wealth of the merchant class often rivaled that of the scholar-officials who administered the affairs of government. For their organizational skills, Ebrey, Walthall, and Palais state that Song Dynasty merchants:

> ... set up partnerships and joint stock companies, with a separation of owners (shareholders) and managers. In large cities, merchants were organized into guilds according to the type of product sold; they periodically set prices and arranged sales from wholesalers to shop owners. When the government requisitioned goods or assessed taxes, it dealt with the guild heads.

Unfortunately, like their counterparts in Europe, these guilds restricted economic growth through collaboration with government to restrict competition.

Large privately-owned enterprises dominated the market system of urban Song China. There was a large black market, which grew after the Jur'chen conquest of North China in 1127 CE. Around 1160 CE, black marketeers smuggled some 70 to 80 thousand cattle.

There were many successful small kilns and pottery shops owned by local families, along with oil presses, wine-making shops, and paper-making businesses. The "... inn keeper, the petty diviner, the drug seller, the cloth trader," also experienced increased economic success.

Song abolition of trade restrictions greatly aided the economy. Commerce increased in frequency and could be conducted anywhere, in contrast to earlier periods where trade was restricted to the 'Fang' and 'Shi' areas. In all the major cities of the Song Dynasty, many shops opened. Often, shops selling the same product were concentrated into one urban area. For example, all the rice shops would occupy one street, and all the fish shops another. Unlike the later Ming Dynasty, most businesses during the Song Dynasty were producers and retailers, selling the products they produced, thus creating a mixture of handicraft and commerce. Although the Song Dynasty saw some large enterprises, the majority of enterprises were small.

Overseas commerce also prospered with the invention of the compass and the encouragement of Song rulers. Developments in shipping and navigation technologies allowed trade and investment on a large scale. The Song-era Chinese could conduct large amounts of overseas trade, bringing some merchants great fortune. Song-era commercial enterprises became very complex. The accumulated wealth of merchants often rivalled that of the scholar-officials who administered the affairs of government.

Developments in currency

The prosperous Song economy resulted in an increase in the minting of currency. By 1085 CE, the output of copper currency reached 6 billion coins a year, compared to 5.86 billion in 1080 CE. 327 million coins were minted annually in the Tang Dynasty's prosperous Tianbao period of 742–755 CE, and only 220 million coins minted annually from 118 BCE to 5 CE during the Han Dynasty.

Paper receipts of deposit first appeared in the 10th century, but the first officially sponsored bills were introduced in Sichuan Province, where the currency was metallic and extremely heavy. Although businesses began to issue private bills of exchange, by the mid-11th century the central government introduced its paper money, produced using woodblock printing and backed by bronze coins. The Song government had also been amassing large amounts of paper tribute. Each year before 1101 CE, the prefecture of Xinan (modern Xi-xian, Anhui) alone sent 1,500,000 sheets of paper in seven different varieties to the capital at Kaifeng. In the Southern Song, standard currency bearing a marked face value, was used. However, a lack of standards caused face values to wildly fluctuate. A nationwide standard paper currency was not produced until 1274 CE, two years before the Southern Song's fall.

Jiaozhi, the world's first paper money. It was introduced during the Song Dynasty

Song fiscal administration

The Song government instituted a taxation system on agriculture in which a property value tax was collected twice every year, amounting to roughly 10% of income. However, the actual level was higher due to numerous surcharges. Commercial taxes were around 2%. In an important change from Tang practices, however, the Song did not attempt to regulate prices and markets, with the exception of the time of Wang Anshi, though it also instituted an indirect monopoly in salt, in which merchants had to deliever grain to the state before being allowed to sell salt.

In 1069 CE, Wang Anshi, whose ideas were similar to the modern welfare state, became chancellor. Believing that the state must provide for the people, and pressed by the need for revenues to wage an irrentist war against the Xi Xia and Liao, he initiated a series of reforms. These reforms included nationalizing industries such as tea, salt and liquor, and adopting a policy of directly transporting goods in abundance in one region to another, which Wang believed would eliminate the need for merchants. Other policies included a rural credit program for peasants, the replacement of corvee labor with a tax, lending peasants military horses for use in peacetime, compulsory military training for civilians, and a "market exchange bureau" to set prices. These policies were extremely controversial, especially to Orthodox Confucians who favored laissez faire, and were largely repealed after Wang Anshi's death, except during the reign of Emperor Huizong.

A second, more serious attempt to intervene in the economy occurred in the late 13th century CE, when the Song Dynasty suffered from fiscal problems while trying to defend themselves against Mongol invasions. The Song chancellnor Jia Sidao attempted to solve the problem through land nationalization, a policy that was heavily opposed and later withdrawn.

Fall of the Song

The prosperity of the Song was interrupted by the invasion of Jur'chen Jin in 1127 CE. After a successful alliance with the Jin in which the Song destroyed its old enemy the Khitan, the Jin attacked the Song and sacked its capital in Kaifeng. The invasion preceded 15 years of constant warfare which ended when the Song court surrendered territory north of the Huai River in exchange for peace, despite victories by the Song general Yue Fei, who had almost defeated the Jur'chens. The southern Chinese provinces became the center of commerce. Millions of Chinese fled Jur'chen rule to the South, which the Song Dynasty still held.

Due to the new military pressure of the Jur'chens, the Southern Song massively increased the tax burden to several times of that of the Northern Song. The Southern Song maintained an uneasy truce with the Jin until the rise of the Mongols, with whom Song allied to destroy the Jin in 1234 CE. Taking advantage of this, the Song army briefly recaptured their lost territory south of the Yellow River as the Mongols withdrew. However, a flood of the Yellow River, coupled with Mongol attacks, eventually forced the Song to withdraw.

Seeking to conquer China, the Mongol Empire launched a series of attacks on the Song. By the 1270s, the Song economy had collapsed from the burden of taxes and inflation which the Song government used to finance its war against the Mongols. In 1275 CE, helped by Frankish counterweight trebuchets designed by Muslim engineers, the Mongols defeated the Song army near Xiangyang and captured Hangzhou, the Song capital, the following year. Song resistance ended at the Battle of Yamen, in which the last Song emperor drowned with the remnants of his navy. The destruction caused by the barbarian invasions in the later half of the Song represented a major setback in China's development.

Yuan (Mongol) Dynasty (1279–1368 CE)

The Mongol Yuan Dynasty was the first foreign dynasty to rule the whole of China. As the largest khanate in the Mongol Empire, the emperors of Yuan had nominal authority over the other three Mongol Empires. This period of Pax Mongolica stimulated trade. However, millions of Chinese died because of the Mongol conquest. Under Mongol rule, approximately 65 million people were registered in 1290 CE; in 1215 CE, the dynasties of Jur'chen Jin and Song had registered populations of between 110 and 120 million. In addition, the Mongol government imposed high taxes and extensively nationalized major sectors of the economy, greatly damaging what was left of China's economic development.

A set of waterwheels used to operate a blast furnace producing iron, an illustration from the *Nong Shu* (農書) published by the official Wang Zhen in 1313 CE

In their conquest of China, particularly the north under Jur'chen Jin, the Mongols resorted to scorched earth policies, destroying entire provinces. Mongol forces carried out massacres in cities they captured, and one Khan proposed that all Chinese under Mongol rule be killed and their lands turned to pasture, but was persuaded against this by his minister Yelu Chucai, who proposed that taxing the region's inhabitants was more advantageous than killing them.

Kublai Khan, after becoming ruler of China, extended the Grand Canal, connecting the Yellow and Yangtze rivers, to the capital, Beijing. This eased transportation between the south, now the hub of economic activity, and Beijing. This enhanced Beijing's status, it having formerly been a peripheral city, and was important to later regimes' decisions to have it remain the capital.

Kublai and his fellow rulers encouraged trade between China and other Khanates of the Mongol Empire. During this era, trade between China and the Middle East increased, and many Arabs, Persians, and other foreigners entered China, some permanently immigrating. It was during this period that Marco Polo visited China. Although Kublai Khan wished to identify with his Chinese subjects, Mongol rule was strict and foreign to the Chinese. Civil service examinations, the traditional way that Chinese elites entered the government, was ended, and most government positions were held by non-Chinese, especially the financial administration of the state. Over-spending by Kublai and his successor caused them to resorted to high taxes and extensive state monopolization of major sectors of the economy to fund their extravagant spending and military campaigns, which became a major burden on the Chinese economy. State monopolies were instituted in salt, iron, sugar, porcelain, tea, vinegar, alcohol and other industries. The most controversial of Kublai's policies, however, was opening the tombs of the Song emperors to gain treasure for the treasury, and issuing large amounts of money which caused hyperinflation. These policies greatly conflicted with Confucian ideals of frugal government and light taxation. As a result of Kublai's policies, and the discrimination of the Mongols towards the Chinese, South China was beset by violent insurrections against Mongol rule. Many Chinese refused to serve or associate themselves with the Yuan administration, who they viewed as barbarian despots.

During the 1340s CE, frequent famines, droughts, and plagues encouraged unrest among the Chinese. In 1341 CE, a peasant rebel leader, who claimed he was the descendant of the Song Emperor Huizong, sought to restore the Song by driving out the Mongols. By 1351 CE, much of South China was free of Mongol rule and had been divided into regional states, such as Zhu Yuanzhang's Ming, Zhang Shichen's Wu and Chen Yolian's Han. In the north, the Mongol Empire became divided between regional warlords who were only nominally loyal to the Yuan. In 1368 CE, after reunifying South China, the Ming Dynasty advanced northward and captured Beijing, ending the Yuan.

Ming Dynasty (1368–1662 CE)

Main article: Economy of the Ming Dynasty

Following the ruin of the Mongol Empire, the peasant Zhu Yuanzhang led a rebellion against Mongol rule. He founded the Ming Dynasty, whose reign is considered the last of China's three Golden Ages. Private industries replaced those managed by the state. Vibrant foreign trade allowed contact to become established between East and West. Cash crops were more frequently grown, specialized industries were founded, and the economic growth caused by privatization of state industries resulted in one of the most prosperous periods in Chinese history, exceeding that of the earlier Song Dynasty.

The Ming was also a period of technological progress, though less so than the earlier Song. Ming China had a population of almost 200 million.

Recovery under Hongwu and Yongle

Zhu Yuanzhang, also called the Hongwu Emperor, was born of a peasant family and was sympathetic towards peasants. Zhu enacted a series of policies designed to favor agriculture at the expense of other industries. The

Portrait of the Hongwu Emperor (r. 1368–1398)

state gave aid to farmers, providing land and agricultural equipment and revising the taxation system. The state also repaired many long-neglected canals and dikes that had aided agriculture. In addition, the Ming Dynasty reinstated the examination system.

Hongwu's successor and grandson, the Jianwen Emperor, was overthrown by his uncle, Zhu Di, called the Yongle Emperor, in a bloody civil war that lasted three years. Zhu Di was more liberally-minded than his father and he repealed many of the controls on gentry and merchants. Thus, his reign is sometimes regarded as a 'second founding' of the Ming Dynasty. The expeditions of his eunuch Zheng He created new trade routes. Under Yongle's rule, Ming armies enjoyed continued victories against the Mongols, who were forced to acknowledge him as their ruler. He also moved the capital to Beijing. By Yongle's reign, China had recovered the territories of Eastern Xinjiang, Manchuria, Tibet, and those lost during the Five Dynasties and Ten Kingdoms Era.

The Ming fiscal administration

The Ming government has been described as "... one of the greatest achievements of Chinese civilization". Although it began as a despotic regime, the Ming government evolved into a system of power-sharing between the emperor and the civil service.

The Ming government collected far fewer revenues than the Song Dynasty. Regional tax quotas set up by the Ming emperor Tai-Tzu would be collected, though in practice Ming revenues were markedly lower than the quotas declared. The gentry class won concessions from the government and resisted tax increases. Throughout the Ming Dynasty, the state was constantly underfunded. Unlike earlier dynasties such as the Tang and Song, and later dynasties such as the Qing, the Ming did not regulate the economy, but had a laissez-faire policy similar to that of the Han Dynasty. The Cambridge history of China volume on the Ming Dynasty stated that:

> Ming government allowed those Chinese people who could attain more than mere subsistence to employ their resources mostly for the uses freely chosen by them, for it was a government that, by comparison with others throughout the world then and later, taxed the people at very low levels and left most of the wealth generated by its productive people in the regions where that wealth was produced.

Key Ming taxes included the land tax (21 million taels), the service levy (direct requisitioning of labor services and goods from civilians, valued at about 10 million taels), and the revenue from the Ming salt monopoly (2 million taels). Other miscellaneous sources of revenue included the inland customs duty (343,729 taels), sale of rank (500,000 taels), licensing fees for monks (200,000 taels), and fines (300,000 taels) and others, which all added up to about 4 million taels. The overall Ming tax rate was very low, at around 3 to 4%. However, by the end of the dynasty, this situation had changed dramatically. Zhang Juzheng instituted the one whip reform, in which the arbitrary service levy was merged into the land tax. The Ming government's salt monopoly was undermined by private sellers, and had collapsed completely by the 15th century; government officials estimated that three-quarters of salt produced was being sold privately.

Developments in Commerce and currency

The Ming's overseas trade began when Zhu Di launched extensive expeditions to southern India and Africa, increasing China's contacts in those areas and establishing state-regulated trade there.

The Ming government often intervened in foreign trade. Under the reigns of Emperors Hongwu, Yongle and Jiajing, foreign trade by private merchants was prohibited completely. Merchants became discontent and engaged in an illegal trade network, which the Ming state could not curtail. Merchants pressured the government repeatedly to lift the prohibition, or to at least ignore it. In 1567 CE, the Hai Jin, or prohibition on overseas trade, was lifted completely, and an extensive expansion of trade followed, with only trade to nations at war with China prohibited. This trade was estimated by Joseph Needham at about 300 million taels from 1567 CE to 1644 CE.[*citation needed*] At that time, Twitchett claims that China, apart from being a lucrative market for Europeans, was the largest and wealthiest nation on Earth, although the economic historian Angus Maddison estimates its GDP per capita to correspond to the Asian average and lower than Europe's. One of the most important parts of this trade was the importation of silver.

A porcelain jar from the reign of the Jiajing Emperor (r. 1521–1567 CE); Chinese export porcelain in the late Ming targeted foreign markets such as those in Europe.

Initially, Hongwu issued paper fiat currency as the standard currency, while private providers issued currency based on metals. Eventually, the state stopped issuing currency because the population lost faith in the fiat paper, which was frequently inflated by Hongwu. By 1425 CE, paper currency was worth approximately 0.014% of its original value. Although the Ming government attempted to stop the inflow of silver, it proved too profitable to halt. Overseas trade brought great prosperity to China, as Japanese and European importers paid for Chinese products with silver, thus monetizing China's economy. The demand for silver was so great that it overwhelmed the earlier paper currency used by the Ming, and silver soon became the common medium of exchange.

In the mid-15th century, a severe decline in the production of silver caused a severe monetary contraction and forced the Ming economy to operate under a monetary constraint, where even counterfeiters' supply of metal decreased.

Developments in industry

After 1400, Ming China's economic recovery led to high economic growth and the revival of heavy industries such as coal and iron. Industrial output reached new heights surpassing that of the Song. Unlike the Song, however, the new industrial centres were located in the south, rather than in North China, and did not have ready access to coal, a factor that may have contributed to the Great Divergence. Iron output increased to triple Song levels, at well over 300,000 tons. Further innovations helped improve industrial capability to above Song levels. Many Ming-era innovations were recorded in the Tiangong Kaiwu, an encyclopedia compiled in 1637.

Developments in agriculture

Under the Ming, some rural areas were reserved exclusively for the production of cash crops. Agricultural tools and carts, some water-powered, allowed the production of a sizable agricultural surplus, which formed the basis of the rural economy. Alongside other crops, rice was grown on a large scale. The population growth and the decrease in fertile land made it necessary that farmers produce cash crops to earn a living. Landed, managed estates grew substantially; while in 1379 only 14,241 households had over 700 mou, by the end of the Ming some large landowners had over 70,000 mou. Increasing commercialization caused huge advances in productivity during the Ming Dynasty, allowing a greater population.

Many markets, with three main types, were established in the countryside. In the simplest markets, goods were exchanged or bartered. In 'urban-rural' markets, rural goods were sold to urban dwellers; landlords residing in cities used income from rural landholdings to facilitate exchange in the cities. Merchants bought rural goods in large quantities and sold them in these markets. The 'national market' developed during the Song Dynasty became more important during the Ming. In addition to the merchants and barter, this type of market involved products produced directly for the market. Many Ming peasants no longer relied upon subsistence farming; they produced products for the market, which they sold for a profit. The Cambridge history states about the Ming that:

> "The commercialization of Ming society within the context of expanding communications may be regarded as a distinguishing aspect of the history of this dynasty. In the matter of commodity production and circulation, the Ming marked a turning point in Chinese history, both in the scale at which goods were being produced for the market, and in the nature of the economic relations that governed commercial exchange."

Economic history of China (pre-1911)

Spring morning in a Han palace, by Qiu Ying (1494–1552); excessive luxury and decadence were hallmarks of the late Ming period, spurred by the enormous state bullion of incoming silver and private transactions involving silver.

Collapse of the Ming economy

At the end of the Ming Dynasty, the Little Ice Age severely curtailed Chinese agriculture in the northern provinces. From 1626 CE, famine, drought, and other disasters befell northern China, bringing peasant revolts. The Ming government's inability to collect taxes resulted in troops frequently not being paid. Many troops joined the rebels, worsening the situation. In 1644 CE, the rebels under Li Zicheng took Beijing, ending Ming rule in the north. The Ming state continued to reign in southern China until 1662 CE.

Qing (Manchu) Dynasty (1644–1911 CE)

China's last imperial dynasty, the Qing Dynasty, was not founded by Han Chinese but the Jur'chens, later called the Manchus, which had been subjects of the Ming and had earlier founded the Jurchen Jin Dynasty. In 1616 CE, under Nurhaci, the Manchus rebelled against the Ming. In 1644 Beijing was sacked by Li Zicheng's rebel forces and the last Ming Emperor Chongzhen committed suicide when the city fell. The Manchu Qing dynasty then allied with Ming Dynasty general Wu Sangui and seized control of Beijing and quickly overthrew Li's short-lived Shun Dynasty. After a long, bloody war lasting until 1683 CE, the Qing took control of the whole of China and suppressed dissent by killing scholars, banning Chinese clothes, and forcing Chinese men to tie pigtails in the Manchu fashion. During the course of the Qing Dynasty, the Qing court imposed some restrictions on industry, commerce, and agriculture, such as prohibiting new mines except in exceptional cases. The Qing reversed the style of government where the emperors relied on consultation with ministers to make decisions. Instead, an absolute monarchy was established, with the emperor at its helm. Although the Qing economy recovered and significantly developed during the 18th century, it failed to keep pace with the economies of European countries in the Industrial Revolution.

Economic effects of the Manchu invasion

After they captured Beijing in 1644, the Qing forces requisitioned large amounts of land from Chinese landowners around the capital, and enslaved thousands of Han Chinese as Booi Aha to work on the captured estates. In Hebei Province alone, some 16.6 million mou of agricultural land was seized. In addition, attacks by overseas Ming loyalist forces prompted the Manchu to adopt a policy of clearing the shore line, in which all cities and towns along China's coast were destroyed and their inhabitants moved inland. This policy ended almost all of China's maritime activity and overseas trade. These policies, and Manchu laws that banned Han dress and mandated the queue, encouraged the Han Chinese to bring heavy resistance against the Manchu, who responded by massacring those who opposed them. The Yangzhou massacre, for example, was estimated to have killed between 800,000 people, including women and children.

The destructive effects of the Manchu invasion were felt economically for decades. In the 1690s, Tang Chen, a retired Chinese scholar and failed merchant wrote:

> More than fifty years have passed since the founding of the Ch'ing dynasty, and the empire grows poorer each day. Farmers are destitute, artisans are destitute, merchants are destitute, and officials too are destitute. Grain is cheap, yet it is hard to eat one's fill. Cloth is cheap, yet it is hard to cover one's skin. Boatloads of goods travel from one marketplace to another, but the cargoes must be sold at a loss. Officials upon leaving their posts discover they have no wherewithal to support their households. Indeed the four occupations are all impoverished!

Economic history of China (pre-1911)

Recovery of the "Kang–Qian Age"

Following the completion of the Manchu conquest in 1683 CE, the Kangxi Emperor revoked destructive measures, such as princely estates and the clearing of the shoreline. Under his successors' reigns, the Qing Dynasty reached its peak in the Kang–Qian Age between the reigns of the Kangxi Emperor and the Qianlong Emperor. Kangxi and his successors subjugated the areas of Xinjiang and Tibet, conquered the Dzungar Khanate and exercised tighter control over these regions than the Ming Dynasty had. This removed a major threat to China and incorporated the regions of Xinjiang and Mongolia into the Chinese economy.

During the Qing Dynasty, foreign food crops, like the potato, were introduced during the 18th century on a large scale. These crops encouraged a dramatic increase in population, from approximately 150–200 million during the Ming to over 400 million during the Qing. During the 18th century, the Qing economy recovered to levels the Ming had achieved in the early 17th century; by 1750, the amount of registered land under cultivation equalled the level the Ming had reached in 1600.

Pine, Plum and Cranes, 1759 AD, by Shen Quan (1682–1760). Hanging scroll, ink and color on silk. The Palace Museum, Beijing.

Reversing one of the Ming's trends, the Qing government interfered greatly in the economy. The monopoly on Salt was restored and became one of the greatest sources of revenue for the state. Qing officials tried to discourage cultivation of cash crops in favor of grain. The Manchu regime restricted the number of merchants that could operate and prohibited new mines except in exceptional cases. In addition, the Manchus purged thousands of scholars through "literary inquisitions" which wished to destroy all anti-Manchu thought and suppressed unorthodox scientific theories. These policies greatly hampered the Qing economy, and was a key reason why it fell behind the West in the 18th century.

Isolationist trade policy

The Qing Dynasty viewed foreign trade with suspicion. Emperor Qianlong proclaimed that:

> Our land is so wealthy and prosperous, that we possess all things. Therefore there is no need to exchange the produce of foreign barbarians for our own.

During the 18th and 19th centuries, however, foreign trade increased massively after the economy recovered from the disruptions of the Manchu invasions, and after the prohibition on foreign trade was lifted in 1684. Despite the Qing government's regulations discouraging trade (during emperor Qianlong's reign, the number of ports allowed to trade was reduced from 4 to 1), trade between China and Europe grew at the rate of 4 percent a year between 1719 CE and 1806 CE, doubling the volume of trade every 18 years. This helped China's interior markets and its coastal city ports, providing additional demand for domestic products.

The Opium wars and the Taiping Rebellion

Considering China to be a large, untapped market, the British tried several times to persuade the Chinese to trade with them, sending an ambassador to the court of the Qianlong Emperor. When they were rejected, the British started smuggling opium into China. The result was disastrous for the Chinese. It is estimated that between 1821 CE and 1840 CE, as much as one-fifth of the silver circulating in China was used to purchase opium, the abuse of which incapacitated able men throughout the country.

The Fuzhou arsenal at Mawei (马尾) harbor, c. 1880, where the Battle of Fuzhou would take place in 1884 during the Sino-French War

When the Qing government tried to stop the opium trade, the result was the Opium Wars, in which the Qing government was defeated through superior firearms. The resulting treaty saw concessions given to European nations in China, undermining Chinese authority. The Opium Wars began a pattern of war, defeat, concessions, and silver payments to foreign powers, which further weakened the Chinese government and economy through outflow of silver. Nevertheless, the Qing government was eager to appease the foreigners.

Anger at the Qing rulers grew after the Opium Wars. In 1851 CE, Hong Xiuquan revolted against the Qing Dynasty, proclaimed Qing's rulers to be "filthy barbarians and beasts" who had " led China into despair". His rebels, called the Taipings, quickly took control of much of southern China. With aid from the British and French, the Qing defeated the rebels, but not before the rebellion claimed over 20 million lives. Lasting until 1871 CE, the Taiping Rebellion was one of the bloodiest wars in history, and it devastated the Qing economy.

Self-Strengthening Movement and Qing's collapse

Following the Taiping Rebellion, some Manchu nobles acknowledged that reforms were necessary. They instituted the Self-Strengthening Movement, in which limited modernization occurred, such as re-equipping the army, creating a standing navy, and industrialization. Although some of these reforms were successful, most of the Manchu nobility opposed them. The Chinese economy underwent a somewhat limited industrialization during this period. After defeat by the Japanese in 1894 CE, the movement became discredited. In 1911 CE, the Xinhai Revolution overthrew Manchu rule and established the Republic of China. The collapse of the Qing accelerated the decline of the Chinese economy, which was rapidly declining in comparison to the world gross domestic product.

See also

- Economy of the Han Dynasty
- Economy of the Song Dynasty
- Economy of the Ming Dynasty
- Economy of the People's Republic of China
- Economy of the Republic of China
- Economy of Tibet
- Taxation in premodern China

Sources

- Compilation Group for the "History of Modern China" Series. (2000). *The Opium War*. Honolulu: University Press of the Pacific; reprint from 1976 edition. ISBN 0898751500.
- Allen, Robert (2009), "Agricultural productivity and rural incomes in England and the Yangtze Delta, c.1620–c.1820"[1], *The Economic History Review* **62** (3): 525–550, doi:10.1111/j.1468-0289.2008.00443.x [2]
- Atwell, William (1998), "Ming China and the emerging world economy, c. 1470–1650", in Twitchett, Denis and Mote, Frederick W. (eds.), *The Cambridge History of China: Volume 8: The Ming Dynasty: 1368–1644*, Cambridge: Cambridge University Press, pp. 376–416, ISBN 0521243335
- Atwell, William S. (2002), "Time, Money, and the Weather: Ming China and the "Great Depression" of the Mid-Fifteenth Century"[3], *The Journal of Asian Studies* **61** (1): 83–113, doi:10.2307/2700190 [4]
- Bagley, Robert (1999), "Shang Archaeology", in Loewe, Michael and Shaughnessy, Edward L. (eds.), *From the Origins of Civilization to 221 B.C.*, The Cambridge History of Ancient China, **1**, Cambridge: Cambridge University Press, pp. 124–231, ISBN 9780521470308
- Benn, Charles (2002), *China's Golden Age: Everyday Life in the Tang Dynasty*, Oxford: Oxford University Press, ISBN 0-19-517665-0

- Bielenstein, Hans (1987), "Wang Mang, the Restoration of the Han Dynasty, and Later Han", in Twitchett, Denis and Fairbank, John K. (eds.), *The Ch'in and Han Empires, 221 B.C. – A.D. 220*, The Cambridge History of China, **1**, Cambridge: Cambridge University Press, pp. 223–290, ISBN 0521243270
- Bodde, Derk (1956), "Feudalism in China", in Coulborn, Rushton (ed.), *Feudalism in History*, Princeton, NJ: Princeton University Press, pp. 49–92, 404–7
- Bodde, Derk (1987), "The State and Empire of Qin", in Twitchett, Denis and Fairbank, John K. (eds.), *The Ch'in and Han Empires, 221 B.C. – A.D. 220*, The Cambridge History of China, **1**, Cambridge: Cambridge University Press, pp. 20–103, ISBN 0521243270
- Bray, Francesca (1984), *Biology and Biological Technology: Agriculture*, Science and Civilisation in China, **VI:2**, Cambridge: Cambridge University Press
- Brook, Timothy (1998), *The Confusions of Pleasure: Commerce and Culture in Ming China*, Berkeley: University of California Press, ISBN 0-520-22154-0
- Chang, Kwang-chih (1999), "China on the Eve of the Historical Period", in Loewe, Michael and Shaughnessy, Edward L. (eds.), *From the Origins of Civilization to 221 B.C.*, The Cambridge History of Ancient China, **1**, Cambridge: Cambridge University Press, pp. 37–73, ISBN 9780521470308
- Dardess, John (1995), "Shun-Ti and the end of Yuan rule in China", in Twitchett, Denis and Franke, Herbert (eds.), *Alien regimes and Border States, 710–1368*, The Cambridge History of China, **6**, Cambridge: Cambridge University Press, pp. 561–588, ISBN 9780521243315
- Dreyer, Edward H. (1988), "Military origins of Ming China", in Twitchett, Denis and Mote, Frederick W. (eds.), *The Ming Dynasty, part 1*, The Cambridge History of China, **7**, Cambridge: Cambridge University Press, pp. 58–107, ISBN 9780521243322
- Du, Wenyu (1998), "Tang Song Jingji Shili Bijiao Yanjiu" [5], *Researches in Chinese Economic History* **1998** (4), ISSN 1002-8005 [6]
- Ebrey, Patricia Buckley (1986), "The Economic and Social History of Later Han", in Twitchett, Denis and Fairbank, John K. (eds.), *The Ch'in and Han Empires, 221 B.C. – A.D. 220*, Cambridge History of China, **1**, Cambridge: Cambridge University Press, pp. 608–648, ISBN 0521243270
- Ebrey, Patricia Buckley (1993), *Chinese Civilization: A Sourcebook*, New York: Simon and Schuster, ISBN 978-0029087527
- Ebrey, Patricia Buckley (1999), *The Cambridge Illustrated History of China*, Cambridge: Cambridge University Press, ISBN 0-521-43519-6
- Ebrey, Patricia Buckley (2001), Shiyu, Zhao et al (translators), ed., *The Cambridge Illustrated History of China*, Shandong illustrated publishing corp, ISBN 7-80603-493-5/K.115
- Ebrey, Patricia; Walthall, Anne; Palais, James (2006), *East Asia: A Cultural, Social, and Political History*, Boston: Houghton Mifflin Company, ISBN 0-618-13384-4
- Embree, Ainslie Thomas (1997), *Asia in Western and World History: A Guide for Teaching*, Armonk: ME Sharpe, Inc

- Fairbank, John K. (1978), "Introduction: The old order", in Fairbank, John K. (ed.), *Late Ch'ing 1800–1911, Part 1, The Cambridge History of China*, **10**, Cambridge: Cambridge University Press, pp. 1–35, ISBN 9780521214476
- Fairbank, John K. (1978), "The Canton trade and the Opium War", in Fairbank, John K. (ed.), *Late Ch'ing 1800–1911, Part 1*, The Cambridge History of China, **10**, Cambridge: Cambridge University Press, pp. 163–213, ISBN 9780521214476
- Fairbank, John K. (1978), "The creation of the Treaty System", in Fairbank, John K. (ed.), *Late Ch'ing 1800–1911, Part 1*, The Cambridge History of China, **10**, Cambridge: Cambridge University Press, pp. 213–264, ISBN 9780521214476
- Fairbank, John K.; Goldman, Merle (2006), *China: A New History* (2nd Enlarged ed.), Harvard: Harvard University Press, ISBN 0-674-01828-1
- Franke, Herbert (1994), "The Chin Dynasty", in Franke, Herbert and Twitchett, Denis (eds.), *Alien Regimes and Border States, 710–1368*, The Cambridge History of China, **6**, Cambridge: Cambridge University Press, pp. 215–319, ISBN 9780521243315
- Gernet, Jacques (1962), *Daily Life in China on the Eve of the Mongol Invasion, 1250–1276*, Stanford: Stanford University Press, ISBN 0-8047-0720-0
- Heijdra, Martin (1998), "The socio-economic development of rural China during the Ming", in Mote, Frederick W. And Twitchett, Denis (eds.), *The Ming Dynasty, 1368–1644, Part 1*, The Cambridge History of China, **8**, Cambridge: Cambridge University Press, pp. 417–578, ISBN 0521243335
- Hinsch, Bret (2002), *Women in Imperial China*, Lanham: Rowman & Littlefield, ISBN 0742518728
- Hobson, John M. (2004), *The Eastern Origins of Western Civilisation*, Cambridge University Press, ISBN 0-521-54724-5
- Hsiao, Ch'i-Ch'ing (1994), "Mid-Yuan politics", in Franke, Herbert and Twitchett, Denis (eds.), *Alien Regimes and Border States, 710–1368*, The Cambridge History of China, **6**, Cambridge: Cambridge University Press, pp. 490–561, ISBN 9780521243315
- Hsu, Cho-yun (1999), "The Spring and Autumn Period", in Loewe, Michael and Shaughnessy, Edward L. (eds.), *From the Origins of Civilization to 221 B.C.*, The Cambridge History of Ancient China, Cambridge: Cambridge University Press, pp. 545–586, ISBN 9780521470308
- Huang, Ray (1998), "The Ming fiscal administration", in Twitchett, Denis and Fairbank, John K. (eds.), *The Ming Dynasty, 1 398–1644, Part 2*, The Cambridge History of China, **8**, Cambridge: Cambridge University Press, pp. 106–172, ISBN 9780521243339
- Ji, Jianghong; et al (2005a) (in Chinese), *Encyclopedia of China History*, **1**, Beijing publishing house, ISBN 7900321543
- Ji, Jianghong; et al (2005b) (in Chinese), *Encyclopedia of China History*, **2**, Beijing publishing house, ISBN 7900321543
- Ji, Jianghong; et al (2005) (in Chinese), *Encyclopedia of China History*, **3**, Beijing publishing house, ISBN 7900321543

- Ji, Xianlin (1997), *History of Cane Sugar in China*, Eastern Culture and economy publishers, ISBN 7-80127-284-6/K
- Keightley, David N. (1999), "The Shang: China's First Historical Dynasty", in Loewe, Michael and Shaughnessy, Edward L. (eds.), *From the Origins of Civilization to 221 B.C.*, The Cambridge History of Ancient China, **1**, Cambridge: Cambridge University Press, pp. 232–291, ISBN 9780521470308
- Kuhn, Dieter (1982), "The Silk Workshops of the Shang Dynasty (16th–11th Century B.C.)", in Guohao, Li et al., *Explorations in the History of Science and Technology in China, in Honour of the Eightieth Birthday of Dr. Joseph Needham*, Shanghai: Guji chubanshe, pp. 367–408
- Kuhn, Dieter (1988), *Textile Technology: Spinning and Reeling*, Science and Civilisation in China, **V:9**, Cambridge: Cambridge University Press
- Lewis, Mark Edward (1999), "Warring States: Political History", in Loewe, Michael and Shaughnessy, Edward L. (eds.), *From the Origins of Civilization to 221 B.C.*, The Cambridge History of Ancient China, Cambridge: Cambridge University Press, pp. 587–650, ISBN 9780521243339
- Li, Bo; Zheng, Yin (2001) (in Chinese), *5000 years of Chinese history*, Inner Mongolian People's publishing corp, ISBN 7-204-04420-7
- Li, Xueqin 李學勤 (editor-in-chief) (2007), *Xizhou shi yu Xizhou wenming* 西周史與西周文明 ["The History and Culture of the Western Zhou"], Shanghai: Shanghai kexue jishu wenxian chubanshe 上海科學技術問現出版社
- Liang, Fangchong (1981), 十四世纪上半叶中国手工业的生产力和生产关系的矛盾 [7], Shaanxi People's publishers
- Loewe, Michael (1986), "Former Han Dynasty", in Twitchett, Denis and Fairbank, John K. (eds.), *The Ch'in and Han Empires, 221 B.C. – A.D. 220*, Cambridge History of China, **1**, Cambridge: Cambridge University Press, pp. 103–223, ISBN 0521243270
- Maddison, Angus (2007), *Chinese economic performance in the long run* [8], Organisation for Economic Co-operation and Development. Development Centre, ISBN 9789264037625
- Milanovic, Branco (2003), *Against globalization as we know it*, Elsevier Science Ltd. World Development Vol. 31, No. 4, pp. 667–683
- Mote, Frederick W. (1988), "Introduction", in Twitchett, Denis and Mote, Frederick W. (eds.), *The Ming Dynasty, part 1*, The Cambridge History of China, **7**, Cambridge: Cambridge University Press, pp. 1–11, ISBN 9780521243322
- Myers, H. Ramon; Wang, Yeh-Chien (2002), "Economic developments, 1644-1800", in Peterson, Willard J. (ed.), *Part One: The Ch'ing Empire to 1800*, The Cambridge History of China, **9**, Cambridge: Cambridge University Press, pp. 563–647, ISBN 9780521243346
- Needham, Joseph; Tsuen-Hsuin, Tsien (1985), *Science and Civilisation in China*, **5:1**, Cambridge: Cambridge University Press, ISBN 9780521086905

- Nishijima, Sadao (1986), "The Economic and Social History of Former Han", in Twitchett, Denis and Fairbank, John K. (eds.), *The Ch'in and Han Empires, 221 B.C. – A.D. 220*, Cambridge History of China, **1**, Cambridge: Cambridge University Press, pp. 545–607, ISBN 0521243270
- Pomeranz, Kenneth (2000), *The Great Divergence: China, Europe, and the Making of the Modern World Economy*, Princeton University Press, ISBN 978-0-691-09010-8
- Qi, Xia 漆侠 (1999) (in Chinese), *Zhongguo jing ji tong shi. Song dai jing ji juan* 中国经济通史. 宋代经济卷 *["General Economic History of China - The Economy of the Song Dynasty"]*, **1:2**, Economic Daily Publishers, ISBN 7-80127-462-8
- Rickett, Adele (1987), "Biography of Derk Bodde", in Le Blanc, Charles and Blader, Susan (eds.), *Chinese Ideas about Nature and Society: Studies in Honour of Derk Bodde*, Hong Kong: Hong Kong University Press, pp. 1–20
- Rossabi, Morris (1988), *Khubilai Khan: His Life and Times*, Berkeley: University of California Press, ISBN 0-520-05913-1
- Rossabi, Morris (1995), "The reign of Khubilai Khan", in Twitchett, Denis and Franke, Herbert (eds.), *Alien regimes and Border States*, The Cambridge History of China, **6**, Cambridge: Cambridge University Press, pp. 414–490, ISBN 9780521243315
- Schafer, Edward H (1985) [1963], *The Golden Peaches of Samarkand: A study of T'ang Exotics* (1st paperback ed.), Berkeley and Los Angeles.: University of California Press, ISBN 0-520-05462-8
- Shaughnessy, Edward L. (1999), "Western Zhou History", in Loewe, Michael and Shaughnessy, Edward L. (eds.), *From the Origins of Civilization to 221 B.C.*, The Cambridge History of Ancient China, **1**, Cambridge: Cambridge University Press, ISBN 9780521470308
- Smith, Paul J. (1993), "State Power and Economic Activism during the New Policies, 1068–1085' The Tea and Horse Trade and the 'Green Sprouts' Loan Policy", in Hymes, Robert P. (ed.), *Ordering the World : Approaches to State and Society in Sung Dynasty China*, Berkeley: Berkeley University of California Press, pp. 76–128, ISBN 9780520076914
- Spence, Jonathan D. (1999), *The Search For Modern China* (2nd ed.), New York: W. W. Norton & Company, ISBN 0-393-97351-4
- Sun, Jian (2000) (in Chinese), *Economic history of China, (1840–1949)*, **2**, China People's University Press, ISBN 7300029531
- Tzu, Sun; Griffith, Samuel B. (translator) (2006), *The Art of War*, Blue Heron Books, ISBN 1897035357
- Wagner, Donald B. (2001a), "The Administration of the Iron Industry in Eleventh-Century China", *Journal of the Economic and Social History of the Orient* **44**: 175–197, doi:10.1163/156852001753731033 [9]
- Wagner, Donald B. (2001b), *The State and the Iron Industry in Han China*, Copenhagen: Nordic Institute of Asian Studies Publishing, ISBN 8787062836
- Wakeman, Frederic (1985), *The Great Enterprise: The Manchu Reconstruction of Imperial Order in Seventeenth-century China*, Berkeley and Los Angeles: University of California Press,

ISBN 0520048040
- Xie, Yuanlu (2005), "Analysis of the Tang-Song socioeconomic transformation" [10], *Research on Chinese economic history* **2**
- Xu, Huan (2005), "The development of South China's economy during the six dynasties", South China's social and economic adevelopment
- Zhan, Zhifei (2006), "Changes in the monetary system in the early Han and its effects", *Economic history* **5**

External links
- Economic History of Premodern China (from 221 BC to c. 1800 AD) [11] Kent Deng, London School of Economics (LSE)

Economic history of modern China

The **economic history of modern China** began with the fall of the Qing Dynasty in 1911. Following the Qing, China underwent a period of instability and disrupted economic activity. Under the Nanjing decade (1927–1937), China advanced several industries, in particular those related to the military, in an effort to catch up with the west and prepare for war with Japan. The Second Sino-Japanese War (1937–1945) and the following Chinese civil war caused the collapse of the Republic of China and formation of the People's Republic of China.

The Lujiazui financial district of Pudong, Shanghai, the financial and commercial hub of modern China

The new ruler of China, Mao Zedong, initially promised to develop "an socialist alliance with petit-bourgeois, workers, and nationalist bourgeois", but enacted collectivization upon consolidation of this regime. Collectivization resulted in the success of the first five-year plan, but Mao's second five-year plan, which included the Great Leap forward, did not meet with the same success. A new party faction who supported private plots eventually challenged Mao's economic policy. Unwilling to give up power, Mao launched the Cultural Revolution, which led to the collapse of the Chinese economy.

Following Mao's death, one of the most senior officials who had advocated private plots in the early 1960s, Deng Xiaoping, initiated gradual market reforms that abolished the communes and collectivized industries of Mao, replacing them with the free-market system. Deng's reforms vastly improved the standard of living of the Chinese people, the competitiveness of the Chinese economy, and caused China to become one of the fastest growing and most important economies in the world. It also led to one of the most rapid industrializations in world history. For this achievement he is sometimes known as "The Venerated Deng" (Chinese:邓公). As a result of Deng's reforms, China is widely regarded as a returning superpower.

Republic of China (1911-1949)

The Republic of China was a period of turmoil for China after the collapse of the Qing dynasty. From 1911 to 1927, China virtually disintegrated into regional warlords, fighting for authority and causing economic misery and contraction. After 1927, Chiang Kai-shek managed to reunify China and bring in the Nanjing decade, a period of relative prosperity despite civil war and Japanese aggression. In 1937, the Japanese invaded and literally laid China to waste in eight years of war. The era also saw the first boycott of Japanese products. Afterwards, the Chinese civil war further devastated China and led to the fall of the Republic in 1949.

A bill from 1930, early ROC

Civil war, famine and turmoil in the early republic

The early republic was marked by frequent wars and factional struggles. From 1911 to 1927, famine, war and change of government was the norm in Chinese politics, with provinces periodically declaring "independence". The collapse of central authority caused the economic contraction that was in place since Qing to speed up, and was only reversed when Chiang reunified China in 1927 and proclaimed himself its leader.

Development of domestic industries

Chinese domestic industries developed rapidly after the downfall of the Manchu Qing dynasty, despite turmoil in Chinese politics. Development of these industries peaked during World War I, which saw a great increase in demand for Chinese goods, which benefitted China's industries. In addition, imports to China fell drastically after total war broke out in Europe. For example, China's textile industry had

482,192 needle machines in 1913, while by 1918 (the end of the war) that number had gone up to 647,570. The number increased even faster to 1,248,282 by 1921. In addition, bread factories went up from 57 to 131.

The May 4th movement, in which Chinese students called China's population to boycott foreign goods, also helped spur development. Foreign imports fell drastically from 1919–1921 and from 1925 to 1927.

Chinese industries continue to develop in the 1930s with the advent of the Nanking decade in the 1930s, when Chiang Kai-shek unified most of the country and brought political stability. China's industries developed and grew from 1927 to 1931. Though badly hit by the Great Depression from 1931 to 1935 and Japan's occupation of Manchuria in 1931, industrial output recovered by 1936. By 1936, industrial output had recovered and surpassed its previous peak in 1931 prior to the Great Depression's effects on China. This is best shown by the trends in Chinese GDP. In 1932, China's GDP peaked at 28.8 billion, before falling to 21.3 billion by 1934 and recovering to 23.7 billion by 1935.

The rural economy of the Republic of China

The rural economy retained much of the characteristics of the Late Qing. While markets had been forming since the Song and Ming dynasties, Chinese agriculture by the Republic of China was almost completely geared towards producing cash crops for foreign consumption, and was thus subject to the say of the international markets. Key exports included glue, tea, silk, sugar canes, tobacco, cotton, corn and peanuts.

The rural economy was hit hard by the Great Depression of the 1930s, in which an overproduction of agricultural goods lead to massive falling prices for China as well as an increase in foreign imports (as agricultural goods produced in western countries were "dumped" in China). In 1931, imports of rice in China amounted to 21 million bushels compared with 12 million in 1928. Other goods saw even more staggering increases. In 1932, 15 million bushels of grain were imported compared with 900,000 in 1928. This increased competition lead to a massive decline in Chinese agricultural prices (which were cheaper) and thus the income of rural farmers. In 1932, agricultural prices were 41 percent of 1921 levels.. Rural incomes had fallen to 57 percent of 1931 levels by 1934 in some areas.

Foreign direct investment in the Republic of China

Foreign direct investment in China soared during the Republic of China. Some 1.5 billion of investment was present in China by the beginning of the 20th century, with Russia, The United Kingdom and Germany being the largest investors. However, with the outbreak of WWI, investment from Germany and Russia stopped while England and Japan took a leading role. By 1930, foreign investment in China totalled 3.5 billion, with Japan leading (1.4 billion) and England at 1 billion. By 1948, however, the capital stock had halted with investment dropping to only 3 billion, with the US and Britain leading.

Currency of the Republic of China

The currency of China was initially silver-backed, but the nationalist government seized control of private banks in the notorious banking coup of 1935 and replaced the currency with the Fabi, a fiat currency issued by the ROC. Particular effort was made by the ROC government to instill this currency as the monopoly currency of China, stamping out earlier Silver and gold-backed notes that had made up China's currency. Unfortunately, the ROC government used this privilege to issue currency en masse; a total of 1.4 billion Chinese yuan was issued in 1936, but by the end of the second Sino-Japanese war some 1.031 trillion in notes was issued. This trend worsened with the outbreak of the Chinese Civil war in 1946. By 1947, some 33.2 trillion of currency was issued as a result of massive budget deficits resulting from war (taxation revenue was just 0.25 billion, compared with 2500 billion in war expenses). By 1949, the total currency in circulation was 120 billion times more than in 1936..

The Chinese war economy (1937-1945)

In 1937, Japan invaded China and the resulting warfare literally laid waste to China. Most of the prosperous east China coast was occupied by the Japanese, who carried out various atrocities such as the Rape of Nanjing in 1937 and random massacres of whole villages. In one anti-guerilla sweep in 1942, the Japanese killed up to 200,000 civilians in a month. The war was estimated to have killed between 20 and 25 million Chinese, and destroyed literally all that Chiang had built up in the preceding decade. Development of industries was severely hampered after the war by devastating conflict as well as the inflow of cheap American goods. By 1946, Chinese industries operated at 20% capacity and had 25% of the output of pre-war China.

Coal mining at Fushun, Liaoning, c. 1940, operating under the control of the Japanese

One effect of the war was a massive increase in government control of industries. In 1936, government-owned industries were only 15% of GDP. However, the ROC government took control of many industries in order to fight the war. In 1938, the ROC established a commission for industries and mines to control and supervise firms, as well as instilling price controls. By 1942, 70% of the capital of Chinese industry were owned by the government.

Hyperinflation, civil war and the relocation of the republic to Taiwan

Following the war with Japan, Chiang acquired Taiwan from Japan and renewed his struggle with the communists. However, the corruption of the KMT, as well as hyperinflation as a result of trying to fight the civil war, resulted in mass unrest throughout the Republic and sympathy for the communists. In addition, the communists' promise to redistribute land gained them support among the massive rural population. In 1949, the communists captured Beijing and later Nanjing as well. The People's Republic of China was proclaimed on 1 October 1949. The Republic of China relocated to Taiwan where Japan had laid an educational groundwork. Taiwan continued to prosper under the Republic of China government and came to be known as one of the Four Asian Tigers due to its "economic miracle", and later became one of the largest sources of investment in mainland China after the PRC economy began its rapid growth following Deng's reforms.

People's Republic of China (1949 onwards)

Main article: Economic history of the People's Republic of China

The People's Republic of China is marked by two distinctly different periods: the Mao Era, characterized by a soviet-style planned economy that extinguished the market and eventually became unresponsive, and the post-Mao Era, more properly called the Deng Era (after the reformer who started it) characterized by a transition to a relatively free market economy which was one of the most prosperous periods in China's history. Many Chinese are hopeful that this newfound prosperity will last and China will reclaim her place at the top of nations.

A 1950 postage stamp of Mao Zedong, Chairman of the Communist Party of China, shaking hands with Joseph Stalin, General Secretary of the Communist Party of the Soviet Union

The Grand socialist experiment: The Mao Era (1949-1976)

The Mao Era was marked by a soviet-style planned economy which was instituted, despite his promises, in 1949-52. A decade of relatively peaceful development and collectivization followed, but in 1959 Mao launched the disastrous Great Leap forward, an attempt to collectivize all aspects of life (even the peasants' cooking pots), a disaster that was exacerbated by famine. Following this, a reformist faction lead by Deng Xiaoping and Liu Shaoqi forced Mao out of office and experimented with market reforms such as giving peasants private plots. However, these reform efforts were disrupted by Mao's Cultural Revolution, a period of virtually total anarchy and street fighting(武鬥) that resulted in the collapse of the Chinese economy and ended with the execution of the Gang of Four.

Initial policies and promises of Mao

Mao initially promised to work with "patriotic capitalists, the petit-bourgeois and other classes" in a period of "New Democracy" in which some capitalism would be allowed. However, in 1952 he broke his promise and accused capitalists of sabotaging China's war effort in Korea. Following this, businesses were collectivized(國有化).

Collectivization of industry and agriculture

Collectivization of industry took place from 1951 to 1954, by which time industry was entirely in state hands. Despite the communist party's original plans not to finish collectivization of agriculture until 1971, Mao pushed ahead with mutual aid teams by 1953, and People's commune (人民公社) by 1955, forcing the collectivization of agriculture.

Economic developments in the fifties

With Soviet aid, Mao set up a basic industrial base that included a small set of industries, mostly related to military matters, that was to become the basis of the later modernization by Deng Xiaoping. New buildings, roads, railroads, and a basic infrastructure was put in place to sustain Chinese development. Illiteracy and a whole host of parasites were eradicated. For these reasons, the 1950s is usually regarded as the high point of the Mao Era.

Great Leap forward

In 1959, Mao launched a disastrous crash industrialization called the Great Leap forward. This involved making many peasants urban workers, collectivizing virtually everything (including cooking tools) and setting up backyard furnaces to improve steel production. However, the program was a disastrous failure; the new collectivization destroyed the incentive of the peasants, who also overate at people's communes. Most of the new "steel" produced from backyard furnaces was useless. Eventually, famine resulted and an estimated 20 million people died from starvation.

Emergence of reformist faction

Reformists, such as Liu Shaoqi and Deng Xiaoping, began to push Mao for reform after the disastrous Great Leap forward. They undid some of Mao's priorities, such as disbanding the People's communes and giving peasants private plots. However, Mao was infuriated and in 1966, he launched a coup against the reformers, calling them Capitalist roader and launching the Cultural Revolution.

Cultural Revolution and the collapse of the economy

The Cultural Revolution is usually thought as one of the greatest catastrophes ever to beset China. At Mao's connivance, youth groups, known as red guards, deposed and frequently shot government officials, and then took control of the cities and provinces they ran. This "revolution" began in Shanghai and quickly spread across the country. By 1966, most of the country was in the hands of these "revolutionary committees" who battled each other for power in the cities and provinces they existed.

This disruption, as well as the purge of millions of intellectuals, workers, and officials as "counter-revolutionaries", was disastrous. Economic output fell some 30% over three years, and stagnated for the rest of the period. In addition, an entire generation was deprived of education and hampered China's development for years to come. When referring to this period, Deng Xiaoping said it had created "an entire generation of mental cripples".

From planned economy to free market powerhouse: The Post-Mao Era (1976 onwards)

Main article: Chinese economic reform

In 1976, at the end of the Cultural Revolution, China's planned economy was in ruins and its people barely surviving. However, in 1978, China was to witness one of the most rapid periods of change in her 5,000 year history as reformer Deng Xiaoping initiated free market reforms that transformed China's economy. Only 30 years later, China had developed from an economically desolate country ruled by a totalitarian government into an industrial powerhouse, rapidly overtaking developed western nations in recession. The agent of this dramatic change, Deng Xiaoping, is sometimes known as "Deng Gong" or the venerated Deng, for his achievements.

Deng Xiaoping's rise

An old party stalwart, Deng had been of the reformist faction in the early 1960s and purged in the Cultural Revolution. After Mao's death, however, a coup overthrew the Gang of Four and instilled old party officials such as Deng back in power. However, it was not until 1978 that Hua Guofeng, Mao's appointed successor, resigned and Deng took power, though he was never officially the leader, instead holding the position of chairman of the Central military commission.

De-collectivization of agriculture

One of Deng's first actions was to break up the People's communes that Mao instated and grant a system of "Bao Chang Dao Hu" (包产到户), in which each plot of land was given to each household to farm. This new, liberalized agriculture was extremely popular, raising grain production tremendously. This system was so successful that in 1983 Deng lifted limits on consumption of many agricultural goods that were instated during the Mao Era due to scarcity. However, these limits were not completely lifted until 1994.

Liberalization and privatization of business

See also: Chengbao system

Private businesses, which were banned in the Mao Era for being "Capitalist exploiters", were reinstated in the Deng Era. Early on, a citizen could opt to become "Ge Ti Hu"(個体户) or self-employed household, and to set up a business instead of taking on state jobs. These "Ge Ti Hu" quickly became extremely wealthy. In the 1990s, many state enterprises were privatized and private individuals were allowed to create companies. In 1990, the Shanghai Stock Exchange was reopened after Mao first closed it 41 years earlier.

A Shanghai branch of Industrial and Commercial Bank of China, largest in the world.

Another innovation instated during this period was the Chengbao system or contracting system, in which state assets were given to private operators, who gave the state the money needed for expenses as well as a share of the profits. This system was also rapidly adopted; in the 1980s and 1990s, many schools, hospitals and even bus lines passed from the state to private operators. However, this system was also criticized as many felt that the change in operation for these schools and hospitals, now for-profit, was detrimental to the poor. In addition, some private contractors were accused of gaining their positions solely because of nepotism.

Although privatizations had occurred in the 1980s, it was sped up in the 1990s by Premier Zhu Rongji, who started a policy of privatizing all state enterprises which were losing money. In 1997, the CPC issued a verdict declaring that state-owned companies were now "people-owned companies" who would be subject to mergers and bankruptcy. Thousands of state companies were privatized or partly floated on the stock exchange. In 1978, more than 90% of GDP was produced in state enterprises, which, up to 1992, dominated China's economy. That figure, not accounting for state assets that were contracted, had fallen to 30% by 2009.

Foreign investment and industrialization

In addition to internal liberalization, Deng also established a series of "special economic zones" in which foreigners could invest in China taking advantage of lower labor costs. This investment helped the Chinese economy boom. In addition, the Chinese government established a series of joint ventures with foreign capital to establish companies in industries hitherto unknown in China. By 2001, China became a member of the World Trade Organization, which has boosted its overall trade in exports/imports—estimated at $851 billion in 2003—by an additional $170 billion a year.

Despite a brief period in 1989 in which foreign capital withdrew from China, China continued to be one of the biggest recipients of foreign investment. In 2006, an estimated $699.5 billion of foreign investment was present in China. A great deal of this investment came from Chinese-speaking regions such as Hong Kong and Taiwan, who was the first to invest in China. Japanese and Western investment followed.

Deng's liberalization of the Chinese economy, along with foreign investment, helped to power China's industrialization. From virtually an industrial backwater in 1978, China is now the world's biggest producer of concrete, steel, ships, textiles as well as the world's biggest auto market. For example, from 2000 to 2006, China's steel production rose from 140 million tons to 416 million tons. From 1975 to 1992, China's auto production rose from 139,800 to 1.1 million automobiles before jumping to 9.35 million in 2008.

Developments post-Deng

In 1997, Deng Xiaoping died. However, his reformist policies were continued by his successor, Jiang Zemin. The result was a vibrant, growing economy.

Under Hu and Wen, who became leaders of China in 2003, the Chinese government continued to give up grounds to private enterprise, yet increased its control in other areas. The new premier, Wen Jiabao, reinstated some Mao-Era social systems, such as social security, as well as sponsoring a new

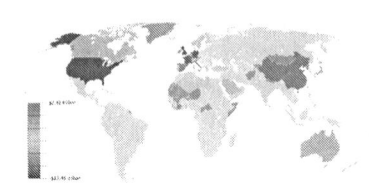

Map of countries by foreign currency reserves and gold minus external debt based on 2009 data from CIA Factbook

initiative in health care in which the state retook control of hospitals from many contractors who had run them for two decades. However, this was reversed in 2009. Nevertheless, China's economy continued to grow. In 2008, however, it was affected by the global financial meltdown and the growth rate fell to 9.0%. As of 2008, China's GDP (PPP) was between 50 and 60 percent of the GDP (PPP) of the US, while over 10 percent of world GDP (PPP).

To offset the effects of the global economic crisis, the government announced a financial stimulus of around 4 trillion yuan spread over two years. However, new spending by the government was actually only about 1 trillion yuan; the rest was already part of the government's budget.

In mid-2005, China began to experience an enormous property bubble, largely caused by loose monetary policy under premier Wen Jiabao. Property prices tripled from 2005 to 2009, and are continuing to rise.

In July 2010 Yi Gang, Deputy Governor of the Bank of China, claimed China`s economy had overtaken Japan as the world`s second biggest economy.[1]

See also

- Economy of the Han Dynasty
- Economy of Hong Kong
- Economy of the Song Dynasty
- Economic history of China (Pre-1911)
- Economy of Macau
- Economy of the Ming Dynasty
- Economic history of the People's Republic of China
- Economy of the People's Republic of China
- Economy of Taiwan

Further reading

- Fengbo Zhang : Analysis of Chinese Macroeconomy .
- Chow, Gregory C. *China's Economic Transformation* (2nd ed. 2007) excerpt and text search [2]
- Duara, Prasenjit, *State Involution: A Study of Local Finances in North China, 1911-1935* [3], in *Comparative Studies in Society and History*, Vol. 29, No. 1 (Jan., 1987), pp. 132–161, Cambridge University Press
- Eastman Lloyd et al. *The Nationalist Era in China, 1927-1949* (1991) excerpt and text search [4]
- Fairbank, John K., ed. *The Cambridge History of China, Vol. 12, Republican China 1912-1949. Part 1.* (1983). 1001 pp., the standard history, by numerous scholars
- Fairbank, John K. and Feuerwerker, Albert, eds. *The Cambridge History of China. Vol. 13: Republican China, 1912–1949, Part 2.* (1986). 1092 pp., the standard history, by numerous scholars
- Ji, Zhaojin. *A History of Modern Shanghai Banking: The Rise and Decline of China's Finance Capitalism.* (2003. 325) pp.
- MacFarquhar, Roderick and Fairbank, John K., eds. *The Cambridge History of China. Vol. 15: The People's Republic, Part 2: Revolutions within the Chinese Revolution, 1966-1982.* Cambridge U. Press, 1992. 1108 pp.
- Naughton, Barry. *The Chinese Economy: Transitions and Growth* (2007)
- Rawski, Thomas G. and Lillian M. Li, eds. *Chinese History in Economic Perspective,* University of California Press, 1992 complete text online free [5]
- Rubinstein, Murray A., ed. *Taiwan: A New History* (2006), 560pp
- Sheehan, Jackie. *Chinese Workers: A New History.* Routledge, 1998. 269 pp.
- Shiroyama, Tomoko. *China during the Great Depression: Market, State, and the World Economy, 1929-1937* (2008)
- Young, Arthur Nichols. *China's nation-building effort, 1927-1937: the financial and economic record* (1971) 553 pages full text online [6]

Sources

- Brandt, Loren et al., China's Great Transformation, ISBN 978-0-511-39680-9 (ebook), April 2008
- Sun, Jian, (Chinese) Economic history of China, Vol 2 (1840–1949), China People's University Press, ISBN 7300029531, 2000.
- Zhou, Enlai: Twenty years since the building of the nation, Ch.1.
- Spence, Jonathan D. (1999). The Search For Modern China. Second Edition. New York: W. W. Norton & Company. ISBN 0-393-97351-4 (Paperback).
- Donald, Stephanie Hemelryk and Robert Benewick. (2005). *The State of China Atlas: Mapping the World's Fastest Growing Economy*. Berkeley, Los Angeles, London: University of California Press. ISBN 0520246276.
- Chan, Alfred (2001). *Mao's Crusade: Politics and Policy Implementation in China's Great Leap Forward*. Oxford University Press. ISBN 0199244065.

External links

- THE ECONOMIC HISTORY AND THE ECONOMY OF CHINA [7]

Economic history of the People's Republic of China

China's economic system before the late 1990's, with state ownership of certain industries and central control over planning and the financial system, has enabled the government to mobilize whatever surplus was available and greatly increase the proportion of the national economic output devoted to investment.

Analysts estimated that investment accounted for about 25 percent of GNP in 1979, a rate surpassed by few other countries. Because of the comparatively low level of GNP, however, even this high rate of investment secured only a small amount of resources relative to the size of the country and the population. In 1978, for instance, only 16 percent of the GNP of the United States went into gross investment, but this amounted to US$345.6 billion, whereas the approximately 25 percent of China's GNP that was invested came to about the equivalent of US$111 billion and had to serve a population 4.5 times the size of that in the United States. The limited resources available for investment prevented China from rapidly producing or importing advanced equipment. Technological development proceeded gradually, and outdated equipment continued to be used as long as possible. Consequently, many different levels of technology were in use simultaneously (see Science and technology in the People's Republic of China). Most industries included some plants that were comparable to modern Western facilities, often based on imported equipment and designs. Equipment produced by Chinese factories was generally some years behind standard Western designs. Agriculture received a smaller share of state investment than industry and remained at a much lower average level of technology and productivity. Despite a significant increase in the availability of tractors, trucks, electric pumps, and mechanical threshers, most agricultural activities were still performed by people or animals.

Although the central administration coordinated the economy and redistributed resources among regions when necessary, in practice most economic activity was very decentralized, and there was relatively little flow of goods and services between areas. About 75 percent of the grain grown in China, for instance, was consumed by the families that produced it. One of the most important sources of growth in the economy was the improved ability to exploit the comparative advantages of each locality by expanding transportation capacity. The communications and transportation sectors were growing and improving but still could not carry the volume of traffic required by a modern economy because of the scarcity of investment funds and advanced technology.

Because of limited interaction among regions, the great variety of geographic zones in China, and the broad spectrum of technologies in use, areas differed widely in economic activities, organizational forms, and prosperity. Within any given city, enterprises ranged from tiny, collectively owned handicraft units, barely earning subsistence-level incomes for their members, to modern state-owned factories, whose workers received steady wages plus free medical care, bonuses, and an assortment of other benefits. The agricultural sector was diverse, accommodating well-equipped, "specialized households" that supplied scarce products and services to local markets; wealthy suburban villages specializing in the production of vegetables, pork, poultry, and eggs to sell in free markets in the nearby cities; fishing villages on the seacoast; herding groups on the grasslands of Inner Mongolia; and poor, struggling grain-producing villages in the arid mountains of Shaanxi and Gansu provinces. The economy had progressed in major ways since 1949, but after four to five decades experts in China and abroad agreed that it had a great distance yet to go.

Despite formidable constraints and disruptions, the Chinese economy was never stagnant. Production grew substantially between 1800 and 1949 and increased fairly rapidly after 1949. Before the 1980s, however, production gains were largely matched by population growth, so that productive capacity was unable to outdistance essential consumption needs significantly, particularly in agriculture. Grain output in 1979 was about twice as large as in 1952, but so was the population. As a result, little surplus was produced even in good years. Further, few resources could be spared for investment in capital goods, such as machinery, factories, mines, railroads, and other productive assets. The relatively small size of the capital stock caused productivity per worker to remain low, which in turn perpetuated the economy's inability to generate a substantial surplus.

Economic policies, 1949-80

When the Communist Party of China came to power in 1949, its leaders' fundamental long-range goals were to transform China into a modern, powerful, socialist nation. In economic terms these objectives meant industrialization, improvement of living standards, narrowing of income differences, and production of modern military equipment. As the years passed, the leadership continued to subscribe to these goals. But the economic policies formulated to achieve them were dramatically altered on several occasions in response to major changes in the economy, internal politics, and international political and economic developments.

An important distinction emerged between leaders who felt that the socialist goals of income equalization and heightened political consciousness should take priority over material progress and those who believed that industrialization and general economic modernization were prerequisites for the attainment of a successful socialist order. Among the prominent leaders who considered politics the prime consideration were Mao Zedong, Lin Biao, and the members of the Gang of Four. Leaders who more often stressed practical economic considerations included Liu Shaoqi, Zhou Enlai, and Deng Xiaoping. For the most part, important policy shifts reflected the alternating emphasis on political and economic goals and were accompanied by major changes in the positions of individuals in the political power structure. An important characteristic in the development of economic policies and the underlying economic model was that each new policy period, while differing significantly from its predecessor, nonetheless retained most of the existing economic organization. Thus the form of the economic model and the policies that expressed it at any given point in Chinese history reflected both the current policy emphasis and a structural foundation built up during the earlier periods.

Recovery from war, 1949-52

In 1949 China's economy was suffering from the debilitating effects of decades of warfare. Many mines and factories had been damaged or destroyed. At the end of the war with Japan in 1945, Soviet troops had dismantled about half the machinery in the major industrial areas of the northeast and shipped it to the Soviet Union. Transportation, communication, and power systems had been destroyed or had deteriorated because of lack of maintenance. Agriculture was disrupted, and food production was some 30 percent below its pre-war peak level. Further, economic ills were compounded by one of the most virulent inflations in world history.

The chief goal of the government for the 1949-1952 period was simply to restore the economy to normal working order. The administration moved quickly to repair transportation and communication links and revive the flow of economic activity. The banking system was nationalized and centralized under the People's Bank of China. To bring inflation under control by 1951, the government unified the monetary system, tightened credit, restricted government budgets at all levels and put them under central control, and guaranteed the value of the currency. Commerce was stimulated and partially regulated by the establishment of state trading companies (commercial departments), which competed with private traders in purchasing goods from producers and selling them to consumers or enterprises. Transformation of ownership in industry proceeded slowly. About a third of the country's enterprises had been under state control while the Guomindang government was in power (1927-1949), as was much of the modernized transportation sector. The Communist Party of China immediately made these units state-owned enterprises upon taking power in 1949. The remaining privately owned enterprises were gradually brought under government control, but 17 percent of industrial units were still completely outside the state system in 1952.

In agriculture a major change in landownership was carried out. Under a nationwide land reform program, titles to about 45 percent of the arable land were redistributed from landlords and more prosperous farmers to the 60 to 70 percent of farm families that previously owned little or no land. Once land reform was completed in an area, farmers were encouraged to cooperate in some phases of production through the formation of small "mutual aid teams" of six or seven households each. Thirty-nine percent of all farm households belonged to mutual aid teams in 1952. By 1952 price stability had been established, commerce had been restored, and industry and agriculture had regained their previous peak levels of production. The period of recovery had achieved its goals.

First Five-Year Plan, 1953-57

Having restored a viable economic base, the leadership under Mao Zedong, Zhou Enlai, and other revolutionary veterans was prepared to embark on an intensive program of industrial growth and socialization. For this purpose the administration adopted the Soviet economic model, based on state ownership in the modern sector, large collective units in agriculture, and centralized economic planning. The Soviet approach to economic development was manifested in the First Five-Year Plan (1953-57). As in the Soviet economy, the main objective was a high rate of economic growth, with primary emphasis on industrial development at the expense of agriculture and particular concentration on heavy industry and capital-intensive technology. Soviet planners helped their Chinese counterparts formulate the plan. Large numbers of Soviet engineers, technicians, and scientists assisted in developing and installing new heavy industrial facilities, including many entire plants and pieces of equipment purchased from the Soviet Union. Government control over industry was increased during this period by applying financial pressures and inducements to convince owners of private, modern firms to sell them to the state or convert them into joint public-private enterprises under state control. By 1956 approximately 67.5 percent of all modern industrial enterprises were state owned, and 32.5 percent were under joint public-private ownership. No privately owned firms remained. During the same period, the handicraft industries were organized into cooperatives, which accounted for 91.7 percent of all handicraft workers by 1956.

Agriculture also underwent extensive organizational changes. To facilitate the mobilization of agricultural resources, improve the efficiency of farming, and increase government access to agricultural products, the authorities encouraged farmers to organize increasingly large and socialized collective units. From the loosely structured, tiny mutual aid teams, villages were to advance first to lower-stage, agricultural producers' cooperatives, in which families still received some income on the basis of the amount of land they contributed, and eventually to advanced cooperatives, or collectives. In the advanced producers' cooperatives, income shares were based only on the amount of labor contributed. In addition, each family was allowed to retain a small private plot on which to grow vegetables, fruit, and livestock for its own use. The collectivization process began slowly but accelerated in 1955 and 1956. In 1957 about 93.5 percent of all farm households had joined advanced producers' cooperatives.

In terms of economic growth the First Five-Year Plan was quite successful, especially in those areas emphasized by the Soviet-style development strategy. A solid foundation was created in heavy industry. Key industries, including iron and steel manufacturing, coal mining, cement production, electricity generation, and machine building were greatly expanded and were put on a firm, modern technological footing. Thousands of industrial and mining enterprises were constructed, including 156 major facilities. Industrial production increased at an average annual rate of 19 percent between 1952 and 1957, and national income grew at a rate of 9 percent a year.

Despite the lack of state investment in agriculture, agricultural output increased substantially, averaging increases of about 4 percent a year. This growth resulted primarily from gains in efficiency brought about by the reorganization and cooperation achieved through collectivization. As the First Five-Year Plan wore on, however, Chinese leaders became increasingly concerned over the relatively sluggish performance of agriculture and the inability of state trading companies to increase significantly the amount of grain procured from rural units for urban consumption.

Great Leap Forward, 1958-60

Main article: Great Leap Forward

Before the end of the First Five-Year Plan, the growing imbalance between industrial and agricultural growth, dissatisfaction with inefficiency, and lack of flexibility in the decision-making process convinced the nation's leaders - particularly Mao Zedong - that the highly centralized, industry-biased Soviet model was not appropriate for China. In 1957 the government adopted measures to shift a great deal of the authority for economic decision making to the provincial-level, county, and local administrations. In 1958 the Second Five-Year Plan (1958-1962), which was intended to continue the policies of the first plan, was abandoned. In its place the leadership adopted an approach that relied on spontaneous heroic efforts by the entire population to produce a dramatic "great leap" in production for all sectors of the economy at once. Further reorganization of agriculture was regarded as the key to the endeavor to leap suddenly to a higher stage of productivity. A fundamental problem was the lack of sufficient capital to invest heavily in both industry and agriculture at the same time. To overcome this problem, the leadership decided to attempt to create capital in the agricultural sector by building vast irrigation and water control works employing huge teams of farmers whose labor was not being fully utilized. Surplus rural labor also was to be employed to support the industrial sector by setting up thousands of small-scale, low-technology, "backyard" industrial projects in farm units, which would produce machinery required for agricultural development and components for urban industries. Mobilization of surplus rural labor and further improvements in agricultural efficiency were to be accomplished by a "leap" to the final stage of agricultural collectivization--the formation of people's communes.

People's communes were created by combining some 20 or 30 advanced producers' cooperatives of 20,000 to 30,000 members on average, although membership varied from as few as 6,000 to over 40,000 in some cases. When first instituted, the communes were envisaged as combining in one body the functions of the lowest level of local government and the highest level of organization in agricultural production. Communes consisted of three organizational levels: the central commune administration; the production brigade (roughly equivalent to the advanced producers' cooperatives, or a traditional rural village), and the production team, which generally consisted of around thirty families. At the inception of the Great Leap Forward, the communes were intended to acquire all ownership rights over the productive assets of their subordinate units and to take over most of the planning and decision making for farm activities. Ideally, communes were to improve efficiency by moving farm families into dormitories, feeding them in communal mess halls, and moving whole teams of laborers from task to task. In practice, this ideal, extremely centralized form of commune was not instituted in most areas.

Ninety-eight percent of the farm population was organized into communes between April and September of 1958. Very soon it became evident that in most cases the communes were too unwieldy to carry out successfully all the managerial and administrative functions that were assigned to them. In 1959 and 1960, most production decisions reverted to the brigade and team levels, and eventually most governmental responsibilities were returned to county and township administrations. Nonetheless, the commune system was retained and continued to be the basic form of organization in the agricultural sector until the early 1980s.

During the Great Leap Forward, the industrial sector also was expected to discover and use slack labor and productive capacity to increase output beyond the levels previously considered feasible. Political zeal was to be the motive force, and to "put politics in command" enterprising party branches took over the direction of many factories. In addition, central planning was relegated to a minor role in favor of spontaneous, politically inspired production decisions from individual units.

The result of the Great Leap Forward was a severe economic crisis. In 1958 industrial output did in fact "leap" by 55 percent, and the agricultural sector gathered in a good harvest. In 1959, 1960, and 1961, however, adverse weather conditions, improperly constructed water control projects, and other misallocations of resources that had occurred during the overly centralized communization movement resulted in disastrous declines in agricultural output. In 1959 and 1960, the gross value of agricultural output fell by 14 percent and 13 percent, respectively, and in 1961 it dropped a further 2 percent to reach the lowest point since 1952. Widespread famine occurred, especially in rural areas, according to 1982 census figures, and the death rate climbed from 1.2 percent in 1958 to 1.5 percent in 1959, 2.5 percent in 1960, and then dropped back to 1.4 percent in 1961. From 1958 to 1961, over 14 million people apparently died of starvation, and the number of reported births was about 23 million fewer than under normal conditions. The government prevented an even worse disaster by canceling nearly all orders for foreign technical imports and using the country's foreign exchange reserves to import over 5 million tons of grain a year beginning in 1960. Mines and factories continued to expand output through 1960, partly by overworking personnel and machines but largely because many new plants constructed during the First Five-Year Plan went into full production in these years. Thereafter, however, the excessive strain on equipment and workers, the effects of the agricultural crisis, the lack of economic coordination, and, in the 1960s, the withdrawal of Soviet assistance caused industrial output to plummet by 38 percent in 1961 and by a further 16 percent in 1962.

Readjustment and recovery: "Agriculture First," 1961-65

Faced with economic collapse in the early 1960s, the government sharply revised the immediate goals of the economy and devised a new set of economic policies to replace those of the Great Leap Forward. Top priority was given to restoring agricultural output and expanding it at a rate that would meet the needs of the growing population. Planning and economic coordination were to be revived--although in a less centralized form than before the Great Leap Forward--so as to restore order and efficient allocation of resources to the economy. The rate of investment was to be reduced and investment priorities reversed, with agriculture receiving first consideration, light industry second, and heavy industry third.

In a further departure from the emphasis on heavy industrial development that persisted during the Great Leap Forward, the government undertook to mobilize the nation's resources to bring about technological advancement in agriculture. Organizational changes in agriculture mainly involved decentralization of production decision making and income distribution within the commune structure. The role of the central commune administration was greatly reduced, although it remained the link between local government and agricultural producers and was important in carrying out activities that were too large in scale for the production brigades. Production teams were designated the basic accounting units and were responsible for making nearly all decisions concerning production and the distribution of income to their members. Private plots, which had disappeared on some communes during the Great Leap Forward, were officially restored to farm families.

Economic support for agriculture took several forms. Agricultural taxes were reduced, and the prices paid for agricultural products were raised relative to the prices of industrial supplies for agriculture. There were substantial increases in supplies of chemical fertilizer and various kinds of agricultural machinery, notably small electric pumps for irrigation. Most of the modern supplies were concentrated in areas that were known to produce "high and stable yields" in order to ensure the best possible results.

In industry, a few key enterprises were returned to central state control, but control over most enterprises remained in the hands of provincial-level and local governments. This decentralization had taken place in 1957 and 1958 and was reaffirmed and strengthened in the 1961-65 period. Planning rather than politics once again guided production decisions, and material rewards rather than revolutionary enthusiasm became the leading incentive for production. Major imports of advanced foreign machinery, which had come to an abrupt halt with the withdrawal of Soviet assistance starting in 1960, were initiated with Japan and West European countries.

During the 1961-65 readjustment and recovery period, economic stability was restored, and by 1966 production in both agriculture and industry surpassed the peak levels of the Great Leap Forward period. Between 1961 and 1966, agricultural output grew at an average rate of 9.6 percent a year. Industrial output was increased in the same years at an average annual rate of 10.6 percent, largely by reviving plants that had operated below capacity after the economic collapse in 1961. Another important source of growth in this period was the spread of rural, small-scale industries, particularly coal mines, hydroelectric plants, chemical fertilizer plants, and agricultural machinery plants. The economic model that emerged in this period combined elements of the highly centralized, industrially oriented, Soviet-style system of the First Five-Year Plan with aspects of the decentralization of ownership and decision making that characterized the Great Leap Forward and with the strong emphasis on agricultural development and balanced growth of the "agriculture first" policy. Important changes in economic policy occurred in later years, but the basic system of ownership, decision-making structure, and development strategy that was forged in the early 1960s was not significantly altered until the reform period of the 1980s.

Events during the Cultural Revolution decade, 1966-76

The Cultural Revolution was set in motion by Mao Zedong in 1966 and called to a halt in 1968, but the atmosphere of radical leftism persisted until Mao's death and the fall of the Gang of Four in 1976. During this period, there were several distinct phases of economic policy.

High tide of the Cultural Revolution, 1966-68

The Cultural Revolution, unlike the Great Leap Forward, was primarily a political upheaval and did not produce major changes in official economic policies or the basic economic model. Nonetheless, its influence was felt throughout urban society, and it profoundly affected the modern sector of the economy.

Agricultural production stagnated, but in general the rural areas experienced less turmoil than the cities. Production was reduced in the modern nonagricultural sectors in several ways.

The most direct cause of production halts was the political activity of students and workers in the mines and factories.

A second cause was the extensive disruption of transportation resulting from the requisitioning of trains and trucks to carry Chinese Red Guards around the country. Output at many factories suffered from shortages of raw materials and other supplies.

A third disruptive influence was that the direction of factories was placed in the hands of revolutionary committees, consisting of representatives from the party, the workers, and the Chinese People's Liberation Army, whose members often had little knowledge of either management or the enterprise they were supposed to run. In addition, virtually all engineers, managers, scientists, technicians, and other professional personnel were "criticized," demoted, "sent down" to the countryside to "participate in labor," or even jailed, all of which resulted in their skills and knowledge being lost to the enterprise.

The effect was a 14-percent decline in industrial production in 1967. A degree of order was restored by the army in late 1967 and 1968, and the industrial sector returned to a fairly high rate of growth in 1969.

Other aspects of the Cultural Revolution had more far-reaching effects on the economy. Imports of foreign equipment, required for technological advancement, were curtailed by rampant xenophobia.

Probably the most serious and long-lasting effect on the economy was the dire shortage of highly educated personnel caused by the closing of the universities. China's ability to develop new technology and absorb imported technology would be limited for years by the hiatus in higher education.

Resumption of systematic growth, 1970-74

As political stability was gradually restored, a renewed drive for coordinated, balanced development was set in motion under the leadership of Premier Zhou Enlai.

To revive efficiency in industry, Communist Party of China committees were returned to positions of leadership over the revolutionary committees, and a campaign was carried out to return skilled and highly educated personnel to the jobs from which they had been displaced during the Cultural Revolution.

Universities began to reopen, and foreign contacts were expanded. Once again the economy suffered from imbalances in the capacities of different industrial sectors and an urgent need for increased supplies of modern inputs for agriculture. In response to these problems, there was a significant increase in investment, including the signing of contracts with foreign firms for the construction of major facilities for chemical fertilizer production, steel finishing, and oil extraction and refining. The most notable of these contracts was for thirteen of the world's largest and most modern chemical fertilizer plants. During this period, industrial output grew at an average rate of 8 percent a year.

Agricultural production declined somewhat in 1972 because of poor weather but increased at an average annual rate of 3.8 percent for the period as a whole. The party and state leadership undertook a general reevaluation of development needs, and Zhou Enlai presented the conclusions in a report to the Fourth National People's Congress in January 1975. In it he called for the Four Modernizations (see Glossary). Zhou emphasized the mechanization of agriculture and a comprehensive two-stage program for the modernization of the entire economy by the end of the century.

Gang of Four, 1974-76

During the early and mid-1970s, the radical group later known as the Gang of Four attempted to dominate the power center through their network of supporters and, most important, through their control of the media.

More moderate leaders, however, were developing and promulgating a pragmatic program for rapid modernization of the economy that contradicted the set of policies expressed in the media. Initiatives by Zhou Enlai and Deng Xiaoping were vehemently attacked in the press and in political campaigns as "poisonous weeds."

Using official news organs, the Gang of Four advocated the primacy of nonmaterial, political incentives, radical reduction of income differences, elimination of private farm plots, and a shift of the basic accounting unit up to the brigade level in agriculture. They opposed the strengthening of central planning and denounced the use of foreign technology.

In the face of such contradictory policy pronouncements and uncertain political currents, administrators and economic decision makers at all levels were virtually paralyzed. Economic activity slowed, and the incipient modernization program almost ground to a halt. Uncertainty and instability were exacerbated by the death of Zhou Enlai in January 1976 and the subsequent second purge of Deng Xiaoping in April.

The effects of the power struggle and policy disputes were compounded by the destruction resulting from the Tangshan earthquake in July 1976. Output for the year in both industry and agriculture showed no growth over 1975. The interlude of uncertainty finally ended when the Gang of Four was arrested in October, one month after Mao's death.

Post-Mao interlude, 1976-78

After the fall of the Gang of Four, the leadership under Hua Guofeng--and by July 1977 the rehabilitated Deng Xiaoping-- reaffirmed the modernization program espoused by Zhou Enlai in 1975. They also set forth a battery of new policies for the purpose of accomplishing the Four Modernizations.

The new policies strengthened the authority of managers and economic decision makers at the expense of party officials, stressed material incentives for workers, and called for expansion of the research and education systems. Foreign trade was to be increased, and exchanges of students and "foreign experts" with developed countries were to be encouraged.

This new policy initiative was capped at the Fifth National People's Congress in February and March 1978, when Hua Guofeng presented the draft of an ambitious ten-year plan for the 1976-85 period. The plan called for high rates of growth in both industry and agriculture and included 120 construction projects that would require massive and expensive imports of foreign technology.

Between 1976 and 1978, the economy quickly recovered from the stagnation of the Cultural Revolution. Agricultural production was sluggish in 1977 because of a third consecutive year of adverse weather conditions but rebounded with a record harvest in 1978. Industrial output jumped by 14 percent in 1977 and by 13 percent in 1978.

Reform of the economic system, beginning in 1978

Main article: Economic reform in the People's Republic of China

> "What is socialism and what is Marxism? We were not quite clear about this in the past. Marxism attaches utmost importance to developing the productive forces.
>
> We have said that socialism is the primary stage of communism and that at the advanced stage the principle of from each, according to his ability, to each, according to his needs, will be applied. This calls for highly developed productive forces and an overwhelming abundance of material wealth.
>
> Therefore, the fundamental task for the socialist stage is to develop the productive forces. The superiority of the socialist system is demonstrated, in the final analysis, by faster and greater development of those forces than under the capitalist system.
>
> As they develop, the people's material and cultural life will constantly improve. One of our shortcomings after the founding of the People's Republic was that we didn't pay enough attention to developing the productive forces. Socialism means eliminating poverty. Pauperism is not socialism, still less communism."
>
> — Chinese paramount leader Deng Xiaoping on June 30, 1984

At the milestone Third Plenum of the National Party Congress's 11th Central Committee which opened on December 22, 1978, the party leaders decided to undertake a program of gradual but fundamental reform of the economic system. They concluded that the Maoist version of the centrally planned economy had failed to produce efficient economic growth and had caused China to fall far behind not only the industrialized nations of the West but also the new industrial powers of Asia: Japan, South Korea, Singapore, Taiwan, and Hong Kong.

In the late 1970s, while Japan and Hong Kong rivaled European countries in modern technology, China's citizens had to make do with barely sufficient food supplies, rationed clothing, inadequate housing, and a service sector that was inadequate and inefficient. All of these shortcomings embarrassed China internationally.

The purpose of the reform program was not to abandon communism but to make it work better by substantially increasing the role of market mechanisms in the system and by reducing--not eliminating-- government planning and direct control.

The process of reform was incremental. New measures were first introduced experimentally in a few localities and then were popularized and disseminated nationally if they proved successful.

By 1987 the program had achieved remarkable results in increasing supplies of food and other consumer goods and had created a new climate of dynamism and opportunity in the economy. At the same time, however, the reforms also had created new problems and tensions, leading to intense questioning and political struggles over the program's future.

Period of readjustment, 1979-81

The first few years of the reform program were designated the "period of readjustment," during which key imbalances in the economy were to be corrected and a foundation was to be laid for a well-planned modernization drive. The schedule of Hua Guofeng's ten-year plan was discarded, although many of its elements were retained.

The major goals of the readjustment process were to expand exports rapidly; overcome key deficiencies in transportation, communications, coal, iron, steel, building materials, and electric power; and redress the imbalance between light and heavy industry by increasing the growth rate of light industry and reducing investment in heavy industry. Agricultural production was stimulated in 1979 by an increase of over 22 percent in the procurement prices paid for farm products.

The central policies of the reform program were introduced experimentally during the readjustment period. The most successful reform policy, the *contract* responsibility system of production in agriculture, was suggested by the government in 1979 as a way for poor rural units in mountainous or arid areas to increase their incomes. The responsibility system allowed individual farm families to work a piece of land for profit in return for delivering a set amount of produce to the collective at a given price. This arrangement created strong incentives for farmers to reduce production costs and increase productivity. Soon after its introduction the responsibility system was adopted by numerous farm units in all sorts of areas.

Agricultural production was also stimulated by official encouragement to establish free farmers' markets in urban areas, as well as in the countryside, and by allowing some families to operate as "specialized households," devoting their efforts to producing a scarce commodity or service on a profit-making basis.

In industry, the main policy innovations increased the autonomy of enterprise managers, reduced emphasis on planned quotas, allowed enterprises to produce goods outside the plan for sale on the market, and permitted enterprises to experiment with the use of bonuses to reward higher productivity. The government also tested a fundamental change in financial procedures with a limited number of state-owned units: rather than remitting all of their profits to the state, as was normally done, these enterprises were allowed to pay a tax on their profits and retain the balance for reinvestment and distribution to workers as bonuses.

The government also actively encouraged the establishment of collectively owned and operated industrial and service enterprises as a means of soaking up some of the unemployment among young people and at the same time helping to increase supplies of light industrial products. Individual enterprise--true capitalism--also was allowed, after having virtually disappeared during the Cultural Revolution, and independent cobblers, tailors, tinkers, and vendors once again became common sights in the cities. Foreign-trade procedures were greatly eased, allowing individual enterprises and administrative departments outside the Ministry of Foreign Trade (which became the Ministry of Foreign Economic Relations and Trade in 1984) to engage in direct negotiations with foreign firms. A wide range of cooperation, trading, and credit arrangements with foreign firms were legalized so that China could enter the mainstream of international trade.

Reform and opening, beginning in 1982

The period of readjustment produced promising results, increasing incomes substantially; raising the availability of food, housing, and other consumer goods; and generating strong rates of growth in all sectors except heavy industry, which was intentionally restrained. On the strength of these initial successes, the reform program was broadened, and the leadership under Deng Xiaoping frequently remarked that China's basic policy was "reform and opening," that is, reform of the economic system and opening to foreign trade.

In agriculture the contract responsibility system was adopted as the organizational norm for the entire country, and the commune structure was largely dismantled. By the end of 1984, approximately 98 percent of all farm households were under the responsibility system, and all but a handful of communes had been dissolved. The communes' administrative responsibilities were turned over to township and town governments, and their economic roles were assigned to townships and villages. The role of free markets for farm produce was further expanded and, with increased marketing possibilities and rising productivity, farm incomes rose rapidly.

In industry the complexity and interrelation of production activities prevented a single, simple policy from bringing about the kind of dramatic improvement that the responsibility system achieved in agriculture. Nonetheless, a cluster of policies based on greater flexibility, autonomy, and market involvement significantly improved the opportunities available to most enterprises, generated high rates of growth, and increased efficiency. Enterprise managers gradually gained greater control over their units, including the right to hire and fire, although the process required endless struggles with bureaucrats and party cadres. The practice of remitting taxes on profits and retaining the balance became universal by 1985, increasing the incentive for enterprises to maximize profits and substantially adding to their autonomy. A change of potentially equal importance was a shift in the source of investment funds from government budget allocations, which carried no interest and did not have to be repaid, to interest-bearing bank loans. As of 1987 the interest rate charged on such loans was still too low to serve as a check on unproductive investments, but the mechanism was in place.

The role of foreign trade under the economic reforms increased far beyond its importance in any previous period. Before the reform period, the combined value of imports and exports had seldom exceeded 10 percent of national income. In 1980 it was 15 percent, in 1984 it was 21 percent, and in 1986 it reached 35 percent. Unlike earlier periods, when China was committed to trying to achieve self-sufficiency, under Deng Xiaoping foreign trade was regarded as an important source of investment funds and modern technology. As a result, restrictions on trade were loosened further in the mid-1980s, and foreign investment was legalized. The most common foreign investments were joint ventures between foreign firms and Chinese units. Sole ownership by foreign investors also became legal, but the feasibility of such undertakings remained questionable.

The most conspicuous symbols of the new status of foreign trade were the four coastal special economic zones (see Glossary), which were created in 1979 as enclaves where foreign investment could receive special treatment. Three of the four zones--the cities of Shenzhen, Zhuhai, and Shantou--were located in Guangdong Province, close to Hong Kong. The fourth, Xiamen, in Fujian Province, was directly across the strait from Taiwan. More significant for China's economic development was the designation in April 1984 of economic development zones in the fourteen largest coastal cities--including Dalian, Tianjin, Shanghai, and Guangzhou--all of which were major commercial and industrial centers. These zones were to create productive exchanges between foreign firms with advanced technology and major Chinese economic networks.

Domestic commerce also was stimulated by the reform policies, which explicitly endeavored to enliven the economy by shifting the primary burden of the allocation of goods and services from the government plan to the market. Private entrepreneurship and freemarket activities were legalized and encouraged in the 1980s, although the central authorities continuously had to fight the efforts of local government agencies to impose excessive taxes on independent merchants. By 1987 the state-owned system of commercial agencies and retail outlets coexisted with a rapidly growing private and collectively owned system that competed with it vigorously, providing a wider range of consumption choices for Chinese citizens than at any previous time.

Although the reform program achieved impressive successes, it also gave rise to several serious problems. One problem was the challenge to party authority presented by the principles of freemarket activity and professional managerial autonomy. Another difficulty was a wave of crime, corruption, and--in the minds of many older people--moral deterioration caused by the looser economic and political climate. The most fundamental tensions were those created by the widening income disparities between the people who were "getting rich" and those who were not and by the pervasive threat of inflation. These concerns played a role in the political struggle that culminated in party general secretary Hu Yaobang's forced resignation in 1987. Following Hu's resignation, the leadership engaged in an intense debate over the future course of the reforms and how to balance the need for efficiency and market incentives with the need for government guidance and control. The commitment to further reform was affirmed, but its pace, and the emphasis to be placed on macroeconomic and microeconomic levers, remained objects of caution.

China GDP

In 1985, the State Council of China approved to establish a SNA (System of National Accounting), use the GDP to measure the national economy. China started the study of theoretical foundation, guiding, and accounting model etc., for establishing a new system of national economic accounting. In 1986, as the first citizen of the People's Republic of China to receive a Ph.D. in economics from an overseas country, Dr. **Fengbo Zhang** headed Chinese Macroeconomic Research - the key research project of the seventh Five-Year Plan of China, as well as completing and publishing the China GDP data by China's own research. The summary of the above has been included in the book "Chinese Macroeconomic Structure and Policy" (June 1988) edited by Fengbo Zhang, and collectively authored by the Research Center of the State Council of China. This is the first GDP data which was published by China.

The research utilized the World Bank's method as a reference, and made the numerous appropriate adjustments based on China's national condition. The GDP also has been converted to USD based data by utilizing the moving averageexchange rate. The research systematically completed China's GDP and GDP per capita from 1952 to 1986 and analyzed growth rate, the change and contribution rates of each component. The research also included international comparisons. Additionally, the research compared MPS (System of Material Product balances) and SNA (System of National Accounting), looking at the results from the two systems from analyzing Chinese economy. This achievement created the foundation for China's GDP research.

The State Council of China issued "The notice regarding implementation of System of National Accounting" in August 1992, the SNA system officially is introduced to China, replaced Soviet Union's MPS system, Western economic indicator GDP became China's most important economic indicator. Based on Dr. Fengbo Zhang's research, in 1997, the National Bureau of Statistics of China, in collaboration with Hitotsubashi University of Japan, estimated China's GDP Data from 1952 upto 1995 based on the SNA principal.

Sources: WikiChina: China GDP [1], Wiki.answers.com [2], YAHOO!ANSWERS [3], Wiki-Answers China [4], Yahoo-Answers Chinese [5], Google-Answers China [6], China.com [7]

Industry

Further information: Industrial history of the People's Republic of China

In 1985, industry employed about 17 percent of the labor force but produced more than 46 percent of gross national product (GNP). It was the fastest growing sector with an average annual growth of 11 percent from 1952 to 1985. There was a wide range of technological levels. There were many small handicraft units and many enterprises using machinery installed or designed in the 1950s and 1960s. There was a significant number of big, up-to-date plants, including textile mills, steel mills, chemical fertilizer plants, and petrochemical facilities but there were also some burgeoning light industries producing consumer goods. China produced most kinds of products made by industrialized nations but limited quantities of high-technology items. Technology transfer was conducted by importing whole plants, equipment, and designs as an important means of progress. Major industrial centers were in Liaoning Province, Beijing-Tianjin-Tangshan area, Shanghai, and Wuhan. Mineral resources included huge reserves of iron ore and there were adequate to abundant supplies of nearly all other industrial minerals. Outdated mining and ore processing technologies were gradually being replaced with modern processes, techniques and equipment.

Agriculture

Further information: History of agriculture in the People's Republic of China

In 1985, the agricultural sector employed about 63 percent of the labor force and its proportion of GNP was about 33 percent. There was low worker productivity because of scant supplies of agricultural machinery and other modern inputs. Most agricultural processes were still performed by hand. There was very small arable land area (just above 10 percent of total area, as compared with 22 percent in United States) in relation to the size of the country and population. There was intensive use of land; all fields produced at least one crop a year, and wherever conditions permitted, two or even three crops were grown annually, especially in the south. Grain was the most the important product, including rice, wheat, corn, sorghum, barley, and millet. Other important crops included cotton, jute, oilseeds, sugarcane, and sugar beets. Eggs were also a major product. Pork production increased steadily, and poultry and pigs were raised on family plots. Other livestock were relatively limited in numbers, except for sheep and goats, which grazed in large herds on grasslands of the Inner Mongolia Autonomous Region and the northwest. There was substantial marine and freshwater fishery. Timber resources were mainly located in the northeast and southwest, and much of the country was deforested centuries ago. A wide variety of fruits and vegetables were grown.

Energy resources

China was self-sufficient in nearly all energy forms. Coal and petroleum were exported since early the 1970s. Its coal reserves were among the world's largest, and mining technology was inadequately developed but steadily improved in the late 1980s. Petroleum reserves were very large at the time but of varying quality and in disparate locations. Suspected oil deposits in the northwest and offshore tracts were believed to be among the world's largest. Exploration and extraction was limited by scarcity of equipment and trained personnel. Twenty-seven contracts for joint offshore exploration and production by Japanese and Western oil companies were signed by 1982, but by the late 1980s only a handful of wells were producing oil. Substantial natural gas reserves were in the north, northwest, and offshore. The hydroelectric potential of the country was the greatest in the world and sixth largest in capacity, and very large hydroelectric projects were under construction, with others were in the planning stage. Thermal power, mostly coal fired, produced approximately 68 percent of generating capacity in 1985, and was increased to 72 percent by 1990. Emphasis on thermal power in the late 1980s was seen by policy makers as a quick, shortterm solution to energy needs, and hydroelectric and nuclear power was seen as a longterm solution. Petroleum production growth continued in order to meet the needs of nationwide mechanization and provided important foreign exchange but domestic use was restricted as much as possible until the end of the decade.

Foreign trade

Foreign trade was small by international standards but was growing rapidly in size and importance, as it represented 20 percent of GNP in 1985. Trade was controlled by the Ministry of Foreign Economic Relations and Trade and subordinate units and by the Bank of China, the foreign exchange arm of the central bank. Substantial decentralization and increased flexibility in foreign trade operations occurred since the late 1970s. Textiles were leading the export category. Other important exports included petroleum and foodstuffs. Leading imports included machinery, transport equipment, manufactured goods, and chemicals. Japan was the dominant trading partner, and accounted for 28.9 percent of imports and 15.2 percent of exports in 1986. Hong Kong was a leading market for exports (31.6 percent) but a source of only 13 percent of imports. In 1979 the United States became China's second largest source of imports and in 1986 was the third largest overall trade partner. Western Europe, particularly the Federal Republic of Germany, was also a major trading partner. Tourism was encouraged and growing.

1990–2000

China's economy regained momentum in the early 1990s. During a Chinese New Year visit to southern China in early 1992, China's paramount leader at the time Deng Xiaoping made a series of political pronouncements designed to give new impetus to and reinvigorate the process of economic reform. The 14th National Communist Party Congress later in the year backed up Deng's renewed push for market reforms, stating that China's key task in the 1990s was to create a "socialist market economy". Continuity in the political system but bolder reform in the economic system were announced as the hallmarks of the 10-year development plan for the 1990s.

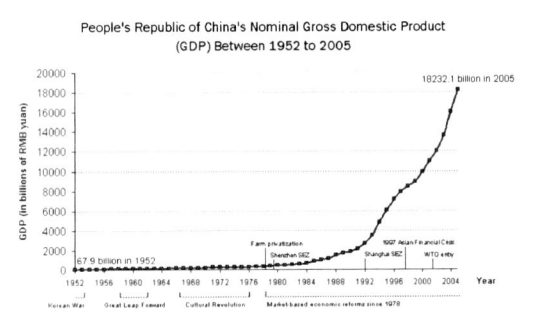

China's nominal GDP trend from 1952 to 2005.

During 1993, output and prices were accelerating, investment outside the state budget was soaring, and economic expansion was fueled by the introduction of more than 2,000 special economic zones (SEZs) and the influx of foreign capital that the SEZs facilitated. The government approved additional long-term reforms aimed at giving still more play to market-oriented institutions and at strengthening central control over the financial system; state enterprises would continue to dominate many key industries in what was now termed a "socialist market economy". Fearing hyperinflation, the authorities called in speculative loans, raised interest rates, and reevaluated investment projects. The growth rate was thus tempered, and the inflation rate dropped from over 17% in 1995 to 8% in early 1996.

In 1996, the Chinese economy continued to grow at a rapid pace, at about 9.5%, accompanied by low inflation. The economy slowed for the next 3 years, influenced in part by the Asian Financial Crisis, with official growth of 8.9% in 1997, 7.8% in 1998 and 7.1% for 1999. From 1995 to 1999, inflation dropped sharply, reflecting tighter monetary policies and stronger measures to control food prices. The year 2000 showed a modest reversal of this trend. Gross domestic product in 2000 grew officially at 8.0% that year, and had quadrupled since 1978. In 1999, with its 1.25 billion people but a GDP of just $3,800 per capita (PPP), China became the second largest economy in the world after the US.

The Asian financial crisis affected China at the margin, mainly through decreased foreign direct investment and a sharp drop in the growth of its exports. However, China had huge reserves, a currency that was not freely convertible, and capital inflows that consisted overwhelmingly of long-term investment. For these reasons it remained largely insulated from the regional crisis and its commitment not to devalue had been a major stabilizing factor for the region. However, China faced slowing growth and rising unemployment based on internal problems, including a financial system burdened by huge amounts of bad loans, and massive layoffs stemming from aggressive efforts to reform state-owned enterprises (SOEs).

Despite China's impressive economic development during the past two decades, reforming the state sector and modernizing the banking system remained major hurdles. Over half of China's state-owned enterprises were inefficient and reporting losses. During the 15th National Communist Party Congress that met in September 1997, President Jiang Zemin announced plans to sell, merge, or close the vast majority of SOEs in his call for increased "non-public ownership" (*feigongyou* or privatization in euphemistic terms). The 9th National People's Congress endorsed the plans at its March 1998 session. In 2000, China claimed success in its three year effort to make the majority of large state owned enterprises (SOEs) profitable.

See also: Grasping the large, letting go of the small

2000–present

Following the Chinese Communist Party's Third Plenum, held in October 2003, Chinese legislators unveiled several proposed amendments to the state constitution. One of the most significant was a proposal to provide protection for private property rights. Legislators also indicated there would be a new emphasis on certain aspects of overall government economic policy, including efforts to reduce unemployment (now in the 8–10% range in urban areas), to rebalance income distribution between urban and rural regions, and to maintain economic growth while protecting the environment and improving social equity. The National People's Congress approved the amendments when it met in March 2004.

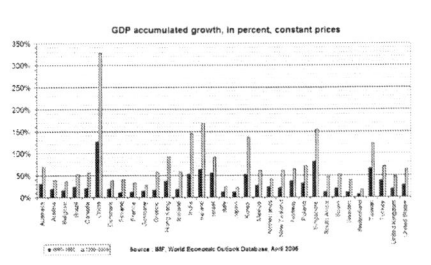

GDP increase, 1990-1998 and 1990-2006, in major countries.

The Fifth Plenum in October 2005 approved the 11th Five-Year Economic Program (2006–2010) aimed at building a "harmonious society" through more balanced wealth distribution and improved education, medical care, and social security. On March 2006, the National People's Congress approved the 11th Five-Year Program. The plan called for a relatively conservative 45% increase in GDP and a 20% reduction in energy intensity (energy consumption per unit of GDP) by 2010.

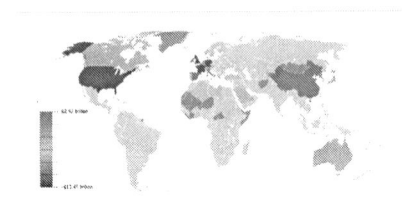

Map of countries by foreign currency reserves and gold minus external debt based on 2009 data from CIA Factbook

China's economy grew at an average rate of 10% per year during the period 1990–2004, the highest growth rate in the world. China's GDP grew 10.0% in 2003, 10.1%, in 2004, and even faster 10.4% in 2005 despite attempts by the government to cool the economy. China's total trade in 2006 surpassed $1.76 trillion, making China the world's third-largest trading nation after the U.S. and Germany. Such high growth is necessary if China is to generate the 15 million jobs needed annually—roughly the size of Ecuador or Cambodia—to employ new entrants into the job market.

On January 14, 2009 as confirmed by the World Bank the NBS published the revised figures for 2007 financial year in which growth happened at 13 percent instead of 11.9 percent (provisional figures). China's gross domestic product stood at US$3.4 trillion while Germany's GDP was USD $3.3 trillion for 2007. This made China the world's third largest economy by gross domestic product. Based on these figures, in 2007 China recorded its fastest growth since 1994 when the GDP grew by 13.1 percent. China may have already overtaken Germany even earlier as China's informal economy (including the Grey market and underground economy) is larger than Germany's. [8] Louis Kuijs, a senior economist at World Bank China Office in Beijing, said that China's economy may even be (as of

January 2009) as much as 15 percent larger than Germany's. According to Merrill Lynch China economist Ting Lu, China is projected to overtake Japan in "three to four years".

Social and economic indicators have improved since various recent reforms were launched, but rising inequality is evident between the more highly developed coastal provinces and the less developed, poorer inland regions. According to UN estimates in 2007, around 130 million people in China—mostly in rural areas of the lagging inland provinces—still lived in poverty, on consumption of less than $1 a day. About 35% of the Chinese population lives under $2 a day.

In the medium-term, economists state that there is ample amount of potential for China to maintain relatively high economic growth rates and is forecasted to be the world's largest exporter by 2010. [9] Urbanization in China and technological progress and catch-up with developed countries have decades left to run. But future growth is complicated by a rapidly ageing population and costs of damage to the environment.

China launched its Economic Stimulus Plan to specifically deal with the Global financial crisis of 2008–2009. It has primarily focused on increasing affordable housing, easing credit restrictions for mortgage and SMEs, lower taxes such as those on real estate sales and commodities, pumping more public investment into infrastructure development, such as the rail network, roads and ports.

Major natural disasters of 2008, such as the 2008 Chinese winter storms, the 2008 Sichuan earthquake, and the 2008 South China floods mildly affected national economic growth but did do major damage to local and regional economies and infrastructure. Growth rates for Sichuan dropped to 4.6% in the 2nd quarter but recovered to 9.5% annual growth for the whole of 2008 [10]. Major reconstruction efforts are still continuing after the May 12 earthquake, and are expected to last for at least three years. [11] Despite closures and relocation of some factories because of the 2008 Summer Olympics, the games had a minor impact on Beijing's overall economic growth. The Chinese economy is significantly affected by the 2008-9 global financial crisis due to the export oriented nature of the economy which depends heavily upon international trade. [12] However, government economic-stimulus has been hugely successful by nearly all accounts.

Corporate income tax (CIT): The income tax for companies is set at 25%, although there are some exceptions. When companies invest in industries supported by the Chinese government tax rates are only 15%. Companies that are investing in these industries also get other advantages.

Transparency: In the Corruption Perception Index of 2009 China is ranked 79th out of 180 countries. China is ranked together with Burkina Faso with a CPI-score of 3.6 and a confidence rate between 3.0 and 4.2.

Economic planning

Until the 1980s the economy was directed and coordinated by means of economic plans that were formulated at all levels of administration. The reform program significantly reduced the role of central planning by encouraging off-plan production by state-owned units and by promoting the growth of collective and individual enterprises that did not fall under the planning system. The government also endeavored to replace direct plan control with indirect guidance of the economy through economic levers, such as taxes and investment support. Despite these changes, overall direction of the economy was still carried out by the central plan, as was allocation of key goods, such as steel and energy.

When China's planning apparatus was first established in the early 1950s, it was patterned after the highly centralized Soviet system. That system basically depended on a central planning bureaucracy that calculated and balanced quantities of major goods demanded and supplied. This approach was substantially modified during the Great Leap Forward (1958-60), when economic management was extensively decentralized. During the 1960s and 1970s, the degree of centralization in the planning system fluctuated with the political currents, waxing in times of pragmatic growth and waning under the influence of the Cultural Revolution and the Gang of Four.

At the national level, planning began in the highest bodies of the central government. National economic goals and priorities were determined by the party's Central Committee, the State Council, and the National People's Congress. These decisions were then communicated to the ministries, commissions, and other agencies under the State Council to be put into effect through national economic plans.

The State Planning Commission worked with the State Economic Commission, State Statistical Bureau, the former State Capital Construction Commission, People's Bank of China, the economic ministries, and other organs subordinate to the State Council to formulate national plans of varying duration and import. Long-range plans as protracted as ten and twelve years also were announced at various times. These essentially were statements of future goals and the intended general direction of the economy, and they had little direct effect on economic activity. As of late 1987 the most recent such long-range plan was the draft plan for 1976-85, presented by Hua Guofeng in February 1978.

The primary form of medium-range plan was the five-year plan, another feature adopted from the Soviet system. The purpose of the five-year plan was to guide and integrate the annual plans to achieve balanced growth and progress toward national goals. In practice, this role was only fulfilled by the First Five-Year Plan (1953-57), which served effectively as a blueprint for industrialization. The second (1958-62), third (1966-70), fourth (1971-75), and fifth (1976-80) five-year plans were all interrupted by political upheavals and had little influence. The Sixth Five-Year Plan (1981-85) was drawn up during the planning period and was more a reflection of the results of the reform program than a guide for reform. The Seventh Five-Year Plan (1986-90) was intended to direct the course of the reforms through the second half of the 1980s, but by mid-1987 its future was already clouded by political struggle.

A second form of medium-range planning appeared in the readjustment and recovery periods of 1949-52, 1963-65, and 1979-81, each of which followed a period of chaos - the civil war, the Great Leap Forward, and the Gang of Four, respectively. In these instances, normal long- and medium-range planning was suspended while basic imbalances in the economy were targeted and corrected. In each case, objectives were more limited and clearly defined than in the five-year plans and were fairly successfully achieved.

The activities of economic units were controlled by annual plans. Formulation of the plans began in the autumn preceding the year being planned, so that agricultural output for the current year could be taken into account. The foundation of an annual plan was a "material balance table." At the national level, the first step in the preparation of a material balance table was to estimate - for each province, autonomous region, special municipality, and enterprise under direct central control - the demand and supply for each centrally controlled good. Transfers of goods between provincial-level units were planned so as to bring quantities supplied and demanded into balance. As a last resort, a serious overall deficit in a good could be made up by imports.

The initial targets were sent to the provincial-level administrations and the centrally controlled enterprises. The provincial-level counterparts of the state economic commissions and ministries broke the targets down for allocation among their subordinate counties, districts, cities, and enterprises under direct provincial-level control. Counties further distributed their assigned quantities among their subordinate towns, townships, and county-owned enterprises, and cities divided their targets into objectives for the enterprises under their jurisdiction. Finally, towns assigned goals to the state-owned enterprises they controlled. Agricultural targets were distributed by townships among their villages and ultimately were reduced to the quantities that villages contracted for with individual farm households.

At each level, individual units received their target input allocations and output quantities. Managers, engineers, and accountants compared the targets with their own projections, and if they concluded that the planned output quotas exceeded their capabilities, they consulted with representatives of the administrative body superior to them. Each administrative level adjusted its targets on the basis of discussions with subordinate units and sent the revised figures back up the planning ladder. The commissions and ministries evaluated the revised sums, repeated the material balance table procedure, and used the results as the final plan, which the State Council then officially approved.

Annual plans formulated at the provincial level provided the quantities for centrally controlled goods and established targets for goods that were not included in the national plan but were important to the province, autonomous region, or special municipality. These figures went through the same process of disaggregation, review, discussion, and reaggregation as the centrally planned targets and eventually became part of the provincial-level unit's annual plan. Many goods that were not included at the provincial level were similarly added to county and city plans.

The final stage of the planning process occurred in the individual producing units. Having received their output quotas and the figures for their allocations of capital, labor, and other supplies, enterprises generally organized their production schedules into ten-day, one-month, three-month, and six-month plans.

The Chinese planning system has encountered the same problems of inflexibility and inadequate responsiveness that have emerged in other centrally planned economies. The basic difficulty has been that it is impossible for planners to foresee all the needs of the economy and to specify adequately the characteristics of planned inputs and products. Beginning in 1979 and 1980, the first reforms were introduced on an experimental basis. Nearly all of these policies increased the autonomy and decision-making power of the various economic units and reduced the direct role of central planning. By the mid-1980s planning still was the government's main mechanism for guiding the economy and correcting imbalances, but its ability to predict and control the behavior of the economy had been greatly reduced.

Prices

Determination of prices

Until the reform period of the late 1970s and 1980s, the prices of most commodities were set by government agencies and changed infrequently. Because prices did not change when production costs or demand for a commodity altered, they often failed to reflect the true values of goods, causing many kinds of goods to be misallocated and producing a price system that the Chinese government itself referred to as "irrational."

The best way to generate the accurate prices required for economic efficiency is through the process of supply and demand, and government policy in the 1980s increasingly advocated the use of prices that were "mutually agreed upon by buyer and seller," that is, determined through the market. The prices of products in the farm produce free markets were determined by supply and demand, and in the summer of 1985 the state store prices of all food items except grain also were allowed to float in response to market conditions. Prices of most goods produced by private and collectively owned enterprises in both rural and urban areas generally were free to float, as were the prices of many items that state-owned enterprises produced outside the plan. Prices of most major goods produced by state-owned enterprises, however, along with the grain purchased from farmers by state commercial departments for retail sales in the cities, still were set or restricted by government agencies and still were not sufficiently accurate.

In 1987 the price structure in China was chaotic. Some prices were determined in the market through the forces of supply and demand, others were set by government agencies, and still others were produced by procedures that were not clearly defined. In many cases, there was more than one price for the same commodity, depending on how it was exchanged, the kind of unit that produced it, or who the buyer was. While the government was not pleased with this situation, it was committed to continued price reform. It was reluctant, however, to release the remaining fixed prices because of potential political and economic disruption. Sudden unpredictable price changes would leave consumers unable to continue buying some goods; some previously profitable enterprises under the old price structure would begin to take losses, and others would abruptly become very wealthy.

Role of prices

As a result of the economic reform program and the increased importance of market exchange and profitability, in the 1980s prices played a central role in determining the production and distribution of goods in most sectors of the economy. Previously, in the strict centrally planned system, enterprises had been assigned output quotas and inputs in physical terms. Under the reform program, the incentive to show a positive profit caused even state-owned enterprises to choose inputs and products on the basis of prices whenever possible. State-owned enterprises could not alter the amounts or prices of goods they were required to produce by the plan, but they could try to increase their profits by purchasing inputs as inexpensively as possible, and their off-plan production decisions were based primarily on price considerations. Prices were the main economic determinant of production decisions in agriculture and in private and collectively owned industrial enterprises despite the fact that regulations, local government fees or harassment, or arrangements based on personal connections often prevented enterprises from carrying out those decisions.

Consumer goods were allocated to households by the price mechanism, except for rationed grain. Families decided what commodities to buy on the basis of the prices of the goods in relation to household income.

Problems in price policy

The grain market was a typical example of a situation in which the government was confronted with major problems whether it allowed the irrational price structure to persist or carried out price reform. State commercial agencies paid farmers a higher price for grain than the state received from the urban residents to whom they sold it. In 1985 state commercial agencies paid farmers an average price of ¥416.4 per ton of grain and then sold it in the cities at an average price of ¥383.3 a ton, for a loss of ¥33.1 per ton. Ninety million tons were sold under this arrangement, causing the government to lose nearly ¥3 billion. If the state reduced the procurement price, farmers would reduce their grain production. Because grain was the staple Chinese diet, this result was unacceptable. If the state increased the urban retail price to equal the procurement price, the cost of the main food item for Chinese families would rise 9 percent, generating enormous resentment. But even this alternative would probably not entirely resolve the problem, as the average free-market price of grain - ¥510.5 a ton in 1987 - indicated that its true value was well above the state procurement price.

There was no clear solution to the price policy dilemma. The approach of the government was to encourage the growth of nonplanned economic activity and thereby expand the proportion of prices determined by market forces. These market prices could then serve as a guide for more accurate pricing of planned items. It was likely that the Chinese economy would continue to operate with a dual price system for some years to come.

Inflation

One of the most striking manifestations of economic instability in China in the 1930s and 1940s was runaway inflation. Inflation peaked during the Chinese civil war of the late 1940s, when wholesale prices in Shanghai increased 7.5 million times in the space of 3 years. In the early 1950s, stopping inflation was a major government objective, accomplished through currency reform, unification and nationalization of the banks, and tight control over prices and the money supply. These measures were continued until 1979, and China achieved a remarkable record of price stability. Between 1952 and 1978, retail prices for consumer goods grew at an average rate of only 0.6 percent a year.

During the reform period, higher levels of inflation appeared when government controls were reduced. The first serious jump in the cost of living for urban residents occurred in 1980, when consumer prices rose by 7.5 percent. In 1985 the increase was 11.9 percent, and in 1986 it was 7.6 percent. There were several basic reasons for this burst of inflation after thirty years of steady prices. First, the years before the reform saw a generally high rate of investment and concentration on the manufacture of producer goods. The resultant shortage of consumer commodities caused a gradual accumulation of excess demand: personal savings were relatively large, and, in the late 1970s and early 1980s, there was a booming market for such expensive consumer durables as watches and television sets. Second, the real value of many items changed as some resources became more scarce and as technology altered both manufacturing processes and products. The real cost of producing agricultural products rose with the increased use of modern inputs. Manufactured consumer goods that were more technologically advanced and more expensive than those previously on the market - such as washing machines and color television sets - became available.

During the early 1980s, both consumer incomes and the amount of money in circulation increased fairly rapidly and, at times, unexpectedly. Consumer incomes grew because of the reform program's emphasis on material incentives and because of the overall expansion in productivity and income-earning possibilities. The higher profits earned and retained by enterprises were passed on to workers, in many cases, in the form of wage hikes, bonuses, and higher subsidies. At the same time, the expanded and diversified role of the banking system caused the amounts of loans and deposits to increase at times beyond officially sanctioned levels, injecting unplanned new quantities of currency into the economy.

National goals

By 1987, under the stimulus of the reform program, the Chinese economy had made major strides toward achieving modernization and improved living standards. The potential for further improvements in efficiency and productivity was greatly increased by the revival of the education system, the opening of the economy to broader trade and cooperation with other countries, the expanded use of the market to enliven commerce and production, and the increased decision-making power of individual economic units.

The country's most important resource was its labor force, the largest in the world. The rapid expansion and improvement of the education system that began in the late 1970s was creating larger numbers of workers who were skilled and well educated, as well as the first substantial numbers of advanced-degree holders to staff the nation's universities and research institutes. In addition, the decentralization of management encouraged the participation in planning and decision making of growing numbers of local and enterprise-level managers, planners, administrators, and scientists. It also trained future economic leaders for higher administrative responsibilities.

In terms of material resources, China was adequately endowed to meet the needs of modernization in all but a few materials. Under the new policy of encouraging cooperation and joint ventures with foreign firms, advanced technology was more widely used to exploit China's large deposits of iron ore and other important minerals, along with the country's vast coal and petroleum reserves and its enormous hydroelectric potential - the largest in the world. Much of the investment in expanding the transportation network in the 1980s was aimed at improving access to previously remote mineral and energy resources for both domestic needs and foreign trade.

The most stringent resource constraint was the limited amount of arable land, which actually declined in the 1980s as cropland was appropriated for new rural housing and urban expansion. Between 1978 and 1985, the total area sown to crops declined by over 4 percent. The loss of farmland, however, was more than compensated for by improved productivity of the land that remained under cultivation. Farmers expanded the irrigated area, increased fertilizer application, acquired improved crop varieties, and made better use of comparative advantage in determining which crops to grow, resulting in an average rate of growth in the value of crop production of better than 5 percent a year over the same 7-year period. Although agricultural growth rates had begun to fall off in the mid-1980s, the incentives of the responsibility system and greater access to international technical advances suggested that the farm sector could continue to meet the needs of the growing economy in the foreseeable future.

The industrial sector, while much less advanced than those of the developed countries, was nonetheless a solid base for modernization. Industrial enterprises were dispersed throughout the country and included units capable of producing all major kinds of machinery, equipment, chemicals, building materials, and light industrial goods. Chinese enterprises could make most of the products required for modernization, and the growing pool of industrial technicians and managers was increasingly capable of effectively integrating advanced foreign technology into Chinese production processes. Key industries were being technologically strengthened by the purchase of advanced foreign equipment and the adoption of modern management techniques. Despite promising potential, formidable obstacles still impeded the drive for modernization. Physical restraints included a renewed increase in birth rates and population growth rates as the number of women of child-bearing age began to rise in 1986 and 1987. Some crucial resources - especially educated personnel and modern equipment - still were in very short supply because of the sheer size of the economy. In the realm of policy, the administration faced the daunting problem of trying to integrate market measures - for efficiency - with government planning and control, the source of stability. In 1987 both kinds of mechanisms exerted extensive influence with the result that market efficiency was hindered by government intervention and government plans were undermined by off-plan activities. Finally, the most serious concern of government leaders was the possibility of future political upheavals. While nearly all Chinese people enjoyed better living conditions as a result of the progress achieved by the reform program, the new policies also had given rise to new social problems and political tensions. Increasing crime and corruption, greater emphasis on the profit motive, widening income disparities, and inflation aroused resistance in many conservative quarters and resulted in the political struggle that caused Hu Yaobang to be forced from his position as Chinese Communist Party general secretary in early 1987. By mid-1987 it was not clear what the outcome of the struggle would be or how it would affect the future course of economic reform (see Economic reform in the People's Republic of China).

See also

- Chinese economic reform
- Economic history of China (pre-1911)
- Economy of the People's Republic of China
- Historical GDP of the People's Republic of China
- Special Economic Zones of the People's Republic of China

Further reading

- Bardhan, Pranab. *Awakening Giants, Feet of Clay: Assessing the Economic Rise of China and India* (Princeton University Press; 2010) 172 pages
- Fengbo Zhang : Analysis of Chinese Macroeconomy
- Chow, Gregory C. *China's Economic Transformation* (2nd ed. 2007) excerpt and text search [2]
- Feenstra, Robert C., and Shang-Jin Wei, eds. *China's Growing Role in World Trade* (University of Chicago Press; 2010) 608 pages; studies of the microstructure of trade, sector-level issues, and foreign direct investment.
- Naughton, Barry. *The Chinese Economy: Transitions and Growth* (2007), important new survey
- Oi, Jean C. *Rural China Takes Off: Institutional Foundations of Economic Reform,* U of California Press, (1999) complete text online free [13]

References

- ⓐ *This article incorporates public domain material from websites or documents* [4] *of the Library of Congress Country Studies.* [5]

External links

- China and the Knowledge Economy [1] - World Bank Institute report
- "This Time, China Is Different" [2] by economist Chen Jing

The Economy of China

Economy of the People's Republic of China

\multicolumn{2}{c	}{**Economy of People's Republic of China**}
\multicolumn{2}{c	}{*Pudong in Shanghai*}
Rank	2nd (nominal) / 2nd (PPP)
Currency	Renminbi (RMB); Unit: Yuan (CNY)
Fixed exchange rates	USD = 6.7872996 RMB (September 06, 2010)
Fiscal year	Calendar year 01 January to 31 December
Trade organizations	WTO, APEC, G-20 and others
\multicolumn{2}{c	}{**Statistics**}
GDP	$4.99 trillion (nominal: 3rd; 2009) $8.77 trillion (PPP: 2nd; 2009)
GDP growth	9.1% (major economies: 1st; 2009)
GDP per capita	$3,677 (nominal: 97th; 2009) $6,567 (PPP: 98th; 2009)
GDP by sector	industry (48.6%), services (40.5%), agriculture (10.9%) (2009)
Inflation (CPI)	3.3% (July 2010)
Gini index	46.9 (List of countries)
Labour force	812.7 million (1st; 2009)

Labour force by occupation	agriculture (39.5%), industry (33.2%), services (27.2%) (2008)
Unemployment	4.2% (July 2010)
Main industries	mining and ore processing, iron, steel, aluminium, and other metals, coal; machine building; armaments; textiles and apparel; petroleum; cement; chemicals; fertilizers; consumer products, including footwear, toys, and electronics; food processing; transportation equipment, including automobiles, rail cars and locomotives, ships, and aircraft; telecommunications equipment, commercial space launch vehicles, satellites
Ease of Doing Business Rank	89th
External	
Exports	$1.2 trillion (1st; 2009)
Export goods	electrical and other machinery, including data processing equipment, apparel, textiles, iron and steel, optical and medical equipment
Main export partners	US 17.7%, Hong Kong 13.3%, Japan 8.1%, South Korea 5.2%, Germany 4.1% (2008)
Imports	$1.01 trillion (2nd; 2009)
Import goods	electrical and other machinery, oil and mineral fuels, optical and medical equipment, metal ores, plastics, organic chemicals
Main import partners	Japan 13.3%, South Korea 9.9%, Taiwan 9.2%, US 7.2%, Germany 4.9% (2008)
FDI stock	$100 billion (2010)
Gross external debt	$347.1 billion (22nd; 2009)
Public finances	
Public debt	18.2% of GDP (107th; 2009)
Revenues	$972.3 billion (2009)
Expenses	$1.137 trillion; (2009)
Economic aid	recipient: $1.12 per capita (2008)
Credit rating	$5.555 trillion (4th; 2008)
Foreign reserves	$2,454,300 million (1st; June 2010)
All values, unless otherwise stated, are in US dollars	

The People's Republic of China is the world's second largest economy after the United States by purchasing power parity ($8.77 trillion in 2009). China is the world's fastest-growing major economy, with average growth rates of 10% for the past 30 years. The country's per capita income was at $6,567 (IMF, 98th) in 2009. China is also the second largest trading nation in the world and the largest exporter and second largest importer of goods.

Overview

In the modern era, China's influence in the world economy was minimal until the late 1980s. At that time, economic reforms initiated after 1978 began to generate significant and steady growth in investment, consumption and standards of living. China now participates extensively in the world market and private sector companies play a major role in the economy. Since 1978 hundreds of millions have been lifted out of poverty: According to China's official statistics, the poverty rate fell from 53% in 1981 to 2.5% in 2005. However, in 2006, 10.8% of people still lived on less than $1 a day (purchasing power parity-adjusted). The infant mortality rate fell by 39.5% between 1990 and 2005, and maternal mortality by 41.1%. Access to telephones during the period rose more than 94-fold, to 57.1%.

China has generally implemented reforms in a gradualist fashion. As its role in world trade has steadily grown, its importance to the international economy has also increased apace. China's foreign trade has grown faster than its GDP for the past 25 years. China's growth comes both from huge state investment in infrastructure and heavy industry and from private sector expansion in light industry instead of just exports, whose role in the economy appears to have been significantly overestimated. The smaller but highly concentrated public sector, dominated by 159 large SOEs, provided key inputs from utilities, heavy industries, and energy resources that facilitated private sector growth and drove investment, the foundation of national growth. In 2008 thousands of private companies closed down and the government announced plans to expand the public sector to take up the slack caused by the global financial crisis. In 2010, there were approximately 10 million small businesses in China.

The PRC government's decision to permit China to be used by multinational corporations as an export platform has made the country a major competitor to other Asian export-led economies, such as South Korea, Singapore, and Malaysia. China has emphasized raising personal income and consumption and introducing new management systems to help increase productivity. The government has also focused on foreign trade as a major vehicle for economic growth. The restructuring of the economy and resulting efficiency gains have contributed to a more than tenfold increase in GDP since 1978. Some economists believe that Chinese economic growth has been in fact understated during much of the 1990s and early 2000s, failing to fully factor in the growth driven by the private sector and that the extent at which China is dependent on exports is exaggerated. Nevertheless, key bottlenecks continue to constrain growth. Available energy is insufficient to run at fully installed industrial capacity, and the transport system is inadequate to move sufficient quantities of such critical items as coal.

The two most important sectors of the economy have traditionally been agriculture and industry, which together employ more than 70 percent of the labor force and produce more than 60 percent of GDP. The two sectors have differed in many respects. Technology, labor productivity, and incomes have advanced much more rapidly in industry than in agriculture. Agricultural output has been vulnerable to the effects of weather, while industry has been more directly influenced by the government. The disparities between the two sectors have combined to form an economic-cultural-social gap between the rural and urban areas, which is a major division in Chinese society. China is the world's largest producer of rice and is among the principal sources of wheat, corn (maize), tobacco, soybeans, peanuts (groundnuts), and cotton. The country is one of the world's largest producers of a number of industrial and mineral products, including cotton cloth, tungsten, and antimony, and is an important producer of cotton yarn, coal, crude oil, and a number of other products. Its mineral resources are probably among the richest in the world but are only partially developed.

China has acquired some highly sophisticated production facilities through trade and also has built a number of advanced engineering plants capable of manufacturing an increasing range of sophisticated equipment, including nuclear weapons and satellites, but most of its industrial output still comes from relatively ill-equipped factories. The technological level and quality standards of its industry as a whole are still fairly low, notwithstanding a marked change since 2000, spurred in part by foreign investment. A report by UBS in 2009 concluded that China has experienced total factor productivity growth of 4 per cent per year since 1990, one of the fastest improvements in world economic history.

China's increasing integration with the international economy and its growing efforts to use market forces to govern the domestic allocation of goods have exacerbated this problem. Over the years, large subsidies were built into the price structure, and these subsidies grew substantially in the late 1970s and 1980s. By the early 1990s these subsidies began to be eliminated, in large part due to China's admission into the World Trade Organization (WTO) in 2001, which carried with it requirements for further economic liberalization and deregulation. China's ongoing economic transformation has had a profound impact not only on China but on the world. The market-oriented reforms China has implemented over the past two decades have unleashed individual initiative and entrepreneurship, whilst retaining state domination of the economy.

Wayne M. Morrison of the Congressional Research Service wrote in 2009 that "Despite the relatively positive outlook for its economy, China faces a number of difficult challenges that, if not addressed, could undermine its future economic growth and stability. These include pervasive government corruption, an inefficient banking system, over-dependence on exports and fixed investment for growth, the lack of rule of law, severe pollution, and widening income disparities." Economic consultant David Smick adds that the recent actions by the Chinese government to stimulate their economy have only added to a huge industrial overcapacity and commercial real estate vacancy problems.

History

Main articles: Economic history of the People's Republic of China, Economic history of China, Five-Year Plans of China, and Historical GDP of the People's Republic of China

1949–1978

See also: Great Leap Forward

In 1949, China followed a socialist heavy industry development strategy, or the "Big Push" strategy. Consumption was reduced while rapid industrialization was given high priority. The government took control of a large part of the economy and redirected resources into building new factories. Entire new industries were created. Most important, economic growth was jump-started. Tight control of budget and money supply reduced inflation by the end of 1950. Though most of it was done at the expense of suppressing the private sector of small to big businesses by the Three-anti/five-anti campaigns between 1951 to 1952. The campaigns were notorious for being anti-capitalist, and imposed charges that allowed the government to punish capitalists with severe fines. In the beginning of the Communist party's rule, the leaders of the party had agreed that for a nation such as China, which does not have any heavy industry and minimal secondary production, capitalism is to be utilized to help the building of the "New China" and finally merged into communism.

1978–1990

See also: Chinese economic reform

Since 1978, China began to make major reforms to its economy. The Chinese leadership adopted a pragmatic perspective on many political and socioeconomic problems, and sharply reduced the role of ideology in economic policy. Political and social stability, economic productivity, and public and consumer welfare were considered paramount and indivisible. In these years, the government emphasized raising personal income and consumption and introducing new management systems to help increase productivity. The government also had focused on foreign trade as a major vehicle for economic growth. In the 1980s, China tried to combine central planning with market-oriented reforms to increase productivity, living standards, and technological quality without exacerbating inflation, unemployment, and budget deficits. Reforms began in the agricultural, industrial, fiscal, financial, banking, price setting, and labor systems.

A decision was made in 1978 to permit foreign direct investment in several small "special economic zones" along the coast. The country lacked the legal infrastructure and knowledge of international practices to make this prospect attractive for many foreign businesses, however. In the early 1980s steps were taken to expand the number of areas that could accept foreign investment with a minimum of red tape, and related efforts were made to develop the legal and other infrastructures necessary to make this work well. This additional effort resulted in making 14 coastal cities and three coastal regions "open areas" for foreign investment. All of these places provide favored tax treatment and other advantages for foreign investment. Laws on contracts, patents, and other matters of concern to foreign businesses were also passed in an effort to attract international capital to spur China's development. The largely bureaucratic nature of China's economy, however, posed a number of inherent problems for foreign firms that wanted to operate in the Chinese environment, and China gradually had to add more incentives to attract foreign capital.

1990–2000

See also: Grasping the large, letting go of the small

In the 1990s, the Chinese economy continued to grow at a rapid pace, at about 9.5%, accompanied by low inflation. The Asian financial crisis affected China at the margin, mainly through decreased foreign direct investment and a sharp drop in the growth of its exports. However, China had huge reserves, a currency that was not freely convertible, and capital inflows that consisted overwhelmingly of long-term investment. For these reasons it remained largely insulated from the regional crisis and its commitment not to devalue had been a major stabilizing factor for the region. However, China faced slowing growth and rising unemployment based on internal problems, including a financial system burdened by huge amounts of bad loans, and massive layoffs stemming from aggressive efforts to reform state-owned enterprises (SOEs).

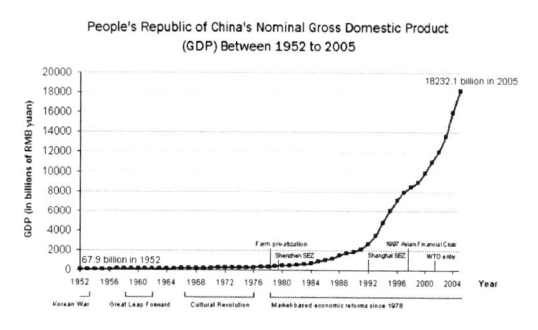

China's nominal GDP trend from 1952 to 2005

Despite China's impressive economic development during the past two decades, reforming the state sector and modernizing the banking system remained major hurdles. Over half of China's state-owned enterprises were inefficient and reporting losses. During the 15th National Communist Party Congress that met in September 1997, President Jiang Zemin announced plans to sell, merge, or close the vast majority of SOEs in his call for increased "non-public ownership" (*feigongyou* or privatization in euphemistic terms). The 9th National People's Congress endorsed the plans at its March 1998 session. In 2000, China claimed success in its three year effort to make the majority of large state owned enterprises (SOEs) profitable.

2000–present

Following the Chinese Communist Party's Third Plenum, held in October 2003, Chinese legislators unveiled several proposed amendments to the state constitution. One of the most significant was a proposal to provide protection for private property rights. Legislators also indicated there would be a new emphasis on certain aspects of overall government economic policy, including efforts to reduce unemployment (now in the 8–10% range in urban areas), to rebalance income distribution between urban and rural regions, and to maintain economic growth while protecting the environment and improving social equity. The National People's Congress approved the amendments when it met in March 2004.

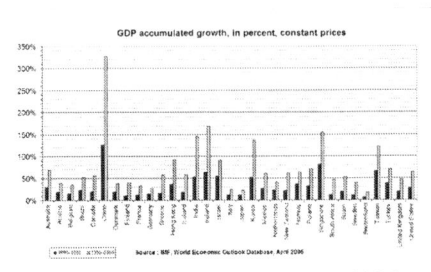

GDP increase, 1990–1998 and 1990–2006, in major countries

The Fifth Plenum in October 2005 approved the 11th Five-Year Economic Program (2006–2010) aimed at building a "harmonious society" through more balanced wealth distribution and improved education, medical care, and social security. On March 2006, the National People's Congress approved the 11th Five-Year Program. The plan called for a relatively conservative 45% increase in GDP and a 20% reduction in energy intensity (energy consumption per unit of GDP) by 2010.

China's economy grew at an average rate of 10% per year during the period 1990–2004, the highest growth rate in the world. China's GDP grew 10.0% in 2003, 10.1%, in 2004, and even faster 10.4% in 2005 despite attempts by the government to cool the economy. China's total trade in 2006 surpassed $1.76 trillion, making China the world's third-largest trading nation after the U.S. and Germany. Such high growth is necessary if China is to generate the 15 million jobs needed annually—roughly the size of Ecuador or Cambodia—to employ new entrants into the job market.

On January 14, 2009, as confirmed by the World Bank the NBS published the revised figures for 2007 fiscal year in which growth happened at 13 percent instead of 11.9 percent (provisional figures). China's gross domestic product stood at US$3.4 trillion while Germany's GDP was USD $3.3 trillion for 2007. This made China the world's third largest economy by gross domestic product. Based on these figures, in 2007 China recorded its fastest growth since 1994 when the GDP grew by 13.1 percent.

China launched its Economic Stimulus Plan to specifically deal with the Global financial crisis of 2008–2009. It has primarily focused on increasing affordable housing, easing credit restrictions for mortgage and SMEs, lower taxes such as those on real estate sales and commodities, pumping more public investment into infrastructure development, such as the rail network, roads and ports. By the end of 2009 it appeared that the Chinese economy was showing signs of recovery. At the 2009 Economic Work Conference in December 'managing inflation expectations' was added to the list of economic objectives, suggesting a strong economic upturn and a desire to take steps to manage it.

By 2010 it was evident to outside observers such as *The New York Times* that China was poised to move from export dependency to development of an internal market. Wages were rapidly rising in all areas of the country and Chinese leaders were calling for an increased standard of living.

In mid-2010, China became the world's second largest economy, surpassing Japan's economy and second only to the economy of the United States. In the second quarter of 2010, China's economy was valued at $1.33 trillion, ahead of the $1.28 trillion that Japan's economy was worth. China could become the world's largest economy (by nominal GDP) sometime as early as 2030.

China is the largest creditor nation in the world and owns over 25% of US Treasury Bonds.

Government role

See also: Government of the People's Republic of China

Since 1949 the government, under socialist political and economic system, has been responsible for planning and managing national economy. In the early 1950s, the foreign trade system was monopolized by the state. Nearly all the domestic enterprises were state-owned and the government had set the prices for key commodities, controlled the level and general distribution of investment funds, determined output targets for major enterprises and branches, allocated energy resources, set wage levels and employment targets, operated the wholesale and retail networks, and steered the financial policy and banking system. In the countryside from the mid-1950s, the government established cropping patterns, set the level of prices, and fixed output targets for all major crops.

Since 1978 when economic reforms were instituted, the government role in the economy has lessened to a great degree. Industrial output by state enterprises slowly declined, although a few strategic industries, such as the aerospace industry have today remained predominantly state-owned. While the role of the government in managing the economy has been reduced and the role of both private enterprise and market forces increased, the government maintains a major role in the urban economy. With its policies on such issues as agricultural procurement the government also retains a major influence on rural sector performance. The State Constitution of 1982 specified that the state is to guide the country's economic development by making broad decisions on economic priorities and policies, and that the State Council, which exercises executive control, was to direct its subordinate bodies in preparing and implementing the national economic plan and the state budget. A major portion of the government system (bureaucracy) is devoted to managing the economy in a top-down chain of command with all but a few of the more than 100 ministries, commissions, administrations, bureaus, academies, and corporations under the State Council are concerned with economic matters.

Each significant economic sector is supervised by one or more of these organizations, which includes the People's Bank of China, National Development and Reform Commission, Ministry of Finance, and the ministries of agriculture; coal industry; commerce; communications; education; light industry; metallurgical industry; petroleum industry; railways; textile industry; and water resources and electric power. Several aspects of the economy are administered by specialized departments under the State Council, including the National Bureau of Statistics, Civil Aviation Administration of China, and the tourism bureau. Each of the economic organizations under the State Council directs the units under its jurisdiction through subordinate offices at the provincial and local levels.

The whole policy-making process involves extensive consultation and negotiation. Economic policies and decisions adopted by the National People's Congress and the State Council are to be passed on to the economic organizations under the State Council, which incorporates them into the plans for the various sectors of the economy. Economic plans and policies are implemented by a variety of direct and indirect control mechanisms. Direct control is exercised by designating specific physical output quotas and supply allocations for some goods and services. Indirect instruments—also called "economic levers"—operate by affecting market incentives. These included levying taxes, setting prices for products and supplies, allocating investment funds, monitoring and controlling financial transactions by the banking system, and controlling the allocation of key resources, such as skilled labor, electric power, transportation, steel, and chemicals (including fertilizers). The main advantage of including a project in an annual plan is that the raw materials, labor, financial resources, and markets are guaranteed by directives that have the weight of the law behind them. In reality, however, a great deal of economic activity goes on outside the scope of the detailed plan, and the tendency has been for the plan to become narrower rather than broader in scope. A major objective of the reform program was to reduce the use of direct controls and to increase the role of indirect economic levers. Major state-owned enterprises still receive detailed plans specifying physical quantities of key inputs and products from their ministries. These corporations, however, have been increasingly affected by prices and allocations that were determined through market interaction and only indirectly influenced by the central plan.

Total economic enterprise in China is apportioned along lines of directive planning (mandatory), indicative planning (indirect implementation of central directives), and those left to market forces. In the early 1980s during the initial reforms enterprises began to have increasing discretion over the quantities of inputs purchased, the sources of inputs, the variety of products manufactured, and the production process. Operational supervision over economic projects has devolved primarily to provincial, municipal, and county governments. The majority of state-owned industrial enterprises, which were managed at the provincial level or below, were partially regulated by a combination of specific allocations and indirect controls, but they also produced goods outside the plan for sale in the market. Important, scarce resources—for example, engineers or finished steel—may have been assigned to this kind of unit in exact numbers. Less critical assignments of personnel and materials would have been authorized in a general way by the plan, but with procurement arrangements left up to the enterprise management.

In addition, enterprises themselves are gaining increased independence in a range of activity. While strategically important industry and services and most of large-scale construction have remained under directive planning, the market economy has gained rapidly in scale every year as it subsumes more and more sectors. Overall, the Chinese industrial system contains a complex mixture of relationships. The State Council generally administers relatively strict control over resources deemed to be of vital concern for the performance and health of the entire economy. Less vital aspects of the economy have been transferred to lower levels for detailed decisions and management. Furthermore, the need to coordinate entities that are in different organizational hierarchies generally causes a great deal of informal bargaining and consensus building.

Consumer spending has been subject to a limited degree of direct government influence but is primarily determined by the basic market forces of income levels and commodity prices. Before the reform period, key goods were rationed when they were in short supply, but by the mid-1980s availability had increased to the point that rationing was discontinued for everything except grain, which could also be purchased in the free markets. Collectively owned units and the agricultural sector were regulated primarily by indirect instruments. Each collective unit was "responsible for its own profit and loss," and the prices of its inputs and products provided the major production incentives.

Vast changes were made in relaxing the state control of the agricultural sector from the late 1970s. The structural mechanisms for implementing state objectives—the people's communes and their subordinate teams and brigades—have been either entirely eliminated or greatly diminished. Farm incentives have been boosted both by price increases for state-purchased agricultural products, and it was permitted to sell excess production on a free market. There was more room in the choice of what crops to grow, and peasants are allowed to contract for land that they will work, rather than simply working most of the land collectively. The system of procurement quotas (fixed in the form of contracts) has been being phased out, although the state can still buy farm products and control surpluses in order to affect market conditions.

Foreign trade is supervised by the Ministry of Commerce, customs, and the Bank of China, the foreign exchange arm of the Chinese banking system, which controls access to the foreign currency required for imports. Ever since restrictions on foreign trade were reduced, there have been broad opportunities for individual enterprises to engage in exchanges with foreign firms without much intervention from official agencies.

Though private sector companies still dominate small and medium sized businesses, the government still plays a large part in the bigger industries. The fact that government accounts for a third of the GDP shows this. Foreign owned companies hold significant stakes. The public sector is mainly made up of State Owned Enterprises (SOE's).

Regional economies

See also: Metropolitan regions of China and List of cities in China

China's unequal transportation system—combined with important differences in the availability of natural and human resources and in industrial infrastructure—has produced significant variations in the regional economies of China.

Economic development has generally been more rapid in coastal provinces than in the interior, and there are large disparities in per capita income between regions. The three wealthiest regions are along the southeast coast, centred on the Pearl River Delta; along the east coast, centred on the Lower Yangtze River; and near the Bohai Gulf, in the Beijing–Tianjin–Liaoning region. It is the rapid development of these areas that is expected to have the most significant effect on the Asian regional economy as a whole, and Chinese government policy is designed to remove the obstacles to accelerated growth in these wealthier regions.

See also: List of administrative regions by GDP, List of administrative regions by GDP per capita, and List of cities by GDP per capita.

Development

See also: List of administrative divisions by Human Development Index (HDI).

China, economically frail before 1978, has again become one of the world's major economic powers with the greatest potential. In the 22 years following reform and opening-up in 1979 in particular, China's economy developed at an unprecedented rate, and that momentum has been held steady into the 21st century.

China adopts the "five-year-plan" strategy for economic development. The 11th Five-Year Plan (2006–2010) is the currently being implemented.

Three-Step Development Strategy

China's overall economic construction objectives were clearly stated in the Three Step Development Strategy set out in 1978: Step One—to double the 1980 GNP and ensure that the people have enough food and clothing—was attained by the end of the 1980s; Step Two—to quadruple the 1980 GNP by the end of the 20th century—was achieved in 1995 ahead of schedule; Step Three—to increase per-capita GNP to the level of the medium-developed countries by 2050—at which point, the Chinese people will be fairly well-off and modernization will be basically realized.

Regional development

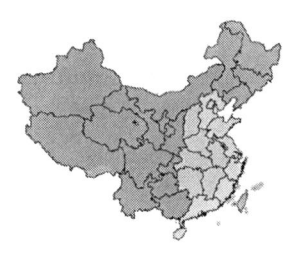

The East Coast
(with existing development programmes)

"Rise of Central China"

"Revitalize Northeast China"

"China Western Development"

These strategies are aimed at the relatively poorer regions in China in an attempt to prevent widening inequalities:

- China Western Development, designed to increase the economic situation of the western provinces through capital investment and development of natural resources.
- Revitalize Northeast China, to rejuvenate the industrial bases in Northeast China. It covers the three provinces of Heilongjiang, Jilin, and Liaoning, as well as the five eastern prefectures of Inner Mongolia.
- Rise of Central China Plan, to accelerate the development of its central regions. It covers six provinces: Shanxi, Henan, Anhui, Hubei, Hunan, and Jiangxi.
- Third Front, focused on the southwestern provinces.

Foreign investment abroad:

- Go Global, to encourage its enterprises to invest overseas.

Key national projects

The "West-to-East Electricity Transmission," the "West-to-East Gas Transmission," and the "South–North Water Transfer Project" are the government's three key strategic projects, aimed at realigning overall economic development and achieving rational distribution of national resources across China. The "West-to-East Electricity Transmission" project is in full swing, involving hydropower and coal resources in western China and the construction of new power transmission channels to deliver electricity to the east. The southern power grid line, transmitting three million kW from Guizhou to Guangdong, was completed in September 2004. The "West-to-East Gas Transmission" project includes a 4,000 km trunk pipeline running through 10 provinces, autonomous regions or municipalities, conveying natural gas to cities in northern and eastern China. This was finished in October 2004 and has a design capacity of 12 billion cu m per year. Construction of the "South-to-North Water Diversion" project was officially launched on 27 December 2002 and completion of Phase I is scheduled for 2010; this will relieve serious water shortfall in northern China and realize a rational distribution of the water resources of the Yangtze, Yellow, Huaihe, and Haihe river valleys.

Hong Kong and Macau

Main articles: One Country, Two Systems, Economy of Hong Kong, and Economy of Macau

In accordance with the One Country, Two Systems policy, the economies of the former European colonies, Hong Kong and Macao, are separate from the rest of the PRC, and each other. Both Hong Kong and Macau are free to conduct and engage in economic negotiations with foreign countries, as well as participating as full members in various international economic organizations such as the World Customs Organization, the World Trade Organization and the Asia-Pacific Economic Cooperation forum, often under the names "Hong Kong, China" and "Macao, China".

See also: Closer Economic Partnership Arrangement with Hong Kong and Macau.

Macroeconomic trends

See also: China's Historical GDP

In 1985, the State Council of China approved to establish a SNA (System of National Accounting), use the GDP (Gross Domestic Product) to measure the national economy. China started the study of theoretical foundation, guiding, and accounting model etc., for establishing a new system of national economic accounting. In 1986, as the first citizen of the People's Republic of China to receive a Ph.D. in economics from an overseas country, Dr. **Fengbo Zhang** headed Chinese Macroeconomic Research - the key research project of the seventh Five-Year Plan of China, as well as completing and publishing the China GDP data by China's own research. The summary of the above has been included in the book "Chinese Macroeconomic Structure and Policy" (June 1988) edited by Fengbo Zhang, and collectively authored by the Research Center of the State Council of China. This is the first GDP data which was published by China.

The table below shows the trend of the GDP of China at market prices estimated by the IMF with figures in millions (Chinese yuan). See also. For purchasing power parity comparisons, the US dollar is exchanged at 2.05 CNY only.

Year	Gross domestic product	US dollar exchange	Inflation index (2000=100)	Per Capita Income (as % of USA)
1955	91,000	2.46	19.2	2.43
1960	145,700	2.46	20.0	3.04
1965	171,600	2.46	21.6	2.63
1970	225,300	2.46	21.3	2.20
1975	299,700	1.86	22.4	2.32
1980	460,906	1.49	25.0	2.52
1985	896,440	2.93	30.0	1.65
1990	1,854,790	4.78	49.0	1.48
1995	6,079,400	8.35	91.0	2.17
2000	9,921,500	8.27	100.0	2.69
2005	18,308,500	8.19	106.0	4.05
2010				

Systemic problems

The government has in recent years struggled to contain the social strife and environmental damage related to the economy's rapid transformation; collect public receipts due from provinces, businesses, and individuals; reduce corruption and other economic crimes; sustain adequate job growth for tens of millions of workers laid off from state-owned enterprises, migrants, and new entrants to the work force; and keep afloat the large state-owned enterprises, most of which had not participated in the vigorous expansion of the economy and many of which had been losing the ability to pay full wages and pensions. From 50 to 100 million surplus rural workers were adrift between the villages and the cities, many subsisting through part-time low-paying jobs. Popular resistance, changes in central policy, and loss of authority by rural cadres have weakened China's population control program. Another long-term threat to continued rapid economic growth has been the deterioration in the environment, notably air and water pollution, soil erosion, growing desertification and the steady fall of the water table especially in the north. China also has continued to lose arable land because of erosion and infrastructure development.

Other major problems concern the labor force and the pricing system. There is large-scale underemployment in both urban and rural areas, and the fear of the disruptive effects of major, explicit unemployment is strong. The prices of certain key commodities, especially of industrial raw materials and major industrial products, are determined by the state. In most cases, basic price ratios were set in the 1950s and are often irrational in terms of current production capabilities and demands. Over the years, large subsidies were built into the price structure, and these subsidies grew substantially in the late 1970s and 1980s. By the early 1990s these subsidies began to be eliminated, in large part due to China's admission into the World Trade Organization (WTO) in 2001, which carried with it requirements for further economic liberalization and deregulation. China's ongoing economic transformation has had a profound impact not only on China but on the world. The market-oriented reforms China has implemented over the past two decades have unleashed individual initiative and entrepreneurship.

By 2010, rapidly rising wages and a general increase in the standard of living had put increased energy use on a collision course with the need to reduce carbon emissions in order to control global warming. There were diligent efforts to increase energy efficiency and increase use of renewable sources; over 1,000 inefficient power plants had been closed, but projections continued to show a dramatic rise in carbon emissions from burning fossil fuels.

Regulatory environment

Though China's economy has expanded rapidly, its regulatory environment has not kept pace. Since Deng Xiaoping's open market reforms, the growth of new businesses has outpaced the government's ability to regulate them. This has created a situation where businesses, faced with mounting competition and poor oversight, take drastic measures to increase profit margins, often at the expense of consumer safety. This issue became more prominent in 2007, with a number of restrictions being placed on problematic Chinese exports by the United States. The Chinese Government recognizes the severity of the problem, recently concluding that up to 20% of the country's products are substandard or tainted.

Inflation

During the winter of 2007–2008, inflation ran about 7% on an annual basis, rising to 8.7% in statistics for February 2008, released in March 2008. The food and fuel sectors were major problem areas, with meat and fuel posing special difficulties.

Shortages of gasoline and diesel fuel developed in the fall of 2007 due to reluctance of refineries to produce fuel at low prices set by the state. These prices were slightly increased in November 2007 with fuel selling for $2.65 a gallon, still slightly below world prices. Price controls were in effect on numerous basic products and services, but were ineffective with food, prices of which were rising at an annual rate of 18.2% in November 2007. The problem of inflation has caused concern at the highest levels of the Chinese government. On January 9, 2008, the government of China issued the following statement on its official website: "The Chinese government decided on Wednesday to take further measures to stabilize market prices and increase the severity of punishments for those guilty of driving up prices through hoarding or cheating."

Pork is an important part of the Chinese economy with a per capita consumption of a fifth of a pound per day. The worldwide rise in the price of animal feed associated with increased production of ethanol from corn resulted in steep rises in pork prices in China in 2007. Increased cost of production interacted badly with increased demand resulting from rapidly rising wages. The state responded by subsidizing pork prices for students and the urban poor and called for increased production. Release of pork from the nation's strategic pork reserve was considered.

By January 2008, the inflation rate rose to 7.1%, which BBC News described as the highest inflation rate since 1997, due to the winter storms that month. China's inflation rate jumped to a new decade high of 8.7 percent in February 2008 after severe winter storms disrupted the economy and worsened food shortages, the government said March 11, 2008.

Throughout the summer and fall, however, inflation fell again to a low of 6.6% in October 2008.

Labor shortages and rising export costs

See also: Labor section below.

By 2005, there were signs of stronger demand for labor with workers being able to choose employment that offered higher wages and better working conditions, enabling some to move away from the restrictive dormitory life and boring factory work that have characterized export industries in provinces such as Guangdong and Fujian. Minimum wages began rising toward the equivalent of 100 U.S. dollars a month as companies scrambled for employees, with some paying as much as $150 a month on average. The labor shortage was partially driven by the demographic trends, as the proportion of people of working age fell as the result of strict family planning.

It was reported in *The New York Times* in April 2006 that labor costs continued to increase and a shortage of unskilled labor had developed with a million or more employees being sought. Operations that relied on cheap labor were contemplating relocations to cities in the interior or to other low-cost countries such as Vietnam or Bangladesh. Many young people were attending college rather than opting for minimum-wage factory work. The demographic shift resulting from the one-child policy continued to reduce the supply of young entry-level workers. Also, government efforts to advance economic development in the interior of the country were beginning to be effective at creating better opportunities there. A follow-up article in *The New York Times* in late August 2007 reported acceleration of this trend. The minimum wage a young unskilled factory worker could be hired at had increased to $200 with experienced workers commanding more. There was strong demand for young workers willing to work long hours and live in dormitory conditions, while older workers, over forty, were considered unsuitable.

Rising wages were being, to a certain extent, offset by increases in productivity, but in 2007, a slight rise in the cost of imports from China was recorded by the United States government: "After falling since its inception in December 2003, the price index for imports from China rose 0.4 percent in July 2007, the largest monthly increase since the index was first published in December 2003. The July increase was the third consecutive monthly advance. Over the past year, import prices from China increased 0.9 percent." By February 2008, concerns were being raised that rising wages and inflation in China were beginning to create inflationary pressure in the United States and Europe, which had depended on cheap prices for consumer goods from China exerting downward pressure on prices.

On January 1, 2008, China introduced a new Labor Law, increasing the rights of the workforce, this caused many foreign and private companies, whose operations in China were based on the exploitation of low wages, to move to countries with lower labor costs, like Thailand, Vietnam or Bangladesh. In the summer of 2008 the growth in export orders began to fall sharply as the sub-prime crisis in export markets reduced demand in Guangdong province, particularly in toy and textile manufacture. According to Chinese Government sources 20 million jobs in 67,000 factories were reported to have been lost. The government initially was happy to see factories close down in labour intensive low wage factories, and the Labor law was seen as a means of helping to eradicate them, but the global financial crisis led to a far more rapid process of private sector collapse in Guangdong than was expected, raising fears of a contagious spread of social unrest.

In early 2010 a labor shortage developed in coastal areas with many migrant workers not returning after the new year holiday. Wages rose rapidly with temp agencies charging over $1.00 US per hour for factory workers in Guangzhou. Following the strikes in 2010 at Japanese auto plants, the shortage continued with many factories unable to fully staff their factories.

According to Fan Gang, professor of economics at Beijing University and director of China's National Economic Research Institute, due to the large volume of workers engaged in relatively unremunerative agricultural work there is considerable room for increased nominal wages in China without changing the competitive position of the Chinese export industry for the next few decades. Lower wages in other countries may not represent productivity comparable to the increasing productivity of Chinese workers.

Financial and banking system

Main articles: Chinese financial system, Banking in China, Foreign exchange reserves of the People's Republic of China, Hedge fund industry in China, and China Venture Capital Association

Most of China's financial institutions are state owned and governed and 98% of banking assets are state owned. The chief instruments of financial and fiscal control are the People's Bank of China (PBC) and the Ministry of Finance, both under the authority of the State Council.

A Shanghai branch of Industrial and Commercial Bank of China (ICBC)

The People's Bank of China replaced the Central Bank of China in 1950 and gradually took over private banks. It fulfills many of the functions of other central and commercial banks. It issues the currency, controls circulation, and plays an important role in disbursing budgetary expenditures. Additionally, it administers the accounts, payments, and receipts of government organizations and other bodies, which enables it to exert thorough supervision over their financial and general performances in consideration to the government's economic plans. The PBC is also responsible for international trade and other overseas transactions. Remittances by overseas Chinese are managed by the Bank of China (BOC), which has a number of branch offices in several countries.

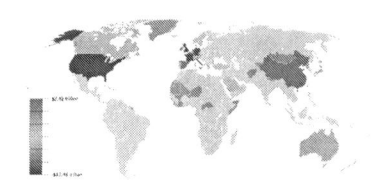

Map of countries by foreign currency reserves and gold minus external debt based on 2009 data from CIA Factbook

Other financial institutions that are crucial, include the China Development Bank (CDB), which funds economic development and directs foreign investment; the Agricultural Bank of China (ABC), which provides for the agricultural sector; the China Construction Bank (CCB), which is responsible for capitalizing a portion of overall investment and for providing capital funds for certain industrial and construction enterprises; and the Industrial and Commercial Bank of China (ICBC), which conducts ordinary commercial transactions and acts as a savings bank for the public.

Shanghai Stock Exchange (SSE)

China's economic reforms greatly increased the economic role of the banking system. In theory any enterprises or individuals can go to the banks to obtain loans outside the state plan, in practice 75% of state bank loans go to State Owned Enterprises. (SOEs) Even though nearly all investment capital was previously provided on a grant basis according to the state plan, policy has since the start of the reform shifted to a loan basis through the various state-directed financial institutions. Increasing amounts of funds are made available through the banks for economic and commercial purposes. Foreign sources of capital have also increased. China has received loans from the World Bank and several United Nations programs, as well as from countries (particularly Japan) and, to a lesser extent, commercial banks. Hong Kong has been a major conduit of this investment, as well as a source itself.

With two stock exchanges (Shanghai Stock Exchange and Shenzhen Stock Exchange), mainland China's stock market had a market value of $1 trillion by January 2007, which became the third largest stock market in Asia, after Japan and Hong Kong. It is estimated to be the world's third largest by 2016.

Currency system

See also: Renminbi, Chinese yuan, and Currency of China

The renminbi ("people's currency") is the currency of China, denominated as the yuan, subdivided into 10 jiao or 100 fen. The renminbi is issued by the People's Bank of China, the monetary authority of the PRC. The ISO 4217 abbreviation is CNY, although also commonly abbreviated as "RMB". The Latinised symbol is ¥. The yuan is generally considered by outside observers to be undervalued by about 30%.

The renminbi is held in a floating exchange-rate system managed primarily against the US dollar. On July 21, 2005, China revalued its currency by 2.1% against the US dollar and, since then has moved to an exchange rate system that references a basket of currencies and has allowed the renminbi to fluctuate at a daily rate of up to half a percent.

The rate of exchange (Chinese yuan per US$1) on July 31, 2008, was RMB 6.846, in mid-2007 was RMB 7.45, while in early 2006 was RMB 8.07:US $1=8.2793 yuan (January 2000), 8.2783 (1999), 8.2790 (1998), 8.2898 (1997), 8.3142 (1996), 8.3514 (1995).

There is a complex relationship between China's balance of trade, inflation, measured by the consumer price index and the value of its currency. Despite allowing the value of the yuan to "float", China's central bank has decisive ability to control its value with relationship to other currencies. Inflation in 2007, reflecting sharply rising prices for meat and fuel, is probably related to the worldwide rise in commodities used as animal feed or as fuel. Thus rapid rises in the value of the yuan permitted in December 2007 are possibly related to efforts to mitigate inflation by permitting the renminbi to be worth more.

Tax system

Main article: Tax system in China

From the 1950s to the 1980s, the central government's revenues derived chiefly from the profits of the state enterprises, which were remitted to the state. Some government revenues also came from taxes, of which the most important was the general industrial and commercial tax.

The trend, however, has been for remitted profits of the state enterprises to be replaced with taxes on those profits. Initially, this tax system was adjusted so as to allow for differences in the capitalization and pricing situations of various firms, but more-uniform tax schedules were introduced in the early 1990s. In addition, personal income and value-added taxes were implemented at that time.

Agriculture

Main article: Agriculture in China

Peanut harvest in Jiangxia District, Hubei

China is one of the world's largest producers and consumers of agricultural products — and some 300 million Chinese farm workers are in the industry, mostly laboring on small pieces of land about the size of U.S farms. Virtually all arable land is used for food crops. China is the world's largest producer of rice and is among the principal sources of wheat, corn (maize), tobacco, soybeans, peanuts (groundnuts), cotton, potatoes, sorghum, peanuts, tea, millet, barley, oilseed, pork, and fish. Major non-food crops, including cotton, other fibers, and oilseeds, furnish China with a small proportion of its foreign trade revenue. Agricultural exports, such as vegetables and fruits, fish and shellfish, grain and meat products, are exported to Hong Kong. Yields are high because of intensive cultivation, for example, China's cropland area is only 75% of the U.S. total, but China still produces about 30% more crops and livestock than the United States. China hopes to further increase agricultural production through improved plant stocks, fertilizers, and technology.

According to the government statistics issued in 2005, after a drop in the yield of farm crops in 2000, output has been increasing annually.

According to the United Nations World Food Program, in 2003, China fed 20 percent of the world's population with only 7 percent of the world's arable land. China ranks first worldwide in farm output, and, as a result of topographic and climatic factors, only about 10–15 percent of the total land area is suitable for cultivation. Of this, slightly more than half is unirrigated, and the remainder is divided roughly equally between paddy fields and irrigated areas.

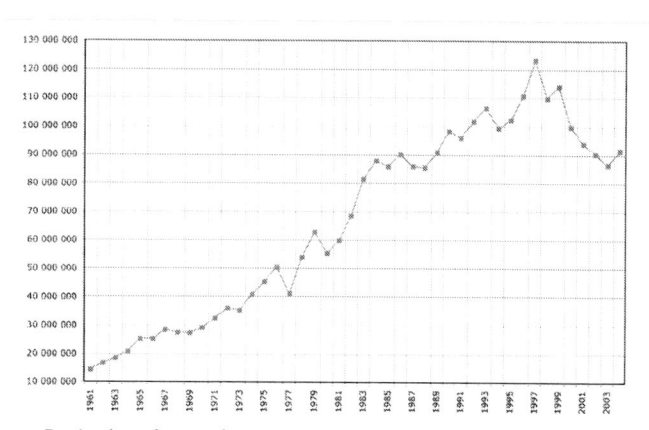

Production of wheat from 1961 to 2004. Data from FAO, year 2005.
Y-axis: Production in metric ton.

Nevertheless, about 60 percent of the population lives in the rural areas, and until the 1980s a high percentage of them made their living directly from farming. Since then, many have been encouraged to leave the fields and pursue other activities, such as light manufacturing, commerce, and transportation;

and by the mid-1980s farming accounted for less than half of the value of rural output. Today, agriculture contributes only 13% of China's GDP.

Animal husbandry constitutes the second most important component of agricultural production. China is the world's leading producer of pigs, chickens, and eggs, and it also has sizable herds of sheep and cattle. Since the mid-1970s, greater emphasis has been placed on increasing the livestock output. China has a long tradition of ocean and freshwater fishing and of aquaculture. Pond raising has always been important and has been increasingly emphasized to supplement coastal and inland fisheries threatened by overfishing and to provide such valuable export commodities as prawns.

Environmental problems such as floods, drought, and erosion pose serious threats to farming in many parts of the country. The wholesale destruction of forests gave way to an energetic reforestation program that proved inadequate, and forest resources are still fairly meagre. The principal forests are found in the Qinling Mountains and the central mountains and on the Sichuan–Yunnan plateau. Because they are inaccessible, the Qinling forests are not worked extensively, and much of the country's timber comes from Heilongjiang, Jilin, Sichuan, and Yunnan.

Western China, comprising Tibet, Xinjiang, and Qinghai, has little agricultural significance except for areas of floriculture and cattle raising. Rice, China's most important crop, is dominant in the southern provinces and many of the farms here yield two harvests a year. In the north, wheat is of the greatest importance, while in central China wheat and rice vie with each other for the top place. Millet and kaoliang (a variety of grain sorghum) are grown mainly in the northeast and some central provinces, which, together with some northern areas, also provide considerable quantities of barley. Most of the soybean crop is derived from the north and the northeast; corn (maize) is grown in the center and the north, while tea comes mainly from the hilly areas of the southeast. Cotton is grown extensively in the central provinces, but it is also found to a lesser extent in the southeast and in the north. Tobacco comes from the center and parts of the south. Other important crops are potatoes, sugar beets, and oilseeds.

There is still a relative lack of agricultural machinery, particularly advanced machinery. For the most part the Chinese peasant or farmer depends on simple, nonmechanized farming implements. Good progress has been made in increasing water conservancy, and about half the cultivated land is under irrigation.

In the late 1970s and early 1980s, economic reforms were introduced. First of all this began with the shift of farming work to a system of household responsibility and a phasing

Fish ponds near Daye, Hubei

out of collectivized agriculture. Later this expanded to include a gradual liberalization of price controls; fiscal decentralization; massive privatization of state enterprises, thereby allowing a wide variety of private enterprises in the services and light manufacturing; the foundation of a diversified banking system (but with large amounts of state control); the development of a stock market; and the opening of the economy to increased foreign trade and foreign investment.

Energy and mineral resources

Energy
Electricity:

- *production:* 2.8344 trillion kWh (2006)
- *consumption:* 2.8248 trillion kWh (2006)
- *exports:* 11.19 billion kWh (2005)
- *imports:* 5.011 billion kWh (2005)

Electricity – production by source:

- *thermal:* 77.8% (68.7% from coal) (2006)
- *hydro:* 20.7% (2006)
- *other:* 0.4% (2006)
- *nuclear:* 1.1% (2006)

Oil:

- *production:* 3.631 million bbl/day (2005)
- *consumption:* 6.534 million bbl/day (2005) and expected 9.3 million bbl/day in 2030
- *exports:* 443,300 bbl/day (2005)
- *imports:* 3.181 million bbl/day (2005)
- *net imports:* 2.74 million barrels per day (2005)
- *proved reserves:* 16.3 billion bbl (1 January 2006)

Natural gas:

- *production:* 47.88 billion m^3 (2005 est.)
- *consumption:* 44.93 billion m^3 (2005 est.)
- *exports:* 2.944 billion m^3 (2005)
- *imports:* 0 m^3 (2005)
- *proved reserves:* 1.448 trillion m^3 (1 January 2006 est.)

See also: Energy policy of China

Since 1980, China's energy production has grown dramatically, as has the proportion allocated to domestic consumption. Some 80 percent of all power generated from fossil fuel at thermal plants, with about 17 percent at hydroelectric installations; only about two percent is from nuclear energy, mainly from plants located in Guangdong and Zhejiang. Though China has rich overall energy potential, most have yet to be developed. In addition, the geographical distribution of energy puts most of these resources relatively far from their major industrial users. Basically the northeast is rich in coal and oil, the central part of north China has abundant coal, and the southwest has immense hydroelectric potential. But the industrialized regions around Guangzhou and the Lower Yangtze region around

Shanghai have too little energy, while there is relatively little heavy industry located near major energy resource areas other than in the southern part of the northeast.

Although electric-generating capacity has grown rapidly, it has continued to fall considerably short of demand. This has been partly because energy prices were long fixed so low that industries had few incentives to conserve. In addition, it has often been necessary to transport fuels (notably coal) great distances from points of production to consumption. Coal provides about 70–75 percent of China's energy consumption, although its proportion has been gradually declining. Petroleum production, which grew rapidly from an extremely low base in the early 1960s, has increased much more gradually from 1980. Natural gas production still constitutes only a small (though increasing) fraction of overall energy production, but gas is supplanting coal as a domestic fuel in the major cities.

In the 1990s, energy demand rocketed in response to the rapid expansion of the economy but energy production was constrained by limited capital. As in other sectors of the state-owned economy, the energy sector suffered from low utilization and inefficiencies in production, transport, conversion, consumption, and conservation. Other problems included declining real prices, rising taxes and production costs, spiraling losses, high debt burden, insufficient investment, low productivity, poor management structure, environmental pollution, and inadequate technological development. To keep pace with demand, China sought to increase electric generating capacity to a target level of 290 gigawatts by 2000.

According to Chinese statistics, China managed to keep its energy growth rate at just half the rate of GDP growth throughout the 1990s. Though these numbers are not reliable, there has been agreement that China had improved its energy efficiency significantly over this period. In the late 1990s, an estimated 10,000 megawatts of generating capacity was added each year, at an annual cost of about $15 billion. China imported new power plants from the West to increase its generation capacity, and these units then accounted for approximately 20% of total generating capacity. More power generating capacity came on line in the mid-2000s as large scale investments were completed. In 2001, China's total energy consumption was projected to double by 2020. Energy consumption grew at nearly 10 percent per year between 2000 and 2005, more than twice the yearly rate of the previous two decades.

In 2003, China surpassed Japan to become the second-largest consumer of primary energy, after the United States. China is the world's second-largest consumer of oil, after the United States, and for 2006, China's increase in oil demand represented 38% of the world total increase in oil demand. China is also the third-largest energy producer in the world, after the United States and Russia. China's electricity consumption is expected to grow by over 4% a year through 2030, which will require more than $2 trillion in electricity infrastructure investment to meet the demand. China expects to add approximately 15,000 megawatts of generating capacity a year, with 20% of that coming from foreign suppliers.

China, due in large part to environmental concerns, has wanted to shift China's current energy mix from a heavy reliance on coal, which accounts for 70–75% of China's energy, toward greater reliance on oil, natural gas, renewable energy, and nuclear power. China has closed thousands of coal mines over the past five to ten years to cut overproduction. According to Chinese statistics, this has reduced coal production by over 25%.

Only one-fifth of the new coal power plant capacity installed from 1995 to 2000 included desulfurization equipment. Interest in renewable sources of energy is growing, but except for hydropower, their contribution to the overall energy mix is unlikely to rise above 1–2% in the near future. China's energy sector continues to be hampered by difficulties in obtaining funding, including long-term financing, and by market balkanization due to local protectionism that prevents more efficient large plants from achieving economies of scale.

Since 1993, China has been a net importer of oil, a large portion of which comes from the Middle East. Imported oil accounts for 20% of the processed crude in China. Net imports are expected to rise to 3.5 million barrels (560,000 m^3) per day by 2010. China is interested in diversifying the sources of its oil imports and has invested in oil fields around the world. China is developing oil imports from Central Asia and has invested in Kazakhstani oil fields. Beijing also plans to increase China's natural gas production, which currently accounts for only 3% of China's total energy consumption and incorporated a natural gas strategy in its 10th Five-Year Plan (2001–2005), with the goal of expanding gas use from a 2% share of total energy production to 4% by 2005 (gas accounts for 25% of U.S. energy production). Analysts expect China's consumption of natural gas to more than double by 2010.

The 11th Five-Year Program (2006–10), announced in 2005 and approved by the National People's Congress in March 2006, called for greater energy conservation measures, including development of renewable energy sources and increased attention to environmental protection. Guidelines called for a 20% reduction in energy consumption per unit of GDP by 2010. Moving away from coal towards cleaner energy sources including oil, natural gas, renewable energy, and nuclear power is an important component of China's development program. Beijing also intends to continue to improve energy efficiency and promote the use of clean coal technology. China has abundant hydroelectric resources; the Three Gorges Dam, for example, will have a total capacity of 18 gigawatts when fully on-line (projected for 2009). In addition, the share of electricity generated by nuclear power is projected to grow from 1% in 2000 to 5% in 2030. China's renewable energy law, which went into effect in 2006, calls for 10% of its energy to come from renewable energy sources by 2020.

In May 2004, then-Secretary of Energy in the United States Spencer Abraham signed a Memorandum of Understanding (MOU) with China's National Development and Reform Commission (NDRC) that launched the U.S.–China Energy Policy Dialogue. The Dialogue strengthened energy-related interactions between China and the United States, the world's two largest energy consumers. The U.S.–China Energy Policy Dialogue has built upon the two countries' existing cooperative ventures in high energy nuclear physics, fossil energy, energy efficiency and renewable energy and energy information exchanges. The NDRC and the Department of Energy also exchange views and expertise on Peaceful Uses of Nuclear Technologies, and convenes an annual Oil and Gas Industry Forum with

China.

Mining

Outdated mining and ore-processing technologies are being replaced with modern techniques, but China's rapid industrialization requires imports of minerals from abroad. In particular, iron ore imports from Australia and the United States have soared in the early 2000s as steel production rapidly outstripped domestic iron ore production. Also China has become increasingly active in several African countries to mine the reserves it requires for economic growth, particularly in countries such as the Democratic Republic of the Congo and Gabon.

The major areas of production in 2004 were coal (nearly 2 billion tons), iron ore (310 million tons), crude petroleum (175 million tons), natural gas (41 million cubic meters), antimony ore (110,000 tons), tin concentrates (110,000 tons), nickel ore (64,000 tons), tungsten concentrates (67,000 tons), unrefined salt (37 million tons), vanadium (40,000 tons), and molybdenum ore (29,000 tons). In order of magnitude, produced minerals were bauxite, gypsum, barite, magnesite, talc and related minerals, manganese ore, fluorspar, and zinc. In addition, China produced 2,450 tons of silver and 215 tons of gold in 2004. The mining sector accounted for less than 0.9% of total employment in 2002 but produced about 5.3% of total industrial production.

Energy and mineral resources

See also: Gold mining in China

Hydroelectric resources

China has an abundant potential for hydroelectric power production due to its considerable river network and mountainous terrain. Most of the total hydroelectric capacity is situated in the southwest of the country, where coal supplies are poor but demand for energy is rising swiftly. The potential in the northeast is fairly small, but it was there that the first hydroelectric stations were built—by the Japanese during its occupation of Manchuria. Due to considerable seasonal fluctuations in rainfall, the flow of rivers tends to drop during the winter, forcing many power stations to operate at less than normal capacity, while in the summer, on the other hand, floods often interfere with generation.

Thirteen years in construction at a cost of $24 billion, the immense Three Gorges Dam across the Yangtze River was essentially completed in 2006 and will revolutionize electrification and flood control in the area.

Coal

China is well endowed with mineral resources, the most important of which is coal. China's mineral resources include large reserves of coal and iron ore, plus adequate to abundant supplies of nearly all other industrial minerals. Although coal deposits are widely scattered (some coal is found in every province), most of the total is located in the northern part of the country. The province of Shanxi, in fact, is thought to contain about half of the total; other important coal-bearing provinces include Heilongjiang, Liaoning, Jilin, Hebei, and Shandong. Apart from these northern provinces, significant quantities of coal are present in Sichuan, and there are some deposits of importance in Guangdong, Guangxi, Yunnan, and Guizhou. A large part of the country's reserves consists of good bituminous coal, but there are also large deposits of lignite. Anthracite is present in several places (especially Liaoning, Guizhou, and Henan), but overall it is not very significant.

To ensure a more even distribution of coal supplies and to reduce the strain on the less than adequate transportation network, the authorities pressed for the development of a large number of small, locally run mines throughout the country. This campaign was energetically pursued after the 1960s, with the result that thousands of small pits have been established, and they produce more than half the country's coal. This output, however, is typically expensive and is used for local consumption. It has also led to a less than stringent implementation of safety measures in these unregulated mines, which cause several thousands of deaths each year.

Coal makes up the bulk of China's energy consumption (70% in 2005), and China is the largest producer and consumer of coal in the world. As China's economy continues to grow, China's coal demand is projected to rise significantly. Although coal's share of China's overall energy consumption will decrease, coal consumption will continue to rise in absolute terms. China's continued and increasing reliance on coal as a power source has contributed significantly to putting China on the path to becoming the world's largest emitter of acid rain-causing sulfur dioxide and greenhouse gases, including carbon dioxide.

See also: Coal power in China

Oil and natural gas

Main article: Petroleum industry in the People's Republic of China

China's onshore oil resources are mostly located in the Northeast and in Xinjiang, Gansu, Qinghai, Sichuan, Shandong, and Henan provinces. Oil shale is found in a number of places, especially at Fushun in Liaoning, where the deposits overlie the coal reserves, as well as in Guangdong. Light oil of high quality has been found in the Pearl River estuary of the South China Sea, the Qaidam Basin in Qinghai, and the Tarim Basin in Xinjiang. The country consumes most of its oil output but does export some crude oil and oil products. China has explored and developed oil deposits in the China Seas, the Yellow Sea, the Gulf of Tonkin, and the Bohai Sea.

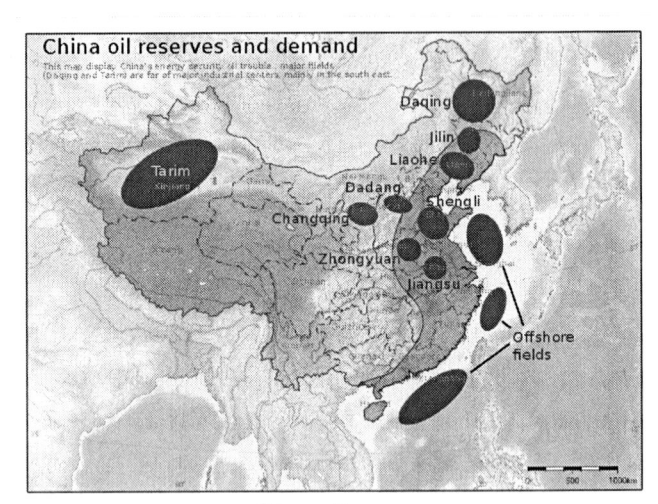

Chinese oil reserves

The total extent of China's natural gas reserves is unknown, as relatively little exploration for natural gas has been done. Sichuan accounts for almost half of the known natural gas reserves and production. Most of the rest of China's natural gas is associated gas produced in the Northeast's major oil fields, especially Daqing oilfield. Other gas deposits have been found in the Qaidam Basin, Hebei, Jiangsu, Shanghai, and Zhejiang, and offshore to the southwest of Hainan Island.

Metals and nonmetals

Iron ore reserves are found in most provinces, including Hainan. Gansu, Guizhou, southern Sichuan, and Guangdong provinces have rich deposits. The largest mined reserves are located north of the Yangtze River and supply neighboring iron and steel enterprises. With the exception of nickel, chromium, and cobalt, China is well supplied with ferroalloys and manganese. Reserves of tungsten are also known to be fairly large. Copper resources are moderate, and high-quality ore is present only in a few deposits. Discoveries have been reported from Ningxia. Lead and zinc are available, and bauxite resources are thought to be plentiful. China's antimony reserves are the largest in the world. Tin resources are plentiful, and there are fairly rich deposits of gold. China is the world's fifth largest producer of gold and in the early 21st century became an important producer and exporter of rare metals needed in high-technology industries. The rare earth reserves at the Bayan Obi mine in Inner Mongolia are thought to be the largest in any single location in the world.

China also produces a fairly wide range of nonmetallic minerals. One of the most important of these is salt, which is derived from coastal evaporation sites in Jiangsu, Hebei, Shandong, and Liaoning, as well as from extensive salt fields in Sichuan, Ningxia, and the Qaidam Basin. There are important deposits of phosphate rock in a number of areas. Pyrites occur in several places; Liaoning, Hebei, Shandong, and Shanxi have the most important deposits. China also has large resources of fluorite (fluorspar), gypsum, asbestos, and cement.

Industry and manufacturing

See also: Industry of China, Made in China, and Industrial history of the People's Republic of China

Industry and construction account for 46.8% of China's GDP. Around 8% of the total manufacturing output in the world comes from China itself. China ranks third worldwide in industrial output. Major industries include mining and ore processing; iron and steel; aluminium; coal; machinery; armaments; textiles and apparel; petroleum; cement; chemical; fertilizers; food processing; automobiles and other transportation equipment including rail cars and locomotives, ships, and aircraft; consumer products including footwear, toys, and electronics; telecommunications and information technology. China has become a preferred destination for the relocation of global manufacturing facilities. Its strength as an export platform has contributed to incomes and employment in China. The state-owned sector still accounts for about 30% of GDP. In recent years, authorities have been giving greater attention to the management of state assets—both in the financial market as well as among state-owned-enterprises—and progress has been noteworthy.

Since the founding of the People's Republic, industrial development has been given considerable attention. Among the various industrial branches the machine-building and metallurgical industries have received the highest priority. These two areas alone now account for about 20–30 percent of the total gross value of industrial output. In these, as in most other areas of industry, however, innovation has generally suffered at the hands of a system that has rewarded increases in gross output rather than improvements in variety, sophistication and quality. China, therefore, still imports significant quantities of specialized steels. Overall industrial output has grown at an average rate of more than 10 percent per year, having surpassed all other sectors in economic growth and degree of modernization. Some heavy industries and products deemed to be of national strategic importance remain state-owned, but an increasing proportion of lighter and consumer-oriented manufacturing firms are privately held or are private-state joint ventures.

The predominant focus of development in the chemical industry is to expand the output of chemical fertilizers, plastics, and synthetic fibers. The growth of this industry has placed China among the world's leading producers of nitrogenous fertilizers. In the consumer goods sector the main emphasis is on textiles and clothing, which also form an important part of China's exports. Textile manufacturing, a rapidly growing proportion of which consists of synthetics, account for about 10 percent of the gross industrial output and continues to be important, but less so than before. The industry tends to be scattered throughout the country, but there are a number of important textile centers, including Shanghai, Guangzhou, and Harbin.

Major state industries are iron, steel, coal, machine building, light industrial products, armaments, and textiles. These industries completed a decade of reform (1979–1989) with little substantial management change. Prior to 1978, most output was produced by state-owned enterprises. As a result of the economic reforms that followed, there was a significant increase in production by enterprises sponsored by local governments, especially townships and villages, and, increasingly, by private entrepreneurs and foreign investors. The 1996 industrial census revealed that there were 7,342,000 industrial enterprises at the end of 1995; total employment in industrial enterprises was approximately 147 million. The 1999 industrial census revealed that there were 7,930,000 industrial enterprises at the end of 1999 (including small-scale town and village enterprises); total employment in state-owned industrial enterprises was about 24 million. The automobile industry has grown rapidly since 2000, as has the petrochemical industry. Machinery and electronic products became China's main exports. China is the world's leading manufacturer of chemical fertilizers, cement, and steel. By 2002 the share in gross industrial output by state-owned and state-holding industries had decreased to 41%, and the state-owned companies themselves contributed only 16% of China's industrial output.

China's construction sector has grown substantially since the early 1980s. In the 21st century, investment in capital construction has experienced major annual increases. In 2001 investments increased 8.5% over the previous year. In 2002 there was a 16.4% increase, followed by a 30% increase in 2003. The manufacturing sector produced 44.1% of GDP in 2004 and accounted for 11.3% of total employment in 2002. Industry and construction produced 53.1% of China's GDP in 2005. Industry (including mining, manufacturing, construction, and power) contributed 52.9% of GDP in 2004 and occupied 22.5% of the workforce.

Energy production has increased rapidly, but it still falls considerably short of demand. This is partly due to artificial energy prices that have been held so low that industries have had few incentives to conserve. Coal provides about 75–80 percent of China's energy consumption. Petroleum production, which began growing rapidly from an extremely low base in the early 1960s, has basically remained at the same level since the late 1970s. There are large petroleum reserves in the inaccessible northwest and potentially significant offshore petroleum deposits, but about half of the country's oil production still comes from the major Daqing oilfield in the northeast. China has much, and partially undeveloped, hydroelectric power potential and natural gas reserves. The government has made plans to develop nuclear power plants in the coastal and western regions (see Nuclear power in China).

Overall, the distribution of industry remains very uneven, despite serious efforts from the mid-1950s to the late 1970s to build up industry in the interior at the cost of the major cities on the east coast. While percentage growth of industry in the interior provinces generally greatly exceeded that of the coastal areas, the far larger initial industrial base of the latter has meant that a few coastal regions have continued to dominate China's industrial economy. The establishment of special economic zones in coastal areas only heightened this disparity. Shanghai by itself accounts for about 8–10 percent of China's gross value of industrial output, and the east coast accounts for about 60 percent of the national industrial output. The rate of industrialization increased and diversified after the early 1990s. Notable were the development of aerospace, aircraft, and automobile manufacturing. In addition, China expanded rapidly into the production of pharmaceuticals, software, semiconductors, electronics, and precision equipment.

Steel industry

China is the largest producer of steel in the world and the steel industry has been rapidly increasing its steel production. Iron ore production kept pace with steel production in the early 1990s but was soon outpaced by imported iron ore and other metals in the early 2000s. Steel production, an estimated 140 million tons in 2000, was increased to 419 million tons in 2006. Much of the country's steel output comes from a large number of small-scale producing centers, one of the largest being Anshan in Liaoning.

China is the top exporter of steel in the world. Export volumes in 2008 were 59.23 million tons, a 5.5% fall over the previous year. The decline ends China's decade-old steel export growth.

Automotive industry

Main article: Automobile industry in China

By 2006 China had become the world's third largest automotive vehicle manufacturer (after US and Japan) and the second largest consumer (only after US). Automobile manufacturing has soared during the reform period. In 1975 only 139,800 automobiles were produced annually, but by 1985 production had reached 443,377, then jumped to nearly 1.1 million by 1992 and increased fairly evenly each year up until 2001, when it reached 2.3 million. In 2002 production rose to nearly 3.25 million and then jumped to 4.44 million in 2003, 5.07 million in 2004, 5.71 million in 2005 and 7.28 million in 2006. In 2007, 9 million automobiles are expected to be produced and the country could become the number-one automaker in the world by 2020. Domestic sales have kept pace with production. After respectable annual increases in the mid- and late 1990s, passenger car sales soared in the early 2000s. In 2006, a total of 7.22 million automobiles have been sold, including 5.18 million units of passenger cars and 2.04 million units of commercial vehicles.

So successful has China's automotive industry been that it began exporting car parts in 1999. China began to plan major moves into the automobile and components export business starting in 2005. A new Honda factory in Guangzhou was built in 2004 solely for the export market and was expected to ship 30,000 passenger vehicles to Europe in 2005. By 2004, 12 major foreign automotive manufacturers had joint-venture plants in China. They produced a wide range of automobiles, minivans, sport utility vehicles, buses, and trucks. In 2003 China exported US$4.7 billion worth of vehicles and components. The vehicle export was 78,000 units in 2004, 173,000 units in 2005, and

340,000 units in 2006. The vehicle and component export is targeted to reach US$70 billion by 2010.

The market for domestically produced cars, under a local name, is likely to continue to grow both inside China and outside. Companies such as Geely and Chery are constantly evaluating new international locations, both in developing and developed countries.

Other industries

See also: Telecommunications industry in China, Electronic information industry in China, Pharmaceutical industry in China, Defense industry in China, and Shipping industry in China

China is the world's biggest sex toy producer and accounts for 70% of the worldwide sex toys production. In the country, 1,000 manufacturers are active in this industry, which generates about two billion dollars a year.

Services

China's services output ranks seventh worldwide, and high power and telecom density has ensured that it has remained on a high-growth trajectory in the long-term. In 2005 the services sector produced 40.3% of China's annual GDP, second only to manufacturing. However, its proportion of GDP is still low compared with the ratio in more developed countries, and the agricultural sector still employs a larger workforce. Prior to the onset of economic reforms in 1978, China's services sector was characterized by state-operated shops, rationing, and regulated prices. With reform came private markets and individual entrepreneurs and a commercial sector. The wholesale and retail trade has expanded quickly, with urban areas now having many shopping malls, retail shops, restaurant chains and hotels. Public administration has still remained a main component of the service sector, while tourism has become a significant factor in employment and as a source of foreign exchange. The potential for growing services in China through franchising is huge.

Tourism

Main article: Tourism in China

China's tourism industry is one of the fastest-growing industries in the national economy and is also one of the industries with a very distinct global competitive edge. The total revenue of China's tourism industry reached USD 67.3 billion in 2002, accounting for 5.44% of the GDP. It dropped, largely due to SARS, to USD 59 billion in 2003. Nevertheless, for areas rich in tourism resources, tourism has become the main source of tax revenue and the key industry for economic development.

The total number of inbound tourists was 91.66 million in 2003, and that of tourists staying overnight was 32.7 million, about 10 times of the number in 1980. International tourism receipts were USD 17.4 billion in 2003. China's ranking for both the overnight tourist arrivals and tourism receipts were among the world's top five in 2003. However, there is unlikely to be a big increase in the inbound tourism market.

China's domestic tourism market makes up more than 90% of the country's tourism traffic, and contributes more than 70% of total tourism revenue. In 2002, domestic tourists reached 878 million and tourism revenue was USD 46.9 billion. The five-days-per-week and long vacation schemes have increased leisure time for the Chinese people and spurred market demand in domestic tourism and led to its prosperity.

A large middle class population with strong consumption power is emerging in China, especially in major cities. China's outbound tourists reached 20.22 million in 2003, overtaking Japan for the first time. Currently there are 65 countries/areas open to Chinese tour groups. Putting aside the threat of SARS and other unexpected events, based on the current economic growth situation and the social development of China, China's outbound tourism is poised to achieve a new growth peak.

Driven by the flourishing tourism industry, China's tourist hotel sector is expanding rapidly. At the end of 2003, China had a total of 10,093 tourist hotels and more than 820,000 rooms. 773 of these tourist hotels were foreign-funded. The number of foreign-funded (inclusive of Hong Kong, Macau and Taiwan investments) four- and five-star tourist hotels made up 26% and 30.02% of the national total, respectively.

In 2003, there were a total of 11,522 travel agencies in China, among which, 1,349 were international ones and 10,203 were domestic ones. While overall tourism market concentration rose, there was a drop in the market position of the traditional three key travel agencies. As competition heightened, China's tourism industry on the whole, had begun to start earning low profits, even while it was expanding its scale of operations.

Currently, there are approximately 15,000 natural, cultural and man-made places of attraction that are above county level. Presently, Hong Kong investors are the main participants in the establishment of tourist attractions in China. In 2001, Sichuan became the first province to propose renting out the operation rights of 10 scenic areas to foreign investors.

According to the plan by China National Tourism Administration, the number of inbound tourists, foreign exchange earnings from tourism and the domestic market size are targeted to have an annual growth of 4%, 8% and 8%, respectively, in the next five to ten years. It is also forecast by the WTO that China's tourism industry will take up to 8.6% of world market share to become the world's top tourism industry by 2020.

Labor and welfare

Main articles: Labor relations in the People's Republic of China and Social welfare in China

One of the hallmarks of China's socialist economy was its promise of employment to all able and willing to work and job-security with virtually lifelong tenure. Reformers targeted the labor market as unproductive because industries were frequently overstaffed to fulfill socialist goals and job-security reduced workers' incentive to work. This socialist policy was pejoratively called the iron rice bowl.

In 1979–1980, the state reformed factories by giving wage increases to workers, which was immediately offset by sharply rising inflation rates of 6–7%. The reforms also dismantled the iron rice bowl, which meant it witnessed a rise in unemployment in the economy. In 1979 there were 20 million unemployed people. Official Chinese statistics reveal that 4.2% of the total urban workforce was unemployed in 2004, although other estimates have reached 10%. As part of its newly developing social security legislation, China has an unemployment insurance system. At the end of 2003, more than 103.7 million people were participating in the plan, and 7.4 million laid-off employees had received benefits.

A window washer on one of skyscrapers in Shanghai

A 10-percent sample tabulation of census questionnaires from the 1982 census provided needed statistical data on China's working population and allowed the first reliable estimates of the labor force's size and characteristics. The estimated mid-1982 labor force was 546 million, or approximately 54 percent of the total population. Males accounted for slightly more than half of the estimated labor force, and the labor force participation rates for persons age fifteen years and older were among the highest in the world.

The 10-percent sample showed that approximately three-fourths of the labor force worked in the agricultural sector. According to the National Bureau of Statistics, in the mid-1980s more than 120 million people worked in the nonagricultural sector. The sample revealed that men occupied the great majority of leadership positions. The average worker was about thirty years old, and three out of every four workers were under forty-five years of age. The working population had a low education level. Less than 40 percent of the labor force had more than a primary school education, and 30 percent were illiterate or semiliterate.

In mid-1982 the overall unemployment rate was estimated to be about 5 percent. Of the approximately 25 million unemployed, 12 million were men and 13 million were women. The unemployment rate was highest in the northeast and lowest in the south. The unemployment rates were higher than those of

East Asian, Southeast Asian, and Pacific island countries for which data were available but were lower than the rates found in North America and Europe. Virtually all of the unemployed persons in cities and towns were under twenty years of age.

By the 1990s and 2000s, agriculture has remained the largest employer, though its proportion of the workforce has steadily declined; between 1991 and 2001 it dropped from about 60% to 40% of the total. The manufacturing labor force has also become smaller at a slower rate, partially because of reforms implemented at many of the state-run enterprises. Such reforms and other factors have increased unemployment and underemployment in both urban and rural areas. Women have been a major labor presence in China since the People's Republic was established. Some 40–45 percent of all women over age 15 are employed.

China's estimated employed labor force in 2005 totaled 791.4 million persons, about 60% of the total population. During 2003, 49% of the labor force worked in agriculture, forestry, and fishing; 22% in mining, manufacturing, energy, and construction industries; and 29% in the services sector and other categories. In 2004 some 25 million persons were employed by 743,000 private enterprises. Urban wages rose rapidly from 2004 to 2007, at a rate of 13 to 19% per year with average wages near $200/month in 2007.

The All-China Federation of Trade Unions (ACFTU) was established in 1925 to represent the interests of national and local trade unions and trade union councils. The ACFTU reported a membership of 130 million, out of an estimated 248 million urban workers, at the end of 2002. Chinese trade unions are organized on a broad industrial basis. Membership is open to those who rely on wages for the whole or a large part of their income, a qualification that excludes most agricultural workers. In theory, membership is not compulsory, but in view of the unions' role in the distribution of social benefits, the economic pressure to join is great. The lowest unit is the enterprise union committee. Individual trade unions also operate at the provincial level, and there are trade union councils that coordinate all union activities within a particular area and operate at county, municipal, and provincial levels. At the top of the movement is the ACFTU, which discharges its functions through a number of regional federations.

In theory the appropriate trade union organizations have been consulted on the level of wages as well as on wage differentials, but in practice their role in these and similar matters has been insignificant. They have not engaged in collective bargaining, as their principal duties have included assisting the party and promoting production. In fulfilling these tasks, they have had a role in enforcing labor discipline. From the point of view of the membership, the most important activities have concerned the social and welfare services. Thus, the unions have looked after industrial safety, organized social and cultural activities, and, provided services such as clinics, rest and holiday homes, hostels, libraries, and clubs. They also administer old-age pensions, workers' insurance, disability benefits, and other welfare schemes. More recently, however, reforms of the social security system have involved moving the responsibility for pensions and other welfare to the provinces.

Chinese labor laws, if fully enforced, would greatly alleviate common abuses such as not paying workers. In 2006 and thereafter there was an organizing campaign orchestrated by the central government to organize Chinese operations of foreign companies. It was reported in 2008 that problems with sweatshops persist.

In 2010, the issues of manufacturing wages caused a strike at a Honda parts plant. This resulted in wage increases both at the struck plant and other industrial plants.

External trade

Main article: History of trade for the People's Republic of China

International trade makes up a sizeable portion of China's overall economy. The course of China's foreign trade has experienced considerable transformations since the early 1950s. In 1950 more than 70 percent of the total trade was with non-Communist countries, but by 1954, a year after the end of the Korean War, the situation was completely reversed, and trade with Communist countries stood at about 75 percent. During the next few years, trade with the Communist world lost some of its standing, but it was only after the Sino-Soviet split of 1960, which resulted in the cancellation of Soviet credits and the withdrawal of Soviet technicians, that the non-Communist world began to see a speedy recovery in its position. In 1965 China's trade with other socialist countries made up only about a third of the total.

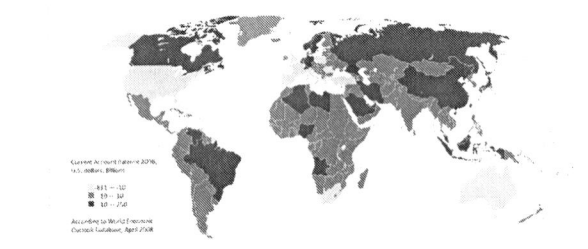

Current account balance 2006

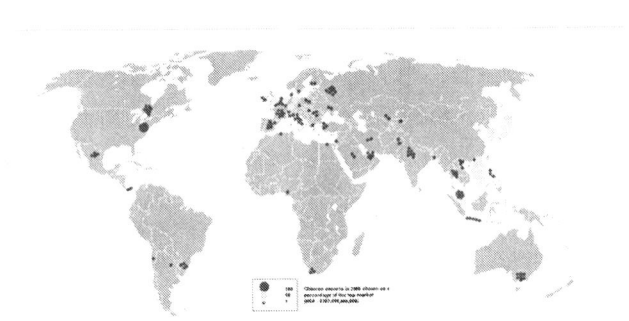

Global distribution of Chinese exports in 2006 as a percentage of the top market

Being a Second World country at the time, a meaningful segment of China's trade with the Third World was financed through grants, credits, and other forms of assistance. At first, from 1953 to 1955, aid went mainly to North Korea and North Vietnam and some other Communist states; but from the mid-1950s large amounts, mainly grants and long-term, interest-free loans, were promised to politically uncommitted developing countries. The principal efforts were made in Asia, especially to Indonesia, Burma, Pakistan, and Ceylon, but large loans were also granted in Africa (Ghana, Algeria, Tanzania) and in the Middle East (Egypt). However, after Mao Zedong's death in 1976, these efforts were scaled back. After which, trade with developing countries became negligible, though during that time, Hong Kong and Taiwan both began to emerge as major trading partners.

Since economic reforms began in the late 1970s, China sought to decentralize its foreign trade system to integrate itself into the international trading system. On November 1991, China joined the Asia-Pacific Economic Cooperation (APEC) group, which promotes free trade and cooperation the in economic, trade, investment, and technology spheres. China served as APEC chair in 2001, and Shanghai hosted the annual APEC leaders meeting in October of that year.

China's global trade totaled $324 billion in 1997 and $151 billion in the first half of 1998; the trade surplus stood at $40.0 billion. China's primary trading partners were Japan, Taiwan, the U.S., South Korea, Hong Kong, Germany, Singapore, Russia, and the Netherlands. China had a trade surplus with the U.S. of $49.7 billion in 1997 and $54.6 billion in 1998. Major imports were power generating equipment, aircraft and parts, computers and industrial machinery, raw materials, and chemical and agricultural products.

In 1998, China was in its 12th year of negotiations for accession to the World Trade Organization (WTO)—formerly the General Agreement on Tariffs and Trade (GATT), and had significantly reduced import tariffs. Previously in 1996, China had already introduced cuts to more than 4,000 tariff lines, reducing average tariffs from 35% to 23%; further tariff cuts that took effect October 1, 1997, decreased average tariffs to 17%. To gain WTO entry, all prospective WTO members were required to comply with certain fundamental trading disciplines and offer substantially expanded market access to other members of the organization. Many major trading entities—among them the United States, the European Union, and Japan—shared concerns with respect to China's accession. These concerns included obtaining satisfactory market access offers for both goods and services, full trading rights for all potential Chinese consumers and end-users, nondiscrimination between foreign and local commercial operations in China, the reduction of monopolistic state trading practices, and the elimination of arbitrary or non-scientific technical standards. China and other WTO members worked to achieve a commercially viable accession protocol.

In 1999, Premier Zhu Rongji signed a bilateral U.S.–China Agricultural Cooperation Agreement, which lifted longstanding Chinese prohibitions on imports of citrus, grain, beef, and poultry. In November 1999, the United States and China reached a historic bilateral market-access agreement to pave the way for China's accession to the WTO. As part of the far-reaching trade liberalization agreement, China agreed to lower tariffs and abolish market impediments after it joins the world trading body. Chinese and foreign businessmen, for example, would gain the right to import and export on their own – and to sell their products without going through a government middleman. After reaching a bilateral WTO agreement with the EU and other trading partners in summer 2000, China worked on a multilateral WTO accession package. China concluded multilateral negotiations on its accession to the WTO in September 2001. The completion of its accession protocol and Working Party

Economy of the People's Republic of China

Report paved the way for its entry into the WTO on December 11, 2001, after 16 years of negotiations, the longest in the history of the General Agreement on Tariffs and Trade.

China's global trade exceeded $2.4 trillion at the end of 2008. It first broke the $100 billion mark in 1988, $200 billion in 1994, $500 billion in 2001 and $1 trillion mark ($1.15 trillion) in 2004. The table below shows the average annual growth (in nominal US dollar terms) of China's foreign trade during the reform era.

With bilateral trade exceeding US$38.6 billion, China is India's largest trading partner. Shown here is a Chinese container ship unloading its cargo at Jawaharlal Nehru Port, Navi Mumbai, India.

Period	Two-way trade	Exports	Imports
1981–85	+12.8%	+8.6%	+16.1%
1986–90	+10.6%	+17.8%	+4.8%
1991–95	+19.5%	+19.1%	+19.9%
1996–2000	+11.0%	+10.9%	+11.3%
2000–05	+24.6%	+25.0%	+24.0%
2006	+27.2%	+19.9%	+23.8%
2007	+25.6%	+20.8%	+23.4%

The vast majority of China's imports consists of industrial supplies and capital goods, notably machinery and high-technology equipment, the majority of which comes from the developed countries, primarily Japan[citation needed] and the United States[citation needed]. Regionally, almost half of China's imports come from East and Southeast Asia, and about one-fourth of China's exports go to the same destinations[citation needed]. About 80 percent of China's exports consist of manufactured goods, most of which are textiles and electronic equipment, with agricultural products and chemicals constituting the remainder. Out of the five busiest ports in the world, three are in China.

The U.S. is one of China's primary suppliers of semiconductors and electronic components, power-generating equipment, aircraft and parts, computers and industrial machinery, raw materials, waste and scrap, and chemical and agricultural products[citation needed]. However, U.S. exporters continue to have concerns about fair market access due to China's restrictive trade policies and U.S.

export restrictionsWikipedia:Disputed statement[citation needed]. Intellectual property theft makes many foreign companies wary of doing business in mainland China.[citation needed] According to U.S. statistics, China had a trade surplus with the U.S. of $170 billion in 2004, more than doubling from 1999. Wal-Mart, the United States' largest retailer, is China's 7th largest export partner, just ahead of the United Kingdom.

Gourmet foods, such as Florida softshell turtle, are among China's imports

The U.S. trade deficit with China reached $232.5 billion in 2006, as imports grew 18%. China's share of total U.S. imports has grown from 7% to 15% since 1996. At the same time, the share of many other Asian countries' imports to the United States fell, from 39% in 1996 to 21.1% in 2005. The share of overall Asian imports (including China) to the United States actually declined from 38.8% in 1996 to 35.7% in 2005. The U.S. global trade deficit with the Asia–Pacific region as a whole also has fallen from 75% in 1995 to 49% in 2005.

Trade volume between China and Russia reached $29.1 billion in 2005, an increase of 37.1% compared with 2004. A spokesman for the Ministry of Commerce, Van Jingsun, said that the volume of trade between China and Russia could exceed 40 billion dollars in 2007. China's export of machinery and electronic goods to Russia grew 70%, which is 24% of China's total export to Russia in the first 11 months of 2005. During the same time, China's export of high-tech products to Russia increased by 58%, and that is 7% of China's total exports to Russia. Also in this time period border trade between the two countries reached $5.13 billion, growing 35% and accounting for nearly 20% of the total trade. Most of China's exports to Russia remain apparel and footwear. Russia is China's eighth largest trade partner and China is now Russia's fourth largest trade partner, and China now has over 750 investment projects in Russia, involving $1.05 billion. China's contracted investment in Russia totaled $368 million during January–September 2005, twice that in 2004.

Chinese imports from Russia are mainly those of energy sources, such as crude oil, which is mostly transported by rail, and electricity exports from neighboring Siberian and Far Eastern regions. In the near future, exports of both of these commodities are set to increase, as Russia is building the Eastern Siberia-Pacific Ocean oil pipeline with a branch to Chinese border, and Russian power grid monopoly UES is building some of its hydropower stations with a view of future exports to China.

Chinese cars at a dealer's lot in Nizhny Novgorod, the traditional capital of the Russian automotive industry

Export growth has continued to be a major component supporting China's rapid economic growth. To increase exports, China pursued policies such as fostering the rapid development of foreign-invested factories, which assembled imported components into consumer goods for export and liberalizing trading rights. In its 11th Five-Year Program, adopted in 2005, China placed greater emphasis on developing a consumer demand-driven economy to sustain economic growth and address imbalances.

The China Council for the Promotion of International Trade (CCPIT) promotes China's international economic and commercial interests. This is accomplished by developing business cooperation and exchanges with foreign countries. It also produces economic data, creates diplomatic ties and is active with trade arbitration issues. Hong Kong remains prominent in domestic trade, notably in its reliance on the mainland for agricultural products.

Trading partners

Main article: List of the largest trading partners of the People's Republic of China

Foreign investment

See also: Qualified Domestic Institutional Investor, Qualified Foreign Institutional Investor, China Investment Promotion Agency, China Council for the Promotion of International Trade, and Ministry of Commerce of the People's Republic of China

China's investment climate has changed dramatically with more than two decades of reform. In the early 1980s, China restricted foreign investments to export-oriented operations and required foreign investors to form joint-venture partnerships with Chinese firms. The Encouraged Industry Catalogue sets out the degree of foreign involvement allowed in various industry sectors. From the beginning of the reforms legalizing foreign investment, capital inflows expanded every year until 1999. Foreign-invested enterprises account for 58–60% of China's imports and exports.

Since the early 1990s, the government has allowed foreign investors to manufacture and sell a wide range of goods on the domestic market, eliminated time restrictions on the establishment of joint ventures, provided some assurances against nationalization, allowed foreign partners to become chairs of joint venture boards, and authorized the establishment of wholly foreign-owned enterprises, now the preferred form of FDI. In 1991, China granted more preferential tax treatment for Wholly Foreign Owned Enterprises and contractual ventures and for foreign companies, which invested in selected economic zones or in projects encouraged by the state, such as energy, communications and transportation.

China also authorized some foreign banks to open branches in Shanghai and allowed foreign investors to purchase special "B" shares of stock in selected companies listed on the Shanghai and Shenzhen Securities Exchanges. These "B" shares sold to foreigners carried no ownership rights in a company. In 1997, China approved 21,046 foreign investment projects and received over $45 billion in foreign direct investment. China revised significantly its laws on Wholly Foreign-Owned Enterprises and China Foreign Equity Joint Ventures in 2000 and 2001, easing export performance and domestic content requirements.

Foreign investment remains a strong element in China's rapid expansion in world trade and has been an important factor in the growth of urban jobs. In 1998, foreign-invested enterprises produced about 40% of China's exports, and foreign exchange reserves totalled about $145 billion. Foreign-invested enterprises today produce about half of China's exports (the majority of China's foreign investment come from Hong Kong, Macau and Taiwan), and China continues to attract large investment inflows. However, the Chinese government's emphasis on guiding FDI into manufacturing has led to market saturation in some industries, while leaving China's services sectors underdeveloped. From 1993 to 2001, China was the world's second-largest recipient of foreign direct investment after the United States. China received $39 billion FDI in 1999 and $41 billion FDI in 2000. China is now one of the leading FDI recipients in the world, receiving almost $80 billion in 2005 according to World Bank statistics. In 2006, China received $69.47 billion in foreign direct investment.

Foreign exchange reserves totaled $155 billion in 1999 and $165 billion in 2000. Foreign exchange reserves exceeded $800 billion in 2005, more than doubling from 2003. Foreign exchange reserves were $819 billion at the end of 2005, $1.066 trillion at the end of 2006, $1.9 trillion by June 2008. In addition, by the end of September 2008 China replaced Japan for the first time as the largest foreign holder of US treasury securities with a total of $585 billion, vs Japan $573 billion. China has now surpassed those of Japan, making China's foreign exchange reserves the largest in the world.

As part of its WTO accession, China undertook to eliminate certain trade-related investment measures and to open up specified sectors that had previously been closed to foreign investment. New laws, regulations, and administrative measures to implement these commitments are being issued. Major remaining barriers to foreign investment include opaque and inconsistently enforced laws and regulations and the lack of a rules-based legal infrastructure. Warner Bros., for instance, withdrew its cinema business in China as a result of a regulation that requires Chinese investors to own at least a 51 percent stake or play a leading role in a foreign joint venture.

Outward foreign direct investment is a new feature of Chinese globalization, where local Chinese firms seek to make investments in both developing and developed countries.

Demographics

Main articles: Demographics of the People's Republic of China, Migration in China, Urbanization in China, and Chinese emigration

See also: Standard of living in the People's Republic of China and Poverty in China

Since the 1950s medical care, public hygiene and sanitation improved considerably, and epidemics were controlled. Consecutive generations continuously experienced better health. The population growth rate surged as the mortality rate dropped more rapidly than the birth rate. China's massive population has always been a major difficulty for the government as it has struggled to provide for it. In the 1950s, food supply was inadequate and the standard of living was generally low. This spurred the authorities to initiate a major birth control program. The Great Leap Forward industrial plan in 1958–60 was partially responsible for a huge famine that caused the death rate to surpass the birth rate, and by 1960, the overall population was declining. A second population control drive began in 1962 with major efforts focused on promoting late marriages and the use of contraceptives. By 1963 the country was in the beginning of recovery from the famine and the birth rate soared to its highest since 1949 with an annual population growth rate of 3%. In 1966, the Cultural Revolution suspended this second family planning program, but resumed four years later with the third attempt by making later marriage and family size limitation an obligation. Since 1970, the efforts have been much more effective. The third family planning program continued until 1979 when the one child per family policy was implemented. By the early 1980s, China's population reached around 1 billion and by the early 2000s, surpassed 1.3 billion. In the 1980s, the average overall population growth was around 1.5%. In the 1990s, this fell to about 1%. Today it is about 0.6%. China's population growth rate is now among the lowest for a developing country, although, due to its large population, annual net population growth is still considerable. One demographic consequence of the one-child policy is that China is now one of the most rapidly ageing countries in the world.

From 100 million to 150 million surplus rural workers are adrift between the villages and the cities, many subsisting through part-time, low-paying jobs.

According to the latest Forbes China Rich List (2007), China had 66 billionaires, the second largest number after the United States, which had 415. In the 2006 Forbes Rich List it stated that there were 15 Chinese billionaires. In the latest 2007 Hurun Report, it lists 106 billionaires in China.

Transportation

Main article: Transport in the People's Republic of China

Development of the country's transportation infrastructure is given a high priority because it is so strategically tied to the national economy and national defense. Regardless, the transportation infrastructure is still not fully developed in many aspects and areas, and it constitutes a major hindrance on economic growth and the efficient logistical movement of goods and people. China's transportation policy, influenced by political, military, and economic concerns, have undergone major changes since 1949.

Immediately after the People's Republic was founded, the primary goal was to repair existing transportation infrastructure in order to meet military transport and logistics needs as well as to strengthen territorial integrity. During most of the 1950s, new road and rail links were built, while at the same time old ones were improved. During the 1960s much of the improvement of regional transportation became the responsibility of the local governments, and many small railways were constructed. Emphasis was also placed on developing transportation in remote rural, mountainous, and forested areas, in order to integrate poorer regions of the country and to help promote economies of scale in the agricultural sector.

Before the reform era began in the late 1970s, China's transportation links were mostly concentrated in the coastal areas and access to the inner regions was generally poor. This situation has been improved considerably since then, as railways and highways have been built in the remote and frontier regions of the northwest and southwest. At the same time, the development of international transportation was also pursued, and the scope of ocean shipping was broadened considerably.

Freight haulage is mainly provided by rail transport. The rail sector is monopolized by China Railways, which is controlled by the Ministry of Railways and there is wide variation in services provided. In late 2007 China became one of the few countries in the world to launch its own indigenously developed high-speed train. As rail capacity is struggling to meet demand for the transport of goods and raw materials such as coal, air routes, roads and waterways are rapidly being developed to provide an increasing proportion of China's overall transportation needs.

Communications

Main article: Telecommunications in the People's Republic of China

China possesses a diversified communications system that links all parts of the country by Internet, telephone, telegraph, radio, and television.

China's number of Internet users or netizens topped 137 million by the end of 2006, an increase of 23.4% from a year before and 162 million by June 2007, making China the second largest Internet user after the United States, according to China's Ministry of Information Industry (MII). China's mobile phone penetration rate is 34% in 2007. In 2006, mobile phone users sent 429 billion text messages, or on average 967 text messages per user. For 2006, the number of fixed-lines grew by 79%, mainly in the rural areas.

Science and technology

Main articles: Science and technology in the People's Republic of China, Higher education in China, and List of Chinese universities

Science and technology have always preoccupied China's leaders and indeed, China's political leadership comes almost exclusively from technical backgrounds and has a high regard for science. Deng Xiaoping called it "the first productive force." In recent times, with Hu Jintao and Wen Jiabao and their predecessors Jiang Zemin and Zhu Rongji all being trained engineers, China's leaders have been described as technocrats.

Since the early 1980s scientific and technological modernization has been given an especially high priority. Plans were made to rebuild the educational structure, continue sending students abroad, negotiate technological purchases and transfer arrangements with the U.S. and others, and develop ways to disseminate scientific and technological information. Areas of most critical interest have included microelectronics, telecommunications, computers, automated manufacturing, and energy. China also has had a space program since the 1960s and, by the late 1990s, had successfully launched more than 25 satellites.

On the other hand, distortions in the economy and society created by party rule have severely hurt Chinese science, according to some Chinese science policy experts. The Chinese Academy of Sciences, modeled on the Soviet system, puts much of China's greatest scientific talent in a large, under-funded apparatus that remains largely isolated from industry, although the reforms of the past decade have begun to address this problem.

Chinese science strategists have seen China's greatest opportunities in newly emerging fields such as biotechnology and computers where there is still a chance for China to become a significant player. A majority of Chinese students who went abroad have not returned, but they have built a dense network of global contacts that have greatly facilitated international scientific cooperation. The United States is often held up as the standard of scientific modernity in China. Indeed, photos of the Space Shuttle often appear in Chinese advertisements as a symbol of advanced technology. China's growing space program, which has put a man in space and successfully completed their second manned orbit in October 2005, is a focus of national pride.

At the end of 1996, China had 5,434 state-owned independent research and development institutions at and above the county level. There were another 3,400 research institutions affiliated with universities, 13,744 affiliated with medium and large industrial enterprises, and 726 affiliated with medium and large construction enterprises. A total of 2.8 million people were engaged in scientific and technological activities in these institutions.

The U.S.–China Science and Technology Agreement remains the framework for bilateral cooperation between the two countries in this field. It was originally signed in 1979. A five-year agreement to extend and amend the accord, including provisions for the protection of intellectual property rights, was signed in May 1991, and the Agreement was again extended for five years in April 1996. Five-year agreements to extend the accord were signed in April 2001 and April 2006. The Agreement is among the longest-standing U.S.–China accords, and includes over eleven U.S. Federal agencies and numerous branches that participate in cooperative exchanges under the S&T Agreement and its nearly 60 protocols, memoranda of understanding, agreements and annexes. The Agreement covers cooperation in areas such as marine conservation, high-energy physics, renewable energy, and health. Biennial Joint Commission Meetings on Science and Technology bring together policymakers from both sides to coordinate joint science and technology cooperation. Executive Secretaries meetings are held biennially to implement specific cooperation programs.

Japan and the European Union also have high profile science and technology cooperative relationships with China.

Luxury goods

A factor that often goes overlooked is the extent of luxury spending the Chinese citizenry are undertaking. There is no greater indication of the newfound wealth of the Chinese than the amount of money now spent on goods and services that were once inaccessible. Foremost among these is the shift towards bottled water. The Chinese bottled water manufacturing industry is forecast to more than double in size in 2008, becoming a $10.5 (US dollars) billion industry in the process. Meanwhile, as those who once had no recourse but poor-quality tap water take advantage of its availability in supermarkets, those who had little or no running water are now capitalising on its availability. The tap water production and supply industry is expected to grow by 29.3% in 2008, to $11.9 billion. This demonstrates the difference in what, exactly, is considered a luxury in Chinese society; many Chinese consider running water a considerable extravagance. Some consumption is more conspicuous. The country's motor vehicle production industry is expected to expand by 29.5% to nearly $200 billion, as many Chinese eschew traditional modes of transport, such as bicycles, for the comforts of modern cars. Also, consumption of chocolate and other confectionery is set to increase by 24.3%, as the industry expands to $4.6 billion, in order to keep up with China's collective sweet tooth. Couple with this is 20.8% growth in China's fast food industry, as major players such as McDonalds enter the country with vigour. Also, the LVMH group, who own major luxury brands including Louis Vuitton apparel, Moet-Chandon wines and champagne and Hennessey cognacs, reported earnings growth of over 25% in 2007 in China, the region now accounting for around 16% of their global business.

Environment and public health

Main articles: Environment of China, Water supply and sanitation in the People's Republic of China, and Public health in the People's Republic of China

One of the serious negative consequences of China's rapid industrial development since the 1980s has been increased pollution and degradation of natural resources. Problems such as soil erosion, desertification and the steady fall of the water table, especially in the north, have posed a threat to the sustainable development of the country. China is an active participant in climate change talks and other multilateral environmental negotiations in organization such as the UN Environment Program (UNEP).

See also

- List of the largest companies of China
- List of companies of the People's Republic of China
- Center for China in the World Economy, Tsinghua University, Beijing
- Central Financial Work Commission
- China Economic Databases (CED) (China Studies Center, National Chengchi University, Taiwan)
- China Circle
- Economy of the Han Dynasty
- Economy of the Song Dynasty
- Economy of the Ming Dynasty
- Energy policy of China
- Hukou system
- Historical GDP
- Fengbo Zhang : Analysis of Chinese Macroeconomy .
- "Grasping the large, letting go of the small" policy
- Imperial Bank of China
- Leading stocks
- Oil shale in China
- Panda bonds
- Rural credit cooperative
- Silk Road
- Township and Village Enterprises (TVEs)
- Three Rural Issues
- Tuangou
- China Beijing Equity Exchange
- China Milan Equity Exchange

References

- China: Country Studies – Federal Research Division, Library of Congress [5]. Lcweb2.loc.gov (2010-07-27). Retrieved on 2010-08-06.

External links and further reading

- National Bureau of Statistics of China [1]
- Chinability [2] News and statistics on China's economy and business climate.
- Chinese Economy statistics [3] NationMaster (All stats [4])
- Asian Development Bank, China [5]
- World Bank, China [6]
- IMF, China [7]
- China Economy [8] (China Economic Information Network). News stories and subscriber-only market analysis for various sectors of the country's economy.
- China's economy [9]. Articles By Subject. Economist.com
- China Economic Net [10]
- China Economic Review [11]
- Far Eastern Economic Review [12] Dow Jones' monthly magazine on Asia. For valuable insights on Asia's business and political development. With search and 58-year archive.
- Chinese Economy [13] China Daily Special Coverage
- Financial Times, China [14]
- The New York Times series "Choking on Growth" [15]
- Asia Business Resources Library [16] – Articles about doing business in China
- The China Perspective [17]
- China Small and Medium Enterprises (SMEs) Information Network [18]
- China Economic Scan [19]
- Chinese Coming Back to Marx Amid Crisis [20] by Bo Gu, *NBC News*, April 8, 2009
- China's Prospects In The Current Global Climate [21] by Louis Kuijs, *International Economics Bulletin*, June 18, 2009.
- Business China [22], up to date economic information and news
- Chinese Economic Development: Chris Bramall, Taylor & Francis, 2008.

Journals

- *China Economic Journal* Taylor & Francis Journals: Welcome [23]. Tandf.co.uk. Retrieved on 2010-08-06.
- *China Economic Quarterly* [24]
- *China & World Economy* China & World Economy – Journal Information [25]. Blackwellpublishing.com (2010-05-07). Retrieved on 2010-08-06.
- *Journal of Chinese Economic and Business Studies* (JCEBS) Taylor & Francis Journals: Welcome [26]. Tandf.co.uk. Retrieved on 2010-08-06. is the official journal of the Chinese Economic Association (UK). CEA Publications – Journal of Chinese Economic and Business Studies [27]. Ceauk.org.uk. Retrieved on 2010-08-06.
- *Journal of Chinese Economic and Foreign Trade Studies* Emerald|Journal of Chinese Economic and Foreign Trade Studies information [28]. Emeraldinsight.com. Retrieved on 2010-08-06.
- *The China Quarterly* http://www.journals.cambridge.org/action/displayJournal?jid=CQY
- *The Chinese Economy* M.E. Sharpe, Inc. – Journal Information [29]. Mesharpe.com. Retrieved on 2010-08-06.
- *Journal of Chinese Economic Studies* (ISSN: 1348-2521)
- *Journal of the Chinese Statistical Association* (ISSN: 0529-6528)
- *China: An International Journal* (ISSN: 0219-7472)
- *China Economic Review* (ISSN: 1043-951X)
- *China Review* (ISSN: 1680-2012)
- *Frontiers of Economics in China* (ISSN: 1673-3444)

1. REDIRECT Template:Navboxes

Economic Reform in China

Great Leap Forward

History of the People's Republic of China
1949–1976, The Mao Era
Revolution
Korean War
Zhen Fan
Three-anti/five-anti campaigns
Hundred Flowers Campaign
Anti-Rightist Movement
Great Leap Forward
Great Chinese Famine
Cultural Revolution
Lin Biao
Gang of Four
Tiananmen Incident
1976–1989, Era of Reconstruction
Economic reform
Sino-Vietnamese War
Tiananmen protests
1989–2002, A Rising Power
One country, two systems
Hong Kong (post 1997)
Macau (post 1999)
Chinese reunification
2002–present, China Today
Sichuan Earthquake
The Beijing Olympics
Ürümqi 7·5 riots
Shanghai 2010 Expo

See also:
Constitutional history **History of China** **History of Beijing** **History of Shanghai**
Paramount leaders Mao - Deng - Jiang - Hu
Other China topics
Culture - Economy **Geography - Politics - Education** *China Portal*

History of China	
ANCIENT	
3 Sovereigns and 5 Emperors	
Xia Dynasty 2100–1600 BCE	
Shang Dynasty 1600–1046 BCE	
Zhou Dynasty 1045–256 BCE	
Western Zhou	
Eastern Zhou	
Spring and Autumn Period	
Warring States Period	
IMPERIAL	
Qin Dynasty 221 BCE–206 BCE	
Han Dynasty 206 BCE–220 CE	
Western Han	
Xin Dynasty	
Eastern Han	
Three Kingdoms 220–280	
Wei, Shu & Wu	
Jin Dynasty 265–420	
Western Jin	**16 Kingdoms** 304–439
Eastern Jin	

Southern & Northern Dynasties 420–589		
Sui Dynasty 581–618		
Tang Dynasty 618–907		
(Second Zhou 690–705)		
5 Dynasties & 10 Kingdoms 907–960	Liao Dynasty 907–1125	
Song Dynasty 960–1279		
Northern Song	W. Xia	
Southern Song	Jin	
Yuan Dynasty 1271–1368		
Ming Dynasty 1368–1644		
Qing Dynasty 1644–1911		
MODERN		
Republic of China 1912–1949		
People's Republic of China 1949–present	Republic of China (Taiwan) 1945–present	

The **Great Leap Forward** (simplified Chinese: 大跃进; traditional Chinese: 大躍進; pinyin: *Dà yuè jìn*) of the People's Republic of China (PRC) was an economic and social campaign of the Chinese Communist Party (CCP), reflected in planning decisions from 1958 to 1961, which aimed to use China's vast population to rapidly transform the country from an agrarian economy into a modern communist society through the process of agriculturalization, industrialization, and collectivization. Mao Zedong led the campaign based on the Theory of Productive Forces, and intensified it after being informed of the impending disaster from grain shortages.

Chief changes in the lives of rural Chinese included the introduction of a mandatory process of agricultural collectivization, which was introduced incrementally. Private farming was prohibited, and those engaged in it were labeled as counter revolutionaries and persecuted. Restrictions on rural people were enforced through public struggle sessions, social pressure, and violence. Food rationing was introduced, in some cases leaving rural Chinese with less than 250g (half a *jin*, 8.82 ounces) of grain per day. Rural industrialization, officially a priority of the campaign, saw "its development ... aborted by the mistakes of the Great Leap Forward." The Great Leap ended in catastrophe, and claimed the lives of some 20 to 45 million people.

The *Cambridge History of China* presents data on economic growth rates in China from 1953 through 1985, calculated by Harvard professor of political economy Dwight H. Perkins. Of all the periods spanning this time frame, only the 1958-1962 period, the period during which the Great Leap Forward campaign was carried out, was a period of economic regress as defined by the growth rate. "As these figures indicate, enormous amounts of investment produced only modest increases in production or none at all," argued Perkins. "The growth of national income for the entire 1958-65 period was less than half of the 1966-78 period, and it took almost twice the level of investment to produce a given increase in output in the former period as in the latter. In short, the Great Leap was a very expensive disaster."

In subsequent conferences in 1960 and 1962, the negative effects of the Great Leap Forward were studied by the CPC, and Mao was criticized in the party conferences. Party members less economically left-wing like Liu Shaoqi and Deng Xiaoping rose to power, and Mao was marginalized within the party, leading him to initiate the Cultural Revolution in 1966.

Background

Main article: History of the People's Republic of China

In October 1949 after the defeat of the Kuomintang, the Chinese Communist Party proclaimed the establishment of the People's Republic of China. Immediately, landlords and wealthier peasants had their land holdings forcibly redistributed to poorer peasants. In the agricultural sectors, crops deemed by the Party to be "full of evil" such as the opium crop, were destroyed and replaced with crops such as rice. Within the Party, there was major debate about redistribution. A moderate faction within the party and Politburo member Liu Shaoqi argued that change should be gradual and any collectivization of the peasantry should wait until industrialization, which could provide the agricultural machinery for mechanized farming. A more radical faction led by Mao Zedong agreed that the best way to finance industrialization was for the government to take control of agriculture, thereby establishing a monopoly over grain distribution and supply. This would allow the state to buy at a low price and sell much higher, thus raising the capital necessary for the industrialization of the country.

It was realized that this policy would be unpopular with the peasants and therefore it was proposed that the peasants should be brought under Party control by the establishment of agricultural collectives which would also facilitate the sharing of tools and draft animals. This policy was gradually pushed through between 1949 and 1958, first by establishing "mutual aid teams" of 5-15 households, then in 1953 "elementary agricultural cooperatives" of 20-40 households, then from 1956 in "higher co-operatives" of 100-300 families. These reforms (sometimes now referred to as *The Great Leap Forward*) were generally unpopular with the peasants and usually implemented by summoning them to meetings and making them stay there for days and sometimes weeks until they "voluntarily" agreed to join the collective.[citation needed]

Besides these economic changes, the Party implemented major social changes in the countryside including the banishing of all religious and mystic institutions and ceremonies and replacing them with political meetings and propaganda sessions. Attempts were made to enhance rural education and the status of women (allowing females to initiate divorce if they desired) and ending foot-binding, child marriage and opium addiction. Internal passports (called the *hukou* system) were introduced in 1956, forbidding travel without appropriate authorization. Highest priority was given to the urban proletariat for whom a welfare state was created.

The first phase of collectivization was not a great success and there was widespread famine in 1956, though the Party's propaganda machine announced progressively higher harvests. Moderates within the Party, including Zhou Enlai, argued for a reversal of collectivization. The position of the moderates was strengthened by Khrushchev's 1956 Secret speech at the 20th Congress which uncovered Stalin's crimes and highlighted the failure of his agricultural policies including collectivization in the USSR.

In 1957 Mao responded to the tensions in the Party by promoting free speech and criticism under the 100 Flowers Campaign. In retrospect, some have come to argue that this was a ploy to allow critics of the regime, primarily intellectuals but also low ranking members of the party critical of the agricultural policies, to identify themselves. Some claim that Mao simply swung to the side of the hard-liners once his policies gained strong opposition. Once he had done so, at least half a million were purged under the Anti-Rightist campaign, which effectively silenced any opposition from within the Party or from agricultural experts to the changes which would be implemented under the Great Leap Forward.

By the completion of the first 5 Year Economic Plan in 1957, Mao had come to doubt that the path to socialism that had been taken by the Soviet Union was appropriate for China. He was critical of Khrushchev's reversal of Stalinist policies and alarmed by the uprisings that had taken place in East Germany, Poland and Hungary, and the perception that the USSR was seeking "Peaceful coexistence" with the Western powers. Mao had become convinced that China should follow its own path to Communism.

According to Jonathan Mirsky, a historian and journalist specializing in Chinese affairs, China's isolation from most of the rest of the world, along with the Korean War, had accelerated Mao's attacks on his perceived domestic enemies. It led him to accelerate his designs to develop an economy where the regime would get maximum benefit from rural taxation.

Before the Great Leap, peasants farmed their own small pockets of land, and observed traditional practices connected to markets—festivals, banquets, and paying homage to ancestors. Starting in 1954, peasants were encouraged to form and join collectives, which would putatively increase their efficiency without robbing them of their own land or restricting their livelihoods. By 1958, however, private ownership was entirely abolished and households all over China were forced into state-operated communes. Mao insisted that the communes must produce more grain for the cities and earn foreign exchange from exports.

Organizational and operational factors

The Great Leap Forward campaign began during the period of the Second Five Year Plan which was scheduled to run from 1958–1963, though the campaign itself was discontinued by 1961. Mao unveiled the Great Leap Forward at a meeting in January 1958 in Nanjing. The central idea behind the Great Leap was that rapid development of China's agricultural and industrial sectors should take place in parallel. The hope was to industrialize by making use of the massive supply of cheap labour and avoid having to import heavy machinery. To achieve this, Mao advocated that a further round of collectivization modeled on the USSR's "Third Period" was necessary in the Chinese countryside where the existing collectives would be merged into huge People's Communes.

People's communes

An experimental commune was established at Chayashan in Henan in April 1958. Here for the first time private plots were entirely abolished and communal kitchens were introduced. At the Politburo meetings in August 1958, it was decided that these people's communes would become the new form of economic and political organization throughout rural China. By the end of the year approximately 25,000 communes had been set up, with an average of 5,000 households each. The communes were relatively self sufficient co-operatives where wages and money were replaced by work points.

Based on his fieldwork, Ralph A. Thaxton Jr. describes the people's communes as a form of "apartheid system" for Chinese farm households. The commune system was aimed at maximizing production for provisioning the cities and constructing offices, factories, schools, and social insurance systems for urban-dwelling workers, cadres and officials. Citizens in rural areas who criticized the system were labeled "dangerous." Escape was also difficult or impossible, and those who attempted were denied by "party-orchestrated public struggle," which further jeopardized their survival. Besides agriculture, communes also incorporated some light industry and construction projects.

Industrialization

Mao saw grain and steel production as the key pillars of economic development. He forecast that within 15 years of the start of the Great Leap, China's steel production would surpass that of the UK. In the August 1958 Politburo meetings, it was decided that steel production would be set to double within the year, most of the increase coming through backyard steel furnaces.[citation needed] Major investments in larger state enterprises were made in 1958-60: 1,587, 1,361, and 1,815 medium- and large-scale state projects were started in 1958, 1959, and 1960 respectively, more in each year than in the first Five Year Plan. Millions of Chinese became state workers as a consequence of this unprecedented industrial investment: in 1958, 21 million were added to non-agricultural state payrolls, and total state employment reached a peak of 50.44 million in 1960, more than doubling the 1957 level; the urban population swelled by 31.24 million people. These new workers placed major stress on China's food-rationing system, which led to increased and unsustainable demands on rural food production.

During this rapid expansion, coordination suffered and material shortages were frequent, resulting in "a huge rise in the wage bill, largely for construction workers, but no corresponding increase in manufactured goods." Facing a massive deficit, the government cut industrial investment from 38.9 to 7.1 billion yuan from 1960 to 1962 (an 82% decrease; the 1957 level was 14.4 billion).

Backyard furnaces

With no personal knowledge of metallurgy, Mao encouraged the establishment of small backyard steel furnaces in every commune and in each urban neighborhood. Mao was shown an example of a backyard furnace in Hefei, Anhui in September 1958 by provincial first secretary Zeng Xisheng[citation needed]. The unit was claimed to be manufacturing high quality steel (though in fact the finished steel had probably been manufactured elsewhere).[citation needed] Huge efforts on the part of peasants and other workers were made to produce steel out of scrap metal. To fuel the furnaces the local environment was denuded of trees and wood taken from the doors and furniture of peasants' houses. Pots, pans, and other metal artifacts were requisitioned to supply the "scrap" for the furnaces so that the wildly optimistic production targets could be met. Many of the male agricultural workers were diverted from the harvest to help the iron production as were the workers at many factories, schools and even hospitals. Although the output consisted of low quality lumps of pig iron which was of negligible economic worth, Mao had a deep distrust of intellectuals and faith in the power of the mass mobilization of the peasants. Moreover, the experience of the intellectual classes following the Hundred Flowers Campaign silenced those aware of the folly of such a plan. According to his private doctor, Li Zhisui, Mao and his entourage visited traditional steel works in Manchuria in January 1959 where he found out that high quality steel could only be produced in large scale factories using reliable fuel such as coal. However, he decided not to order a halt to the backyard steel furnaces so as not to dampen the revolutionary enthusiasm of the masses. The program was only quietly abandoned much later in that year.

Substantial effort was expended during the Great Leap Forward on large-scale, but often on poorly planned capital construction projects, such as irrigation works often built without input from trained engineers. Mao was well aware of the human cost of these water-conservancy campaigns. In early 1958, while listening to a report on irrigation in Jiangsu, he muttered that:

> "Wu Zhipu claims he can move 30 billion cubic metres; I think 30,000 people will die. Zeng Xisheng has said that he will move 20 billion cubic metres, and I think that 20,000 people will die. Weiqing only promises 600 million cubic metres, maybe nobody will die."

Nevertheless, mass mobilization on irrigation works continued unabated for the next several years, and claimed the lives of hundreds of thousands of exhausted, starving villagers. The inhabitants of Qingshui and Gansu referred to these projects as the "killing fields."

Great Leap Forward

On the communes, a number of radical and controversial agricultural innovations were promoted at the behest of Mao. Many of these were based on the ideas of now discredited Soviet biologist Trofim Lysenko and his followers. The policies included close cropping, whereby seeds were sown far more densely than normal on the incorrect assumption that seeds of the same class would not compete with each other. Deep plowing (up to 2m deep) was encouraged on the mistaken belief that this would yield plants with extra large root systems. Moderately productive land was left unplanted with the belief that concentrating manure and effort on the most fertile land would lead to large per-acre productivity gains. Altogether, these untested innovations generally led to decreases in grain production rather than increases.

Meanwhile, local leaders were pressured into falsely reporting ever-higher grain production figures to their political superiors. Participants at political meetings

Chinese propaganda poster showing larger-than-human melon

remembered production figures being inflated up to 10 times actual production amounts as the race to please superiors and win plaudits — like the chance to meet Mao himself — intensified. The state was later able to force many production groups to sell more grain than they could spare based on these false production figures.

The initial impact of the Great Leap Forward was discussed at the Lushan Conference in July/August 1959. Although many of the more moderate leaders had reservations about the new policy, the only senior leader to speak out openly was Marshall Peng Dehuai. Mao used the conference to dismiss Peng from his post as Defence Minister and denounce both Peng (who came from a poor peasant family) and his supporters as "bourgeois," and launch a nationwide campaign against "rightist opportunism." Peng was replaced by Lin Biao, who began a systematic purge of Peng's supporters from the military.

Treatment of villagers

The ban on private holdings ruined peasant life at its most basic level, according to Mirsky. Villagers were unable to secure enough food to go on living, because the traditional means of being able to rent, sell, or use their land as collateral for loans was deprived of them by the commune system. In one village, once the commune was operational the Party boss and his colleagues "swung into manic action, herding villagers into the fields to sleep and to work intolerable hours, and forcing them to walk, starving, to distant additional projects."

Edward Friedman, a political scientist at the University of Wisconsin, Paul Pickowicz, a historian at the University of California at San Diego and Mark Selden, a sociologist at Binghamton University, wrote about the dynamic of interaction between the Party and villagers:

> Beyond attack, beyond question, was the systemic and structured dynamic of the socialist state that intimidated and impoverished millions of patriotic and loyal villagers.

The authors present a similar picture to Thaxton in depicting the Communist Party's destruction of the traditions of Chinese villagers. Traditionally prized local customs were deemed signs of "feudalism" to be extinguished, according to Mirsky. "Among them were funerals, weddings, local markets, and festivals. The Party thus destroyed 'much that gave meaning to Chinese lives. These private bonds were social glue. To mourn and to celebrate is to be human. To share joy, grief, and pain is humanizing.'" Failure to participate in the CCP's political campaigns—though the aims of such campaigns were often conflicting--"could result in detention, torture, death, and the suffering of entire families."

Public criticism sessions were often used to intimidate the peasants into obeying local cadres; they increased the death rate of the famine in several ways, according to Thaxton. "In the first case, blows to the body caused internal injuries that, in combination with physical emaciation and acute hunger, could induce death." In one case, after a peasant stole two cabbages from the common fields, the thief was publicly criticized for half a day. He collapsed, fell ill, and never recovered. Others were sent to labor camps.

Modes of resistance

According to over 20 years of research by Ralph Thaxton, professor of politics at Brandeis University, villagers turned against the CCP during and after the Great Leap, seeing it as autocratic, brutal, corrupt, and mean-spirited. The CCP's policies, which included plunder, forced labor, and starvation, according to Thaxton, led villagers "to think about their relationship with the Communist Party in ways that do not bode well for the continuity of socialist rule."

Often, villagers composed doggerel to show their defiance to the regime, and "perhaps, to remain sane." During the Great Leap, one jingle ran: "Flatter shamelessly—eat delicacies.... Don't flatter—starve to death for sure."

Climate conditions and famine

Main article: Great Chinese Famine

Despite the harmful agricultural innovations, the weather in 1958 was very favorable and the harvest promised to be good. Unfortunately, the amount of labour diverted to steel production and construction projects meant that much of the harvest was left to rot uncollected in some areas. This problem was exacerbated by a devastating locust swarm, which was caused when their natural predators were killed as part of the Great Sparrow Campaign. Although actual harvests were reduced, local officials, under tremendous pressure from central authorities to report record harvests in response to the new innovations, competed with each other to announce increasingly exaggerated results. These were used as a basis for determining the amount of grain to be taken by the State to supply the towns and cities, and to export. This left barely enough for the peasants, and in some areas, starvation set in. During 1958–1960 China continued to be a substantial net exporter of grain, despite the widespread famine experienced in the countryside, as Mao sought to maintain face and convince the outside world of the success of his plans. Foreign aid was refused. When the Japanese foreign minister told his Chinese counterpart Chen Yi of an offer of 100,000 tonnes of wheat to be shipped out of public view, he was rebuffed. John F Kennedy was also aware that the Chinese were exporting food to Africa and Cuba during the famine and said "we've had no indication from the Chinese Communists that they would welcome any offer of food."

In 1959 and 1960 the weather was less favorable, and the situation got considerably worse, with many of China's provinces experiencing severe famine. Droughts, floods, and general bad weather caught China completely by surprise. In July 1959, the Yellow River flooded in East China. According to the Disaster Center, it directly killed, either through starvation from crop failure or drowning, an estimated 2 million people.

In 1960, at least some degree of drought and other bad weather affected 55 percent of cultivated land, while an estimated 60 percent of northern agricultural land received no rain at all.

With dramatically reduced yields, even urban areas suffered much reduced rations; however, mass starvation was largely confined to the countryside, where, as a result of drastically inflated production statistics, very little grain was left for the peasants to eat. Food shortages were bad throughout the country; however, the provinces which had adopted Mao's reforms with the most vigor, such as Anhui, Gansu and Henan, tended to suffer disproportionately. Sichuan, one of China's most populous provinces, known in China as "Heaven's Granary" because of its fertility, is thought to have suffered the greatest absolute numbers of deaths from starvation due to the vigor with which provincial leader Li Jinquan undertook Mao's reforms. During the Great Leap Forward, cases of cannibalism also occurred in the parts of China that were severely affected by drought and famine.

The agricultural policies of the Great Leap Forward and the associated famine would then continue until January 1961, where, at the Ninth Plenum of the Eighth Central Committee, the restoration of agricultural production through a reversal of the Great Leap policies was started. Grain exports were stopped, and imports from Canada and Australia helped to reduce the impact of the food shortages, at least in the coastal cities.

Consequences

As inflated statistics reached planning authorities, orders were given to divert human resources into industry rather than agriculture. The official toll of excess deaths recorded in China for the years of the Great Leap Forward is 14 million, but as of 1987, scholars had estimated the number of victims to be between 20 and 43 million. An article in *The Independent* published in 2010 profiled the finding of Hong Kong historian Frank Dikötter who, according to the article, estimated the total death toll between 1958 and 1962 to be "at least 45 million people", who were "worked, starved or beaten to death", citing a speech presented by him at the Woodstock Literary Festival and a book he had written on the subject based on examination of Chinese archival material that had been sealed until 1996.

The three years between 1959 and 1962 were known as the "Three Bitter Years" and the Three Years of Natural Disasters. Many local officials were tried and publicly executed for giving out misinformation.

Thaxton's final judgement of the effect on villagers of the famine was that "Village people... had come to associate socialism with starvation and the agents of the party-state with the specter of death."

Deaths by starvation

Starting in the early 1980s, critics of the Great Leap added quantitative muscle to their arsenal. U.S. government employee Judith Banister published what became an influential article in the *China Quarterly*, and since then estimates as high as 30 million deaths in the Great Leap became common in the U.S. press. Wim F Wertheim, emeritus professor from the University of Amsterdam, disagrees with the numbers presented on the basis that they lack scientific support. Critics of this position point to the numerous studies by individuals such as Aird in 1982, Ashton et al. in 1984, and Peng in 1987 that specifically sought to quantify the Great Leap's demographic impact. A lingering problem that all scholars point to is the assumptions regarding birth rate used in the most widely cited projections of famine deaths. These assumptions make it difficult to precisely gauge the death toll with a high degree of accuracy.

Dr Ping-ti Ho, professor of history at the University of Chicago and an expert in Chinese Demography, in a book titled *Studies on the Population of China, 1368–1953* (Harvard East Asian Studies No 4, 1959), also mentioned numerous flaws in the 1953 census on which famine death projections are made, though acknowledging the lack of more accurate sources.

Critics of Jung Chang and Jon Halliday's book *Mao: The Unknown Story* often cite these studies as evidence that their body count (38 million) may be exaggerated. One authoritative account of the famine, a 1,100-page study by Yang Jisheng, a long-time communist party member and a reporter for the official Chinese news agency Xinhua, puts the number of deaths from the Great Chinese Famine at 36 million. His book, entitled *Tombstone* (*Mùbēi*, 2008), challenges the official Communist Party line that the famine was largely a result of "Three Years of Natural Disasters" and he puts the blame squarely on Maoist policies, such as diverting agricultural workers to steel production instead of growing crops, and exporting grain at the same time. Another account by the aforementioned historian Frank Dikötter (*Mao's Great Famine*, 2010), which is based on recently accessible Chinese archival sources, places the death toll even higher, at 45 million minimum. He claims that the census figures, which point to a death toll between 15 and 32 million, are largely inadequate, and that public security reports and secret reports collated by party committees towards the end of the Great Leap indicate the human cost was far greater. He also notes that "Some historians speculate that the true figure stands as high as 50 to 60 million people."

Yang notes that local party officials were indifferent to the large number of people dying around them, as their primary concern was the delivery of grain, which Mao wanted to use to pay back debts to the USSR totaling 1.973 billion yuan. In Xinyang, people died of starvation at the doors of grain warehouses. Mao refused to open the state granaries as he dismissed reports of food shortages and accused the peasants of hiding grain.

Mao and the Communist Party knew that some of their policies were contributing to the starvation. Foreign minister Chen Yi said of some of the early human losses in Novermber 1958:

> "Casualties have indeed appeared among workers, but it is not enough to stop us in our tracks. This is the price we have to pay, it's nothing to be afraid of. Who knows how many people have been sacrificed on the battlefields and in the prisons [for the revolutionary cause]? Now we have a few cases of illness and death: it's nothing!"

During a secret meeting in Shanghai in 1959, Mao demanded the state procurement of one-third of all grain to feed the cities and satisfy foreign clients. He stated at the same meeting:

> "When there is not enough to eat people starve to death. It is better to let half of the people die so that the other half can eat their fill."

Like in the USSR during the famine of 1932-33, peasants were confined to their starving villages by a system of household registration, and the worst effects of the famine were directed against enemies of the regime. Those labeled as "black elements" (religious leaders, rightists, rich peasants, etc.) in any previous campaign were given the lowest priority in the allocation of food, and therefore died in the greatest numbers. According to genocide scholar Adam Jones, "no group suffered more than the Tibetans," with perhaps one in five dying from 1959 to 1962. Further, not all deaths during the Great Leap were from starvation, as Frank Dikotter estimates that at least 2.5 million people were beaten or tortured to death and 1 to 3 million committed suicide.

Impact on economy

During the Great Leap, the Chinese economy initially grew. Iron production increased 45% in 1958 and a combined 30% over the next two years, but plummeted in 1961, and did not reach the previous 1958 level until 1964.

In agrarian policy, the failures of food supply during the Great Leap were met by a gradual de-collectivization in the 1960s that foreshadowed further de-collectivization under Deng Xiaoping. Political scientist Meredith Jung-En Woo argues: "Unquestionably the regime failed to respond in time to save the lives of millions of peasants, but when it did respond, it ultimately transformed the livelihoods of several hundred million peasants (modestly in the early 1960s, but permanently after Deng Xiaoping's reforms subsequent to 1978.)"

Despite the risks to their careers, some Communist Party members openly laid blame for the disaster at the feet of the Party leadership and took it as proof that China must rely more on education, acquiring technical expertise and applying bourgeois methods in developing the economy. Liu Shaoqi made a speech in 1962 at Seven Thousand Man's Assembly criticizing that "The economic disaster was 30% fault of nature, 70% human error."

Impact on the government

Mao stepped down as State Chairman of the PRC in 1959, predicting he would take most of the blame for the failure of the Great Leap Forward, though he did retain his position as Chairman of the CCP. Liu Shaoqi (the new PRC Chairman) and reformist Deng Xiaoping (CCP General Secretary) were left in charge to change policy to bring about economic recovery. Mao's Great Leap Forward policy came under open criticism at the Lushan party conference. The attack was led by Minister of National Defense Peng Dehuai, who, initially troubled by the potentially adverse effect of the Great Leap Forward on the modernization of the armed forces, also admonished unnamed party members for trying to "jump into communism in one step." After the Lushan showdown, Mao defensively replaced Peng with Lin Biao.

However, in June 1962, the party held an enlarged Central Work Conference and rehabilitated the majority of the deposed comrades who had criticized Mao in the aftermath of the Great Leap Forward. The event was again discussed, with much self-criticism, with the contemporary government calling it a "serious [loss] to our country and people" and blaming the cult of personality of Mao. Following the 1962 conference, Mao became a "dead ancestor", as he labeled himself: a person who was respected but never consulted, occupying the political background of the Party. He launched a vain attempt for influence in 1966 with the Cultural Revolution, but died ten years later, leaving the forces within the party that opposed the Cultural Revolution and the Great Leap Forward in power.

See also

- Virgin Lands Campaign, contemporary program in the Soviet Union

Bibliography and Further reading

- Bachman, David (1991). *Bureaucracy, Economy, and Leadership in China: The Institutional Origins of the Great Leap Forward*. New York: Cambridge University Press.
- Becker, Jasper (1998). *Hungry Ghosts: Mao's Secret Famine* [1]. Holt Paperbacks. ISBN 0805056688
- Jung Chang and Jon Halliday. (2005) *Mao: The Unknown Story*, Knopf. ISBN 0679422714
- Dikötter, Frank (2010). *Mao's Great Famine: The History of China's Most Devastating Catastrophe, 1958-62* [2]. Walker & Company. ISBN 0802777686
- Li, Wei, and Dennis Tao Yang (2005). *The Great Leap Forward: Anatomy of a Central Planning Disaster*. Journal of Political Economy 113 (4):840-877.
- Li, Zhisui (1996). *The Private Life of Chairman Mao*. Arrow Books Ltd.
- Macfarquhar, Roderick (1983). *Origins of the Cultural Revolution: Vol 2*. Oxford: Oxford University Press.
- Short, Philip (2001). *Mao: A Life* [3]. Owl Books. ISBN 0805066381
- Tao Yang, Dennis. (2008) "China's Agricultural Crisis and Famine of 1959–1961: A Survey and Comparison to Soviet Famines." [4] Palgrave MacMillan, *Comparatrive economic Studies* 50, pp. 1–29.
- Thaxton. Ralph A. Jr (2008). *Catastrophe and Contention in Rural China: Mao's Great Leap Forward Famine and the Origins of Righteous Resistance in Da Fo Village*. Cambridge University Press. ISBN 0521722306
- Wertheim, Wim F (1995). *Third World whence and whither? Protective State versus Aggressive Market*. Amsterdam: Het Spinhuis. 211 pp. ISBN 9055890820
- E. L Wheelwright, Bruce McFarlane, and Joan Robinson (Foreword), *The Chinese Road to Socialism: Economics of the Cultural Revolution*.
- Yang, Dali (1996). *Calamity and Reform in China: State, Rural Society, and Institutional Change since the Great Leap Famine*. Stanford University Press.
- Yang, Jisheng (2008). *Tombstone (Mu Bei - Zhong Guo Liu Shi Nian Dai Da Ji Huang Ji Shi)*. Cosmos Books (Tian Di Tu Shu), Hong Kong.

   This article incorporates public domain text from the United States Library of Congress Country Studies. - China [5]

Chinese economic reform

History of the People's Republic of China
1949–1976, The Mao Era
Revolution
Korean War
Zhen Fan
Three-anti/five-anti campaigns
Hundred Flowers Campaign
Anti-Rightist Movement
Great Leap Forward
Great Chinese Famine
Cultural Revolution
Lin Biao
Gang of Four
Tiananmen Incident
1976–1989, Era of Reconstruction
Economic reform
Sino-Vietnamese War
Tiananmen protests
1989–2002, A Rising Power
One country, two systems
Hong Kong (post 1997)
Macau (post 1999)
Chinese reunification
2002–present, China Today
Sichuan Earthquake
The Beijing Olympics
Ürümqi 7·5 riots
Shanghai 2010 Expo
See also: **Constitutional history** **History of China** **History of Beijing** **History of Shanghai**

Paramount leaders
Mao - Deng - Jiang - Hu
Other China topics
Culture - Economy Geography - Politics - Education *China Portal*

History of China
ANCIENT
3 Sovereigns and 5 Emperors
Xia Dynasty 2100–1600 BCE
Shang Dynasty 1600–1046 BCE
Zhou Dynasty 1045–256 BCE
Western Zhou
Eastern Zhou
Spring and Autumn Period
Warring States Period
IMPERIAL
Qin Dynasty 221 BCE–206 BCE
Han Dynasty 206 BCE–220 CE
Western Han
Xin Dynasty
Eastern Han
Three Kingdoms 220–280
Wei, Shu & Wu
Jin Dynasty 265–420

Western Jin	**16 Kingdoms** 304–439
Eastern Jin	

Southern & Northern Dynasties 420–589
Sui Dynasty 581–618
Tang Dynasty 618–907
(**Second Zhou** 690–705)

5 Dynasties & 10 Kingdoms 907–960	Liao Dynasty 907–1125		
Song Dynasty 960–1279			
Northern Song		W. Xia	
Southern Song	Jin		
Yuan Dynasty 1271–1368			
Ming Dynasty 1368–1644			
Qing Dynasty 1644–1911			
MODERN			
Republic of China 1912–1949			
People's Republic of China 1949–present	Republic of China (Taiwan) 1945–present		

The **Chinese economic reform** (simplified Chinese: 改革开放; traditional Chinese: 改革開放; pinyin: *Găigé kāifàng, literally **Reform and Opening***) refers to the program of economic reforms called "Socialism with Chinese characteristics" in the People's Republic of China (PRC) that were started in December 1978 by reformists within the Communist Party of China (CPC) led by Deng Xiaoping. The goal of Chinese economic reform was to transform China's stagnant, impoverished planned economy into a market economy capable of generating strong economic growth and increasing the well-being of Chinese citizens.

China had one of the world's largest and most advanced economies prior to the nineteenth century, while its wealth remained average in global terms. The economy stagnated since the 16th century and even declined in absolute terms in the nineteenth and much of the twentieth century, with a brief recovery in the 1930s. From 1949 to 1978, Mao's disastrous collectivizations, Great Leap Forward and Cultural revolution devastated the Chinese economy, resulting in the destruction of much traditional culture and a massive drop in living standards. After Mao's death, his main leftist supporters, led by the Gang of Four, were ousted in a coup, and reformists lead by Deng Xiaoping took power.

Economic reforms began in 1978 and occurred in two stages. The first stage, in the late 1970s and early 1980s, involved the decollectivization of agriculture, the opening up of the country to foreign investment, and permission for entrepreneurs to start up businesses. However, most industry remained state-owned, inefficient and acted as a drag on economic growth. The second stage of reform, in the late 1980s and 1990s, involved the privatization and contracting out of much state-owned industry and the lifting of price controls, protectionist policies, and regulations, although state monopolies in sectors such as banking and petroleum remained. The private sector grew remarkably, accounting for as much as 70 percent of China's GDP by 2005, a figure larger in comparison to many Western nations. From 1978 to 2010, unprecedented growth occurred, with the economy increasing by 9.5% a year. China's economy became the second largest after the U.S.. The Conservative Hu-Wen Administration more heavily regulated and controlled the economy after 2005, reversing some reformist gains.

The success of China's economic reforms has resulted in massive changes in Chinese society. Poverty was reduced and both wealth and wealth inequality increased, leading to a backlash lead by the Maoist New Left. In the academic scene, scholars have debated the reason for the success of Chinese economic reforms, and have compared them to attempts to reform socialism in the Eastern bloc and the growth of other developing economies.

Chinese economy prior to reform

During the 1930s, China developed a modern industrial sector, which stimulated modest but significant economic growth. Before the collapse of international trade that followed the onset of the Great Depression, China's share of world trade and its ratio of foreign trade to GDP achieved levels that were not regained for over sixty years. The economy was heavily disrupted by the war against Japan and the Chinese Civil War from 1937 to 1949, after which the victorious Communists installed a planned economy. Afterwards, the economy largely stagnated and was disrupted by the Great Leap Forward famine which killed between 30 and 40 million people, and the purges of the Cultural Revolution further disrupted the economy. Urban Chinese citizens experienced virtually no increase in living standards from 1957 onwards, and rural Chinese had no better living standards in the 1970s than the 1930s. Socialist equality had destroyed the incentive to improve; one study noted that average pay levels in the catering sector exceeded wages in higher education. The economic performance of China was poor in comparison with other East Asian countries, such as Japan, Korea, and even Chiang Kai-Shek's rival Republic of China. The economy was riddled with huge inefficiencies and malinvestments, and with Mao's death, even the CPC leadership turned to market-oriented reforms as the only way to salvage the failing economy.

Course of reforms

Famous billboard of Deng in Shenzhen, one of the most successful Special Economic Zones created by his reforms.

Economic reforms began after Deng Xiaoping and his reformist allies ousted the Gang of Four Maoist faction. By the time Deng took power, there was widespread support among the elite for economic reforms. As de facto leader, Deng's policies faced opposition from party conservatives but were extremely successful in increasing the country's wealth.

1978-84

Deng's first reforms began in agriculture, a sector long neglected by the Communist Party. By the late 1970s, food supplies and production had become so deficient that government officials were warning that China was about to repeat the "disaster of 1959" - the famines which killed tens of millions during the Great Leap Forward. Deng responded by decollectivizing agriculture and emphasizing the Household-responsibility system, which divided the land of the People's communes into private plots. Farmers were able to keep the land's output after paying a share to the state. This move increased agricultural production, increased the living standards of hundreds of millions of farmers and stimulated rural industry.

Reforms were also implemented in urban industry to increase productivity. A dual price system was introduced, in which state-owned industries were allowed to sell any production above the plan quota, and commodities were sold at both plan and market prices, allowing citizens to avoid the shortages of the Maoist era. Private businesses were allowed to operate for the first time since the Communist takeover, and they gradually began to make up a greater percentage of industrial output. Price flexibility was also increased, expanding the service sector.

The country was opened to foreign investment for the first time since the Kuomintang era. Deng created a series of special economic zones for foreign investment that were relatively free of the bureaucratic regulations and interventions that hampered economic growth. These regions became engines of growth for the national economy.

1984-93

During this period, Deng Xiaoping's policies continued beyond the initial reforms. Controls on private businesses and government intervention continued to decrease, and there was small-scale privatization of state enterprises which had become unviable. A notable development was the decentralization of state control, leaving local provincial leaders to experiment with ways to increase economic growth and privatize the state sector. Township and village enterprises, firms nominally owned by local governments but effectively private, began to gain market share at the expense of the state sector.

Conservative elder opposition, lead by Chen Yun, prevented many major reforms which would have damaged the interests of special interest groups in the government bureaucracy. Corruption and increased inflation increased discontent, contributing to the Tiananmen Square protests of 1989 and a conservative backlash after that event which ousted several key reformers and threatened to reverse many of Deng's reforms. However, Deng stood by his reforms and in 1992, he affirmed the need to continue reforms in his southern tour. He also reopened the Shanghai Stock Exchange closed by Mao 40 years earlier. Dr. Fengbo Zhang introduced Western Economics to China, provided methods and theory for Deng Xiaoping leadership promoting economic reform and decision-making.

Although the economy grew quickly during this period, economic troubles in the inefficient state sector increased. Heavy losses had to be made up by state revenues and acted as a drain upon the economy. Inflation became problematic in 1985, 1988 and 1992. Privatizations began to accelerate after 1992, and the private sector surpassed the state sector in share of GDP for the first time in the mid-1990s. China's government slowly expanded recognition of the private economy, first as a "complement" to the state sector (1988) and then as an "important component" (1999) of the socialist market economy.

1993-05

In the 1990s, Deng forced many of the Conservative elders such as Chen Yun into retirement, allowing radical reforms to be carried out. Despite Deng's death in 1997, reforms continued under his handpicked successors, Jiang Zemin and Zhu Rongji, who were ardent reformers. In 1997 and 1998, large-scale privatization occurred, in which all state enterprises, except a few large monopolies, were liquidated and their assets sold to private investors. Between 2001 and 2004, the number of state-owned enterprises decreased by 48 percent. During the same period, Jiang and Zhu also reduced tariffs, trade barriers and regulations, reformed the banking system, dismantled much of the Mao-era social welfare system, forced the PLA to divest itself of military-run businesses, reduced inflation, and joined the World Trade Organization. These moves invoked discontent among some groups, especially laid off workers of state enterprises that had been privatized.

The Lujiazui financial district of Pudong, Shanghai, the financial and commercial hub of modern China

The domestic private sector first exceeded 50% of GDP in 2005 and has further expanded since. However, some state monopolies still remained, such as in petroleum and banking.

Post-2005

The conservative Hu-Wen Administration began to reverse many of Deng Xiaoping's reforms in 2005. Observers note that the government adopted more egalitarian and populist policies. It increased subsidies and control over the health care sector, halted privatization, and adopted a loose monetary policy, which lead to the formation of a U.S.-style property bubble in which property prices tripled. The privileged state sector was the primary recipient of government investment, which under the new administration, promoted the rise of large "national champions" which could compete with large foreign corporations.

Economic performance since reform

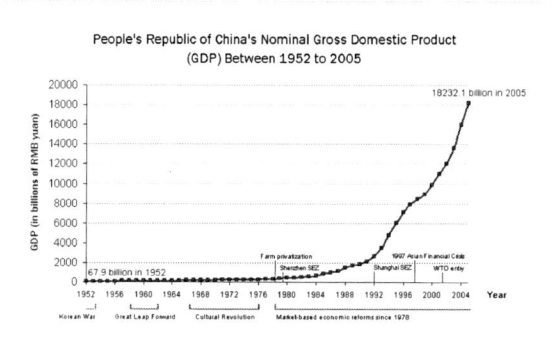

China's nominal GDP trend from 1952 to 2005. Note the rapid increase since reform in the late 1970's.

China's economic growth since Reform has been very rapid, exceeding the East Asian Tigers. Economists estimate China's GDP growth from 1978 to 2005 at 9.5% a year. Since the beginning of Deng Xiaoping's reforms, China's GDP has risen tenfold. The increase in total factor productivity (TFP) was the most important factor, with productivity accounting for 40.1% of the GDP increase, compared with a decline of 13.2% for the period 1957 to 1978 - the height of Maoist policies. For the period 1978-2005, Chinese GDP per capita increased from 2.7% to 15.7% of US GDP per capita, and from 53.7% to 188.5% of Indian GDP per capita. Per capita incomes grew at 6.6% a year. Average wages rose sixfold between 1978 and 2005, while absolute poverty declined from 41% of the population to 5% from 1978 to 2001. Some scholars believed that China's economic growth has been understated, due to large sectors of the economy not being counted.

Impact on world growth

China is widely seen as an engine of world and regional growth.. Surges in Chinese demand account for 50, 44 and 66 percent of export growth of Hong Kong, Japan and Taiwan respectively, and China's trade deficit with the rest of East Asia helped to revive the economies of Japan and Southeast Asia. Asian leaders view China's economic growth as an "...engine of growth for all Asia".

Reforms in specific sectors

After three decades of reform, China's economy experienced one of the world's biggest booms. Agriculture and light industry have largely been privatized, while the state still retains control over some heavy industries. Despite the dominance of state ownership in finance, telecommunications, petroleum and other important sectors of the economy, private entrepreneurs continue to expand into sectors formerly reserved for public enterprise. Prices have also been liberalized.

Agriculture

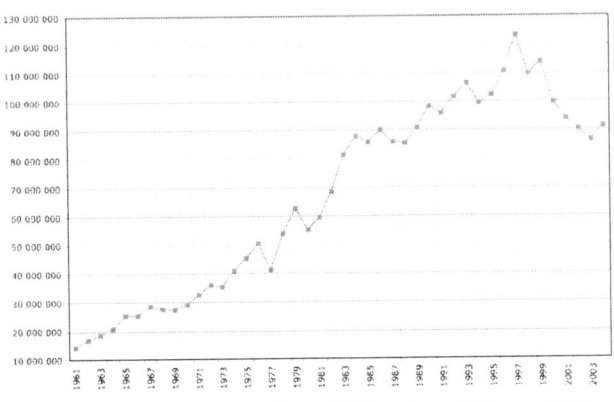

Production of wheat from 1961 to 2004. Data from FAO, year 2005.
Y-axis: Production in metric ton.

During the pre-reform period, Chinese agricultural performance was extremely poor and food shortages were common. After Deng Xiaoping implemented the household responsibility system, agricultural output increased by 8.2 percent a year, compared with 2.7% in the pre-reform period, despite a decrease in the area of land used. Food prices fell nearly 50%, while agricultural incomes rose.

A more fundamental transformation was the economy's growing adoption of cash crops instead of just growing rice and grain. Vegetable and meat production increased to the point that Chinese agricultural production was adding the equivalent of California's vegetable industry every two years. Growth in the sector slowed after 1984, with agriculture falling from 40% of GDP to 16%; however, increases in agricultural productivity allowed workers to be released for work in industry and services, while simultaneously increasing agricultural production. Trade in agriculture was also liberalized and China became an exporter of foodstuffs, a great contrast to its previous famines and shortages.

Industry

In the pre-reform period, industry was largely stagnant and the socialist system presented few incentives for improvements in quality and productivity. With the introduction of the dual price system and greater autonomy for enterprise managers, productivity increased greatly in the early 1980s. Foreign enterprises and newly formed Township and Village Enterprises, owned by local government and often de facto private firms, competed successfully with state-owned enterprises. By the 1990s, large-scale privatizations reduced the market share of both the Township and Village Enterprises and state-owned enterprises and increased the private sector's market share. The state sector's share of industrial output dropped from 81 percent in 1980 to 15 percent in 2005. Foreign capital controls much of Chinese industry and plays an important role.

From virtually an industrial backwater in 1978, China is now the world's biggest producer of concrete, steel, ships and textiles, and has the world's largest automobile market. Chinese steel output quadrupled between 1980 and 2000, and from 2000 to 2006 rose from 128.5 million tons to 418.8 million tons, one-third of global production. Labor productivity at some Chinese steel firms exceeds Western productivity. From 1975 to 1992, China's automobile production rose from 139,800 to 1.1 million, rising to 9.35 million in 2008. Light industries such as textiles saw an even greater increase, due to reduced government interference. Chinese textile exports increased from 4.6% of world exports in 1980 to 24.1% in 2005. Textile output increased 18-fold over the same period.

This increase in production is largely the result of the removal of barriers to entry and increased competition; the number of industrial firms rose from 377,300 in 1980 to nearly 8 million in 1990 and 1996; the 2004 economic census, which excluded enterprises with annual sales below RMB5 million, counted 1.33 million manufacturing firms, with Jiangsu and Zhejiang reporting more firms than the nationwide total for 1980. Compared to other East Asian industrial growth spurts, China's industrial performance exceeded Japan's but remained behind South Korea and Taiwan's economies.

Trade and foreign investment

Scholars find that China has an "...attained a degree of openness that is unprecedented among large and populous nations", with competition from foreign goods in almost every sector of the economy. Foreign investment helped to greatly increase quality, knowledge and standards, especially in heavy industry. China's experience supports the assertion that globalization greatly increases wealth

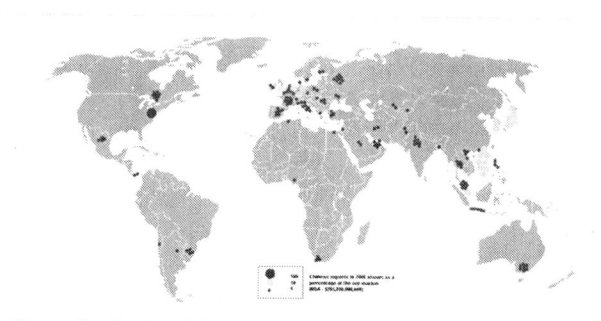

Global distribution of Chinese exports in 2006 as a percentage of the top market.

for poor countries. Throughout the reform period, the government reduced tariffs and other trade barriers, with the overall tariff rate falling from 56% to 15%. By 2001, less than 40% of imports were subject to tariffs and only 9 percent of import were subject to licensing and import quotas. Even during the early reform era, protectionist policies were often circumvented by smuggling. When China joined the WTO, it agreed to considerably harsher conditions than other developing countries. Trade has

increased from under 10% of GDP to 64% of GDP over the same period. China is considered the most open large country; By 2005, China's average statutory tariff on industrial products was 8.9 percent.

For Argentina, Brazil, India, and Indonesia, the respective percentage figures are 30.9, 27.0, 32.4, and 36.9 percent.

China's trade surplus is considered by some in the United States as threatening American jobs. In the 2000s, the Bush administration pursued protectionist policies such as tariffs and quotas to limit the import of Chinese goods. Some scholars argue that China's growing trade surplus is the result of industries in more developed Asian countries moving to China, and not a new phenomenon. China's trade policy, which allows producers to avoid paying the Value Added Tax (VAT) for exports and undervaluation of the currency since 2002, has resulted in an overdeveloped export sector and distortion of the economy overall, a result that could hamper future growth.

Foreign investment was also liberalized upon Deng's ascension. Special economic zones (SEZs) were created in the early 1980s to attract foreign capital by exempting them from taxes and regulations. This experiment was successful and SEZs were expanded to cover the whole Chinese coast. Although FDI fell briefly after the 1989 student protests, it increased again to 160 billion by 2004.

Services

In the 1990s, the financial sector was liberalized. After China joined the World Trade Organization (WTO), the service sector was considerably liberalized and foreign investment was allowed. Restrictions on retail, wholesale and distribution were ended. Banking, financial services, insurance and telecommunications were also opened up to foreign investment.

China's banking sector is dominated by four large state-owned banks, which are largely inefficient and monopolistic. China's largest bank, ICBC, is the largest bank in the world. The financial sector is widely seen as a drag on the economy due to the inefficient state management. Non-performing loans, mostly made to local governments and unprofitable state-owned enterprises for political purposes, are a big drain on the financial system and economy, reaching over 22% of GDP by 2000, with a drop to 6.3% by 2006 due to government recapitalization of these banks. In 2006, the total amount of non-performing loans was estimated at 160 billion USD. Observers recommend privatization of the banking system to solve this problem, a move that was partially carried out when the four banks were floated on the stock market. China's financial markets, the Shanghai Stock Exchange and Shenzhen Stock Exchange, are relatively ineffective at raising capital, as they comprise only 11 percent of GDP.

Shanghai Stock Exchange (SSE)

Due to the weakness of the banks, firms raise most of their capital through an informal, nonstandard financial sector developed during the 1980s and 1990s, consisting largely of underground businesses and private banks. Internal finance is the most important method successful firms use to fund their activities.

Government finances

In the pre-reform era, government was funded by profits from state-owned enterprises, much like the Soviet Union. As the state sector fell in importance and profitability, government revenues, especially that of the central government in Beijing, fell substantially and the government relied on a confused system of inventory taxes. Government revenues fell from 35% of GDP to 11% of GDP in the mid-1990s, excluding revenue from state-owned enterprises, with the central government's budget at just 3% of GDP. The tax system was reformed in 1994 when inventory taxes were unified into a single VAT of 17% on all manufacturing, repair, and assembly activities and an excise tax on 11 items, with the VAT becoming the main income source, accounting for half of government revenue. The 1994 reform also increased the central government's share of revenues, increasing it to 9 percent of GDP.

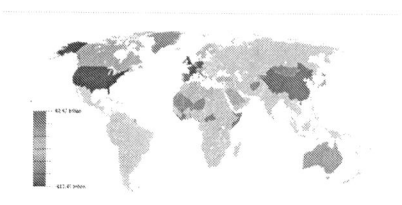

Map of countries by foreign currency reserves and gold minus external debt based on 2009 data from CIA Factbook

Reasons for success

Scholars have proposed a number of theories to explain the success of China's economic reforms in its move from a planned economy to capitalism despite unfavorable factors such as the troublesome legacies of socialism, considerable erosion of the work ethic, decades of anti-market propaganda, and the "lost generation" whose education disintegrated amid the disruption of the Cultural Revolution. One notable theory is that decentralization of state authority allowed local leaders to experiment with various ways to privatize the state sector and energize the economy. Although Deng was not the originator of many of the reforms, he gave approval to them. Another theory focuses on internal incentives within the Chinese government, in which officials presiding over areas of high economic growth were more likely to be promoted. Scholars have noted that local and provincial governments in China were "...hungry for investment" and competed to reduce regulations and barriers to investment to boost economic growth and the officials' own careers. A third explanation believes that the success of the reformists are attributable to Deng's cultivation of his own followers in the government. Herman Kahn (1979) explained the raise of Asian economic power saying the Confucian ethic was playing a "similar but more spectacular role in the modernization of East Asia than the Protestant ethic played in Europe".[citation needed]

Effect on inequality

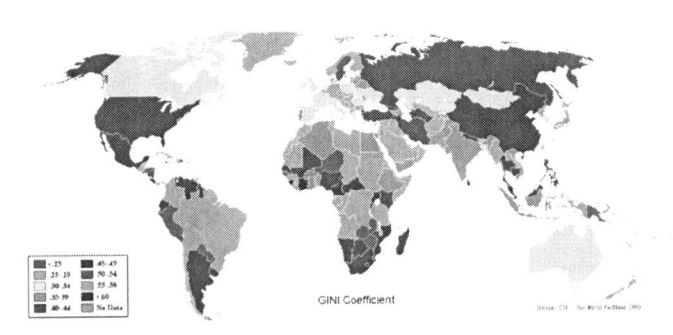

Gini-coefficient of national income distribution around the world (dark green: <0.25, red: >0.60)

The economic reforms have increased inequality dramatically within China. Despite rapid economic growth which has virtually eliminated poverty in urban China and reduced it greatly in rural regions, the Gini coefficient of China is estimated to be above 0.45, comparable to many South American countries. Increased inequality is attributed to the disappearance of the welfare state and differences between coastal and interior provinces, the latter being burdened by a larger state sector. Some Western scholars have suggested that reviving the welfare state and instituting a re-distributive income tax system is needed to relieve inequality, while some Chinese economists, influenced by the Austrian School, have suggested that privatizing state monopolies and distributing the proceeds to the population can reduce inequality. In China businesses do not have the same level of environmental, safety and child labor regulations to comply with, thus they have a competitive advantage compared to business operating in most western nations, but there has been a down-side in the form of many scandals which have hurt sales. In 2008, a court in China refused to hear a lawsuit against a Chinese dairy filed by dozens of families whose children were sickened by tainted milk. In 2007 China manufactured every one of the 24 kinds of toys recalled for safety reasons in the United States so, including the enormously popular Thomas & Friends wooden train sets, a record that is causing alarm among consumer advocates, parents and regulators. The toys were coated at a factory in China with lead paint, which can damage brain cells, especially in children.

A ghoulish fake eyeball toy made in China was recalled after it was found to be filled with kerosene. Sets of toy drums and a toy bear were also recalled because of lead paint, and an infant wrist rattle was recalled because of a choking hazard. These and other examples have somewhat tarnished China's reputation with respect to quality and safety.

Comparison to other developing economies

China's transition from socialism to capitalism has often been compared with economies in Eastern Europe that are undergoing a similar transition. China's performance has been praised for avoiding the major shocks and inflation that plagued the Eastern bloc. The Eastern bloc economies saw declines of 13 to 65% in GDP at the beginning of reforms, while Chinese growth has been very strong since the beginning of reform. China also managed to avoid the hyperinflation of 200 to 1,000% that Eastern Europe experienced. This success is attributed to the gradualist and decentralized approach of the Chinese government, which allowed market institutions to develop to the point where they could replace state planning. This contrasts with the "big bang" approach of Eastern Europe, where the state-owned sector was rapidly privatized with employee buyouts, but retained much of the earlier, inefficient management. Other factors thought to account for the differences are the greater urbanization of the CIS economies and differences in social welfare and other institutions. Another argument is that, in the Eastern European economies, political change is sometimes seen to have made gradualist reforms impossible, so the shocks and inflation were unavoidable.

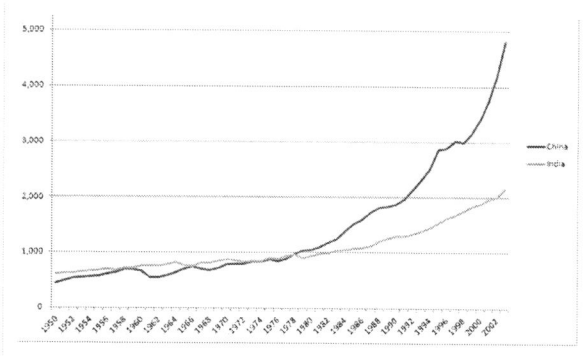

The development trends of Chinese and Indian GDP (1950-2003).

China's economic growth has been compared with other developing countries, such as Brazil, Mexico, and India. GDP growth in China outstrips all other developing countries, with only India after 1990 coming close to China's experience. Scholars believes that high rates of investments, especially increases in capital invested per worker, have contributed to China's superior economic performance. China's relatively free economy, with less government intervention and regulation, is cited by scholars as an important factor in China's superior performance compared to other developing countries.

Legacy and criticism

Although very successful in turning China's economy into one of the world's largest and most dynamic economies, reforms have been incomplete. The government retains monopolies in several sectors, such as petroleum and banking;, the inefficient state banking system has a large number of non-performing loans and loose monetary policy has caused an asset bubble which threatens economic stability. The recent reversal of some reforms have left some observers dubbing 2008 the "...third anniversary of the end of reforms". Nevertheless, observers believe that China's economy can continue growing at rates of 6-8 percent until 2025, though a reduction in state intervention is considered necessary for sustained growth.

Despite reducing poverty and increasing China's wealth, Deng's reforms have been criticized by the Chinese New Left for increasing inequality and allowing private entrepreneurs to purchase state assets at reduced prices. These accusations were especially intense during the Lang-Gu dispute, in which New Left academic Larry Lang accused entrepreneur Gu Sujung of usurping state assets, after which Gu was imprisoned. The Hu-Wen Administration has adopted some New Left policies, such as halting privatizations and increasing the state sector's importance in the economy, Keynesian policies that have been criticized by many Chinese economists who advocate a policy of deregulation, tax cuts, and privatization inspired by the Austrian School.

Other criticisms focus on the effects of industrialization on public health and the environment. Scholars believe that public health issues are unlikely to become major obstacles to the growth of China's economy during the coming decades, and studies have shown that air quality and other environmental measures in China are better than those in developed countries, such as the United States and Japan, at the same level of development.

Sources

- Allen, Franklin et al (2008), "China's Financial system: Past, present and future", *China's Great Transformation*, Cambridge: Cambridge university press
- Benjamin, Dwayne et al (2008), "Income inequality during China's Economic Transition", *China's Great Transformation*, Cambridge: Cambridge university press
- Brandt, Loren et al (2008), "China's Great Transformation", *China's Great Transformation*, Cambridge: Cambridge university press
- Bransetter, Lee et al (2008), "China's embrace of globalization", *China's Great Transformation*, Cambridge: Cambridge university press
- Cai, Fang et al (2008), "The Chinese labor market in the reform era", *China's Great Transformation*, Cambridge: Cambridge university press
- Haggard, Stevens et al (2008), "The political economy of private-sector development in China", *China's Great Transformation*, Cambridge: Cambridge university press
- Herston, Alan et al (2008), "China and Development economics", *China's Great Transformation*, Cambridge: Cambridge university press
- Huang, Jikun et al (2008), "Agriculture in China's Development: Past Disappointments, Recent Successes, and Future Challenges", *China's Great Transformation*, Cambridge: Cambridge university press
- Naughton, Barry et al (2008), "A Political Economy of China's Economic Transition*in* China's Great Transformation", *China's Great Transformation*, Cambridge: Cambridge university press
- Perkins, Dwight et al (2008), "Forecasting China's growth to 2025", *China's Great Transformation*, Cambridge: Cambridge university press

- Rawski, G. Thomas et al (2008), "China's Industrial Development", *China's Great Transformation*, Cambridge: Cambridge university press
- Svejnar, Jan et al (2008), "China in light of other transition economies", in Brandt, Loren and Rawski, G. Thomas, *China's Great Transformation*, Cambridge: Cambridge university press
- Wong, P.W. Christine et al (2008), "China's Fiscal system: a work in progress", *China's Great Tranformation*, Cambridge: Cambridge university press

See also

- Economic history of China (pre-1911)
- Economic history of modern China
- Great Divergence
- Doi Moi

Grasping the large, letting go of the small

The "**grasping the large and letting the small go**" policy (Chinese: 抓大放小; pinyin: *Zhuā dà fàng xiǎo*) was part of a wave of industrial reforms implemented by the central government of the People's Republic of China in 1996. These reforms included efforts to corporatize state-owned enterprises (SOEs) and to downsize the state sector.

The "grasping the large and letting the small go" policy was adopted in September 1997 at the 15th Communist Party Congress. The "grasping the large" component indicated that policy-makers should focus on maintaining state control over the largest state-owned enterprises (which tended to be controlled by the central government).

"Letting the small go" meant that the central government should relinquish control over smaller state-owned enterprises. Relinquishing control over these enterprises took a variety of forms: giving local governments authority to restructure the firms, privatizing them, or shutting them down.

While "grasping the large and letting the small go" represented a significant policy change at the central level, it merely gave legal sanction to changes in SOE ownership structure that had been occurring at the local level since 1992.

See also

- Economy of the People's Republic of China
- SASAC

Notes

- 'Letting Go of the Small': An Analysis of the Privatisation of Rural Enterprises in Jiangsu and Shandong [1] Samuel P.S. Ho; Paul Bowles; Xiaoyuan Dong. Source: Journal of Development Studies, Volume 39, Number 4, April 01, 2003 , pp. 1-26(26)

Economic Development Plans

China Western Development

The East Coast
(with existing development programmes)

"Rise of Central China"

"Revitalize Northeast China"

"China Western Development"

China Western Development (simplified Chinese: 西部大开发; traditional Chinese: 西部大開發; pinyin: *Xībù Dàkāifā*), also **China's Western Development, Western China Development, Great Western Development Strategy,** or the **Open Up the West Program** is a policy adopted by the People's Republic of China to boost its less developed western regions.

The policy covers 6 provinces (Gansu, Guizhou, Qinghai, Shaanxi, Sichuan, and Yunnan), 5 autonomous regions (Guangxi, Inner Mongolia, Ningxia, Tibet, and Xinjiang), and 1 municipality (Chongqing). This region contains 71.4% of mainland China's area, but only 28.8% of its population, as of the end of 2002, and 19.9% of its total economic output, as of 2009.

History

Under the leadership of Deng Xiaoping, the People's Republic of China began to reform its economy in 1978 by changing from a command economy to a market economy. The coastal regions of eastern China benefited greatly from these reforms, and their economies quickly raced ahead. The western half of China, however, lagged behind severely. In order to help the western half of China catch up with the eastern half, a Leadership Group for Western China Development (西部地区开发领导小组) was created by the State Council in January 2000, led by then-Premier Zhu Rongji.

Chronicle of Events

1999: the "Western Development" guidelines are clarified

2000: the "Western Development" plan begins

2001: the official website of the "Western Development" program is launched

2002: construction of the "West-East Gas Pipeline" begins

2003: the policy of "Returning Grazing Land to Grassland" comes into effect

2004: the Law on Promoting Western Development is listed on the legislative plan of the 10th National People's Congress

2005: compulsory education tuition and fees become exempt in western areas

2006: the Qinghai-Tibet Railway begins operation

2007: the Ministry of Finance invests 280 billion yuan in the west to support key projects

Strategy

The main components of the strategy include the development of infrastructure (transport, hydropower plants, energy, and telecommunications), enticement of foreign investment, increased efforts on ecological protection (such as reforestation), promotion of education, and retention of talent flowing to richer provinces. As of 2006, a total of 1 trillion yuan has been spent building infrastructure in western China.

Transportation

The western development bureau affiliated to the state council released a list of 10 major projects to launch in 2008, with a combined budget of 436 billion yuan (64.12 billion U.S. dollars).

These projects included new railway lines connecting Guiyang and Guangzhou, Lanzhou and Chongqing, Kashgar and Hotan in Xinjiang; highways between Wanyuan and Dazhou in Sichuan Province, Shuikou and Duyun in Guizhou Province; airport expansion projects in Chengdu, Chongqing and Xi'an.

They also include the building of hydropower stations, coal mines, gas and oil transmission tube lines as well as public utilities projects in western regions.

By the end of 2007, China has started 92 key construction projects in western regions, with a total investment of more than 1.3 trillion yuan.

Hydraulic projects

The Big Western Line, a possible element of the South–North Water Transfer Project, is a proposal for diverting water from the upstream sections of six rivers in southwestern China, including the Mekong, the Yarlung Tsangpo and the Salween, to the dry areas of northern China through a system of reservoirs, tunnels and natural rivers. This project may be the most controversial plan to date.

Effects

Economic Developments

China's attempt to develop its western regions has had varying effects on the West's economic development. While massive investment has boosted the region's output, effectively raising the GDP in all western regions, the project failed to achieve its goal of eliminating the economic gap between China's East and West. From 1999 to 2001, Xinjiang and Guangxi displayed an annual GDP percent increase of as high as 30%. China's western regions have reported an annual average economic growth rate of 10.6% for six years in a row. The combined GDP of the western regions reached 3.33 trillion yuan in 2005, compared with 1.66 trillion yuan in 2000, while net income grew on average 10% for urban residents in the west and 6.8% for rural residents. Initiatives encouraging Chinese from wealthier and more crowded regions of China to move to the relatively less crowded western regions has resulted in population growth in [a few cities], most notably Qinghai with its increase of 12.6%.

Nevertheless, the economic growth rate of China's East continues to exceed that of the West, causing the western share of domestic product to continue to fall. The West's contribution to the GDP decreased from 20.88% in 1990 to 17.13% in 2000. Relative levels of GDP per capita in the West decreased from 73.30% in 1990 to 60.87% in 2000. In 1990, Shanghai's per capita GDP was 7.3 times that of Guizhou, the poorest province in China; by 2000, the figure had grown to 12.9 times. Evidence from the China Statistical Yearbook also confirms the increasing economic gap between China's West and East, indicating that the east-to-west GDP ratio increased from 2.98 in 1980 to 4.33 in 2000.

Foreign Investment

Since the introduction of economic reform and open-door policy in 1978, the western region has been in a disadvantageous economic position because it promises a less lucrative return to the investors than its eastern competitors. Therefore, one of the major objectives of the Open Up the West initiative was to bring in foreign investment by creating a more stable investing environment through infrastructure construction. This was a success for the western development project at some level, for statistics shows a substantial growth in foreign investment in the western regions, from US $1,837.35 million in 1999 to $1,922.19 million in 2001. However, not all areas in the western region shared in this progress. While foreign direct investment in Chongqing grew US $17.56 million between 1999 and 2001 (from US $238.93 million to $256.49 million), foreign investment in Guizhou, Guangxi and Ningxi declined significantly, dropping about USD $19.71, $250.96 million, and $34.54 million respectively.

The situation in Guizhou reveals a particularly pernicious effect of the Western Development Program. Despite the fact that Guizhou received 53.3 billion yuan in infrastructure construction in 2001 alone, more than the total amount given by the Ninth Five-year Plan (1995-2002), its foreign capital declined from US $40.9 million in 1999 to $29.29 million in 2001, an astonishing 31% decline, reaching its lowest point since 1997. Contrary to what the state had intended, the West-East Electricity Transfer Project in Guizhou only assured the continued increase in foreign investment on the coast, as most of the electricity generated in Guizhou was transmitted to Guangdong.

Tim Oakes, associate professor of geography at the University of Colorado at Boulder, argues that the decline of foreign investment in certain western regions is a consequence of Beijing's attempt to recentralize the province's economy through mega-projects such as Guizhou's west-east electricity transfer project. The strengthening of central control over the economy has eroded the trust of foreign investors. In the case of Guizhou, while the Chinese central government intended to attract foreign investment in the power sector through the West-East Electricity Transfer Project, only 5% of foreign investment entered the energy sector. About 75% of Guizhou's foreign investment was channeled into manufacturing and 15% to real estate development. Because the campaign's economic program is strongly central planned, the campaign has actually discouraged foreign investment, working against its original intent.

Environmental Protection

Foreseeing significant environmental impacts in the massive infrastructure development program, the state highly publicizes environmental preservation in its campaign to open up the West. Farmland conversion to forest and grassland is the dominant strategy for this effort, targeting specifically the regions crucial to the Yangtze's protection. In Sichuan, the government aims to protect the 19.23 million hectares of existing forest and plant an additional 2.93 million hectares of new forest to diminish the amount of silt flowing into the Yangtze. Around 20,000 mu of farmland was converted in Guizhou in 2001, a key region for Yangtze preservation. In Shaanxi, 571,000 hectares of farmland and 427,000 hectares of wasteland were converted to forest or grass between 1999 and 2002. Another 280,000 hectares of farmland and the same expanse of wasteland were converted in 2003. China's environmental program in the west has made China "one of a few countries in the world that have been rapidly increasing their forest cover," according to David Dollar, director of the World Bank in China.

Although the project seems to be going successfully, it creates a potential fiscal burden for the government. Massive farmland conversion requires a tremendous amount of funding for resettling the farmers. In addition, to compensate farmers for their loss in agricultural profit, the state has committed to supplying them with grains and funds for planting trees and grass. This results in a prescribed allotment of 60 yuan per mu by the central policy. A further complication is farmer dissatisfaction when the government fails to deliver on its contract, since the local government usually bases compensation on actual production value, resulting in compensation between 20-50 yuan, plus a 300 jin appropriation of grain.

Farmers who are temporarily benefiting from the compensation will soon rely on governmental subsidy once the tree-planting project is completed. 81,000 tons of grain, 154 million yuan in cash subsidies and 266 million yuan for tree saplings to almost 800,000 farming households have already been spent in Shaanxi. If the provincial government decides to honor its commitment for another 5-8 years, it will cost a total of 11.7 billion yuan in grain and cash subsidies. The heavy financial cost makes the sustainability of the environmental project questionable.

Furthermore, while the environmental project is critically emphasized in the campaign, very little has been discussed on the impact of intensified coal extraction, increased thermal plant operation, reservoir inundation, and transportation and transmission line construction, all of which create a more detrimental impact to the environment that the environmental program can compensate for.

Recent developments

- Chongqing Metro
- Qingzang railway, linking Lhasa and Xining

See also

- Bohai Economic Rim
- Yangtze River Delta Economic Zone
- Northeast China Revitalization
- Rise of Central China Plan
- Economy of the People's Republic of China

Further reading

- Asia Times Online: Asphalt net covers China's west [1]
- China's Campaign to 'Open up the West'National, Provincial and Local Perspectives, *The China Quarterly Special Issues (No. 5)*, Edited by David S. G. Goodman [2]

External links

- China Western Development Network [3]

Northeast Area Revitalization Plan

The East Coast
(with existing development programmes)

"Rise of Central China"

"Revitalize Northeast China"

"China Western Development"

Revitalize The Old Northeast Industrial Bases (simplified Chinese: 振兴东北老工业基地; traditional Chinese: 振興東北老工業基地; pinyin: *Zhènxīng Dōngběi Lǎo Gōngyè Jīdì*), also **Revitalize Northeast China** or **Northeast China Revitalization**, is a policy adopted by the People's Republic of China in 2003 to rejuvenate industrial bases in **Northeast China**. It covers three provinces: Heilongjiang, Jilin, and Liaoning, as well as the five eastern prefectures of Inner Mongolia: Xilin Gol, Chifeng, Tongliao, Hinggan and Hulunbuir. The State Council established a special Leading Group to define and adopt related strategies, which held its first meeting in August 2009 and the second in August 2010. Chairman of the Leading Group is Premier Wen Jiabao.

Following the first meeting of the Leading Group, the revitalization strategy was affirmed and extended in a document of September 9th, 2009. The State Council asked the Northeastern provinces to better coordinate their economic development strategies. As a result, the top party and government leaders of Liaoning, Jilin, Heilongjiang and Inner Mongolia met in Shenyang, capital of Liaoning for the first Northeast Summit in April 2010, and signed a framework agreement of 25 articles for cooperation and integrated regional development. The 2011 Northeast Summit is scheduled to take place in Changchun, capital of Jilin province.

The core of the program is to revitalize the regions's traditional industry, while speeding up development in aspects of structural regulation, regional cooperation, economic reform, the construction of an environment-friendly economy, and increased efforts in education, healthcare, and cultural projects.

Cooperation with Russia, the two Koreas and Mongolia, as well as securing natural gas supplies will become important factors in this revitalisation program.

See also

- Bohai Economic Rim
- Yangtze River Delta Economic Zone
- China Western Development
- Rise of Central China Plan
- Economy of the People's Republic of China

External links

- NE China Revitalization [1] - Special Report
- Asia Times Online: Reviving northeast China [2]

Rise of Central China Plan

The East Coast
(with existing development programmes)

"Rise of Central China"

"Revitalize Northeast China"

"China Western Development"

The **Rise of Central China Plan** (simplified Chinese: 中部崛起计划; traditional Chinese: 中部崛起計劃; pinyin: *Zhōngbù Juéqǐ Jìhuà*) is a policy adopted by the People's Republic of China to accelerate the development of its central regions. It was announced by Premier Wen Jiabao on the 5 March 2004. It covers six provinces: Shanxi, Henan, Anhui, Hubei, Hunan, and Jiangxi.

See also

- Economy of the People's Republic of China
- Bohai Economic Rim
- Beibu Gulf Economic Rim
- Pearl River Delta Economic Zone
- Yangtze River Delta Economic Zone

External links

- China Internet Information Center: China to Boost Rise of Central Region [1]

Third Front (China)

The **Third Front** is a massive Chinese development of industry in its south-western interior, where it would be strategically secure in the event of a war.

Origins

Begun in the 1960s, it was little mentioned at the time. It was loosely linked with the Three Gorges Dam. The basic idea was to have an industrial base that would be secure from foreign attack, unlike the coastal industries or Manchuria (Northeast China).

> The 'Third Front' refers to a large-scale programme the country started in 1964 -- in response to the then volatile international situation -- to build a range of industrial bases in its remote yet strategically secured hinterland.

> By 1980, the programme had created a railway grid linking previously isolated parts of south-western and western China, in addition to a galaxy of power, aviation and electronic plants, said Zhang Yunchuan, minister of the Commission of Science, Technology and Industry for National Defence. (People's Daily Online)

Mao and his generals envisaged three line of defense (coastal, central, and western), and they decided in 1964 on a massive construction of military-industrial complexes in westen China, the third line of defense, popularly translated as the "third front"

To minimize the vulnerability of the third-front industries to air attack, Lin Biao, who was Defense Minister and Mao's designated successor, instructed that these projects be located "in mountains, in dispersion, and in caves".

The area of the Third Front is the hardest part of China for any invading foreign power to access. During the Second Sino-Japanese War of 1937-45, it remained unconquered. The Kuomintang (at that time in alliance with the Chinese Communists based at Yan'an) made Chongqing their capital. Some

Chinese industry was also moved there from the cities. So the 'Third Front' strategy had precedents, though it was immediate politics that was the main cause:

> From the early 1960s, with its Soviet ties deteriorating and the Vietnam War escalating, China became concerned of a possible nuclear attack. As a result, Mao Zedong ordered an evacuation of military and other key state enterprises away from Shanghai and other coastal areas and from the northeastern frontier region bordering the Soviet Union and started moving them in 1964 to the interior in Sichuan, Guizhou, Yunnan and other inland provinces. In those days, the coastal and the northeastern frontier regions were known as the 'first front line' and the inland regions in the southwest as the "third front line," while all the land area in between was designated as the 'second front line.' (*Japan-China relations*)

For a time, Peng Dehuai was in charge of the Third Front, but he was arrested in 1966 during the Cultural Revolution.

Current role

Even today, the composition of the 'third front' remains a mystery. Parts of it have been shown to the outside world, primarily that of factories seeking investment. The mountainous terrain and geographical isolation of the region have added to this concealment.

> Due to the emphasis that China has placed on concealment of its special weapons capabilities, it is doubtful whether any other country, perhaps even including the United States, has identified all of China's special weapons related facilities. (*Chinese Nuclear Weapons*)

From the 1980s, with the post-Mao economic reform, there was a shift to non-military production and an attempt to attract foreign investment. Much of the output is now non-military:

> A number of moribund factories were shut down, many ventures were moved close to urban areas, and technological renovation has enabled them to produce competitive products for civilian use...

> *Part of the achievement is that a batch of 'backbone' enterprises has evolved from the 'Third Front' to develop more than 2,000 products including satellite and automobile parts and civilian aircraft,* said Ji Dawei, a chief co-ordinator for the relocation drive.

> The machinery, metallurgical, chemical and non-ferrous mineral and other companies based in the 'Third Front' have laid a solid foundation for the economic take-off of western China. (*China putting on a brave 'Third Front'*)

See also

- Economy of the People's Republic of China

Media

The 'Third Front' is the setting for a recent Chinese film called *Shanghai Dreams*. Set in the 1980s, it is a bleak and thoughtful drama that shows the life of some ordinary families who had moved there and would like to move back to Shanghai.

External links

- Article [1] in *China Quarterly*
- China's military industry enterprises come out of mountains to world market [2]
- Regional Development Strategies in China [3]
- Paper about Chinese regional development [4] from Harvard University
- Beijing and the Vietnam Conflict, 1964-1965 [5]

Go Out policy

Go Out policy (Chinese: 走出去战略; pinyin: *Zǒuchūqū Zhànlüè*) is the People's Republic of China's current strategy to encourage its enterprises to invest overseas.

Most nations favour actively attracting inward foreign investment, and would only support outward foreign investment passively. The People's Republic of China, however, attaches importance to both inward and outward foreign investment.

Causes

- The People's Republic of China has amassed huge amounts of foreign reserves, thus putting upward pressure on the foreign exchange rate of renminbi, the Chinese currency. Indeed, there have been much demand from the international community for the PRC to float its currency. In order to deflate that demand, the PRC therefore actively seeks to employ its foreign reserves by acquiring assets overseas.
- The PRC is opening up the domestic market in mainland China as a result of its open door policy, which is further accelerated by its commitments when entering the World Trade Organization. Therefore, the PRC can foresee that world class competitors are now competing for business in the Chinese market, and so the PRC is seeking to equip the domestic firms and their management with international experience so that they can take the competition to the home markets of the foreign nations and so that they can compete better at mainland China's own domestic market.

- It is a matter of national pride that the PRC should have world class enterprises.

History

The Go Out Policy (also referred to as the Going Global Strategy) was an effort initiated in 1999 by the Chinese government to promote Chinese investments abroad. The Government, together with the China Council for the Promotion of International Trade (CCPIT), has introduced several schemes to assist domestic companies in developing a global strategy to exploit opportunities in the expanding local and international markets.

The programs launched so far by the Chinese Government have these goals in mind:

1. increase Chinese Direct Foreign Investment (FDI)
2. pursue product diversification
3. improve the level and quality of the projects
4. expand financial channels with respect to the national market
5. promote brand recognition of Chinese companies in EU and US markets

Since the launching of the Going out Strategy, interest in overseas investing by Chinese companies has increased significantly especially among State Owned Enterprises. Statistics indicate that Chinese direct foreign investments rose from US$3 billion in 1991 to US$35 billion in 2003. This trend was underscored in 2007, when Chinese FDI reached US$92 billion. This boost in foreign investment can also be attributed to the Chinese Government's ability and commitment to create the right environment for foreign investment; and China's huge production capacity, coupled with low labor costs. With a dynamic economy, and a strong business-friendly culture, the outlook for Chinese companies will continue to be positive.

As part of its efforts to restructure state-owned enterprises, the Chinese government has established the SASAC (State-Owned Asset Supervision Administration Commission), which develops China's equity exchange market, while supporting Chinese foreign investments. SASAC's responsibilities include:

1. supervision and evaluation of state-owned enterprises
2. oversight of state-owned assets
3. recruiting of top executive talent
4. drafting of laws, administrative rules and regulations that promote increased development of corporate law in China
5. coordination of local state-owned assets as prescribed by law

The SASAC operates through several equity exchanges such as CBEX (China Beijing Equity Exchange), which is the largest and most prestigious in terms of trading volume. It is headquartered in the heart of Beijing financial district. Presently, CBEX has established three international platforms in Italy, Japan and the United States of America. The Italian CMEX (China Milan Equity Exchange), created in 2007, is CBEX's first international partner, operating as a liaison to facilitate the penetration of Chinese companies into the Italian and European markets and of European companies in China. Following the trend of the Go out policy, some of the most prominent Chinese professional institutions are expanding their business on the international markets. King&Wood, the largest Law Firm in China with more than 800 lawyers, has recently opened a branch in Japan and in the US, while Grandall Legal Group (one of the most prominent Chinese Law Firms, with a staff of more than 600 professionals) through its International Department has established a European hub called the "China-Europe Legal Group" to assist Chinese companies in Europe. Carone & Partners is a member law firm of the "China-Europe Legal Group" in Italy.

Recent examples of the Go out policy

The following list of M&A transactions performed by Chinese companies overseas are just some of the most notable examples of the successful implementation of the Go out policy:

- June 2009: Proposed purchase of Hummer by Sichuan Tengzhong Heavy Industrial Machinery Company
- February 2009: Chinalco injected $19.5bn cash into the Australian mining company Rio Tinto, increasing its stake from 9 per cent to 18 per cent
- February 2009: Minmetals unveiled a friendly A$2.6bn ($1.7bn) takeover offer for the Australian Oz Mineral
- September 2008: Zoomlion, controlled by the Hunan provincial government, bought a 60% stake in Compagnia Italiana Forme Acciaio, the Italian construction equipment & machinery company, with full takeover possible 3 years later
- May 2005: Lenovo bought IBM's personal computer division

See also

- Economy of the People's Republic of China
- Foreign policy of the People's Republic of China
- SinoLatin Capital

External links

- National Development and Reform Commission [1]
- Ministry of Commerce [2]
- This Time, China Is Different [2] by Chinese economist Chen Jing
- SASAC State-owned Assets Supervision and Administration Commission [3]
- CBEX - China Beijing Equity Exchange [4]
- CMEX - China Milan Equity Exchange [5]
- CPLEX - Carone & Partners Law Firm [6]

The Financial System of China

Chinese financial system

China's financial system is highly regulated and has recently begun to expand rapidly as monetary policy becomes integral to its overall economic policy. As a result, banks are becoming more important to China's economy by providing increasingly more finance to enterprises for investment, seeking deposits from the public to mop up excess liquidity, and lending money to the government.

Beijing Financial Street, the economic centre of Beijing.

As part of US$586 billion economic stimulus package of November 2008, the government plans to remove loan quotas and ceilings for all lenders, and increase bank credit for priority projects, including rural areas, small businesses, technology companies, iron and cement companies.

Financial reform

For the past few decades, the People's Bank of China has exercised the functions and powers of a central bank, as well as handling industrial and commercial credits and savings business; it was neither the central bank in the true sense, nor a commercial entity conforming to the law of the market economy. But since reform and opening-up began in 1978, China has carried out a series of significant reforms in its banking system, and strengthened its opening to the outside world. Consequently, the finance industry has made steady development. At the end of 2004, the balance of domestic and foreign currency savings deposits stood at 25,318.8 billion yuan and the balance of home and foreign currency loans came to 18,856.6 billion yuan. Now China has basically formed a financial system under the regulation, control and supervision of the central bank, with its state banks as the mainstay, featuring the separation of policy-related finance and commercial finance, the cooperation of various financial institutions with mutually complementary functions.

In 1984, the People's Bank of China stopped handling credit and savings business, and began formally to exercise central bank functions and powers by conducting macro-control and supervision over the nation's banking system. In 1994, the Industrial and Commercial Bank of China, the Bank of China, the Agricultural Bank of China and the China Construction Bank were transformed into state-owned commercial banks; and three policy-related banks were founded, namely, the Agricultural Development Bank of China, the National Development Bank and the China Import and Export Bank. In 1995, the Commercial Bank Law was promulgated, creating the conditions for forming the commercial bank system and organizational structure, and providing a legal basis for changing the specialized state banks to state-owned commercial banks.

Since 1996, the financial organizational system has gradually been improved; the wholly state-owned commercial banks have been transformed into modern financial enterprises handling currencies; over 120 shareholding medium and small-sized commercial banks have been set up or reorganized; and securities and insurance financial institutions have been further standardized and developed. April 2003 saw the formal establishment of the China Banking Regulatory Commission (CBRC). Since then, a financial regulatory system has been formed in which CBRC, China Securities Regulatory Commission (CSRC) and China Insurance Regulatory Commission (CIRC) work in coordination, each body having its own clearly defined responsibilities.

In January 2004, the State Council decided that the Bank of China and the China Construction Bank would start the experiment of transforming the shareholding system. The main tasks are to establish a standardized corporate governance and an internal system of rights and responsibilities in accordance with the requirements for modern commercial banks; to restructure the financial system, speed up the disposal of non-performing assets and to reinforce minimum capital requirement to build up first-class modern financial enterprises. Now, six shareholding commercial banks and urban commercial banks in China have begun to accept overseas investors as shareholders.

Opening up of the financial industry

Over the past 20-odd years, China's financial institutions in the Special Economic Zone, coastal open cities and inland central cities have approved a range of wholly foreign-owned and Chinese-foreign joint venture financial institutions. Every year since 2002, China has increased the number of cities where foreign banks are allowed to handle RMB business, and within five years such banks will be allowed to handle RMB business in any city. At the end of 2004, the total assets of foreign financial institutions in China reached over US$47 billion; foreign banks were allowed to handle RMB business in 16 areas, and 62 foreign banks from 19 countries and regions set up 191 business institutions in China, of which 116 were approved to handle RMB business. There were 211 foreign bank branches in China.

The CSRC has approved the establishment of 13 Sino-foreign equity joint venture fund management companies, and started to formally handle the application of establishment of joint venture fund management companies with a maximum 49 percent foreign share; the CIRC declared that: from December 11, 2004 on, foreign insurance companies could handle health insurance, group insurance, life insurance and annuity insurance businesses; regional restrictions on establishing wholly foreign-funded insurance institutions were canceled and the proportion of the foreign share in joint venture insurance agencies was allowed to reach 51 percent.

Foreign banks have expanded their China-related business scope. In November 2003, the CBRC started to implement new policies, e.g., permitting foreign banks to provide RMB services to all kinds of Chinese enterprises in areas with open RMB business (previously, these banks' RMB services were restricted to foreign-funded enterprises, foreigners and people from Hong Kong, Macao and Taiwan in cities with open RMB business). The new policy also encourages qualified international strategic investors to join the restructuring and reforming of China's banking and financial institutions on a voluntary and commercial basis.

Meanwhile, all China's commercial banks have set up branches overseas, and started an international credit business. The Bank of China ranks first in the number and scale of overseas outlets. In 1980, China resumed membership of the World Bank, and returned to the International Monetary Fund. In 1984, China started business contacts with the Bank for International Settlements. In 1985, China formally joined the African Development Bank and in 1986 formally became a member of the Asian Development Bank.

Economic reform

Main articles: Economy of the People's Republic of China and Chinese economic reform

The ongoing development of China's financial system will play a critical role in the country's effort to narrow social disparities and pursue balanced growth. Reforming the financial system would increase the rate of GDP growth and help spread China's new wealth more evenly. If the reforms directed additional funds to private companies — China's new growth engine — the economy would generate significantly higher returns for the same level of investment and GDP would rise. Such a shift will stimulate mass job creation in the strongest areas of China's economy and increase tax revenues to finance social programs.

After more than a quarter century of reform and opening to the outside world, by 2005 China's economy had become the second largest in the world after the United States when measured on a purchasing power parity (PPP) basis. The government has a goal of quadrupling the gross domestic product (GDP) by 2020 and more than doubling the per capita GDP. Central planning has been curtailed, and widespread market mechanisms and a reduced government role have prevailed since 1978. The government fosters a dual economic structure that has evolved from a socialist, centrally planned economy to a socialist market economic system, or a "market economy with socialist characteristics". Industry is marked by increasing technological advancements and productivity. People's communes were eliminated by 1984 — after more than 25 years — and the system of township-collective-household production was introduced to the agricultural sector. Private ownership of production assets is legal, although some nonagricultural and industrial facilities are still state-owned and centrally planned. Restraints on international trade were relaxed when China acceded to the World Trade Organization in 2001. Joint ventures are encouraged, especially in the coastal Special Economic Zones and open coastal cities. A sign of the affluence that the reformed economy has brought to China might be seen in the number of its millionaires (measured in U.S. dollars): a reported 236,000 millionaires in 2004, an increase of 12 percent over two years earlier.

Chinese officials cite two major trends that have an effect on China's market economy and future development: world multipolarization and regional integration. In relation to these trends, they foresee the roles of China and the United States in world affairs and with one another as very important. Despite successes, China's leaders face a variety of challenges to the nation's future economic development. They have to maintain a high growth rate, deal effectively with the rural workforce, improve the financial system, continue to reform the state-owned enterprises, foster the productive private sector, establish a social security system, improve scientific and educational development, promote better international cooperation, and change the role of the government in the economic system. Despite constraints the international market has placed on China, it nevertheless became the world's third largest trading nation in 2004 after only the United States and Germany.

The Fifth Plenum of the Sixteenth CCP Central Committee took place in October 2005. The Fifth Plenum approved the new Eleventh Five-Year Plan (2006–10), which emphasizes a shift from extensive to intensive growth in order to meet demands for improved economic returns; the conservation of resources to include a 20% reduction in energy consumption by 2010; and an effort to raise profitability. Better coordination of urban and rural development and of development between nearby provincial regions also is emphasized in the new plan.

Government finances and budget

China's government debt is less than 25% of gross domestic product (about 22.10% in 2006). (See *List of countries by public debt.*)

China has a budget deficit of around 1.5% of GDP. China projected a budget deficit of 295 billion yuan in 2006, down 1.7% from 2005. The overall budget deficit in 2004 was approximately US$26 billion, an amount equivalent to about 1.5% of GDP. In 2007, economic planners expect China's already small budget deficit to shrink again. According to economists, this has afforded China to spend more on public services such as education and healthcare.

The government budget for 2004 was US$330.6 billion in revenue and US$356.8 billion in expenditures. 95.5% of revenue was from taxes and tariffs, 54.9% of which was collected by the central government and 45% by local government. The expenditures were for culture, education, science, and health care (18%); capital construction (12%); administration (14%); national defense (7.7%); agriculture, forestry, and water conservancy (5.9%); subsidies to compensate for price increases (2.7%); pensions and social welfare provisions (1.9%); promotion of innovation, science, and technology (4.3%); operating expenses of industry, transport, and commerce (1.2%); geological prospecting (0.4%), and other (31.9%).

Taxation

Main article: Tax system in China

Before the reform and opening, China exercised a single taxation system. Because taxation had no connection with the economic activities of enterprises, this system lacked vitality. In 1981, the Chinese government began to collect income tax from Sino-foreign joint ventures and solely foreign-funded enterprises, taking the first step in taxation system reform. From 1983 to 1984, the reform consisting of the replacement of profits by taxes was carried out in domestic enterprises, and a foreign-related taxation system was set up. As a result, instead of a single tax category, a compound taxation system in which turnover and income taxes were the mainstay and other tax categories were in coordination with it was initially in place and promoted the control of finances and the economy. In 1994, the reform of the taxation system was deepened, and a complete structural adjustment of the taxation system was made by taking the market economy as the norm. In 1996, China lowered the rate of customs duties and export drawback, and exercised import supervision.

Inflation

China's annual rate of inflation averaged 6% per year during the 1990–2002 period. Although consumer prices declined by 0.8% in 2002, they increased by 1.2% in 2003. China's estimated inflation rate in 2006 was 1.8%.

Banking sector

Main articles: Banking in China and History of banking in China

China's banking system is highly regulated with six major banks, each having specific tasks and duties. The People's Bank of China is the largest bank in China and acts as the Treasury. It also issues currency, monitors money supply, regulates monetary organizations and formulates monetary policy for the State Council. The Bank of China manages foreign exchange transactions and manages foreign exchange reserves. The China Development Bank distributes foreign capital from a variety of sources, and the China International Trust and Investment Corporation (CITIC) was previously a financial organization that smoothed the inflow of foreign funds, but is now a full bank, allowing to compete for foreign investment funds with the Bank of China. The China Construction Bank lends funds for capital construction projects from the state budget, and finally the Agricultural Bank of China functions as a lending and deposit taking institution for the agricultural sector.

Banking reform

Financial reform in China's banking sector include the introduction of leasing and insurance, and operational boundaries are being slowly eroded to promote competition for customers who are now permitted to choose banks as well as hold accounts in more than one bank.

Banking reform was initiated in China in 1994, and the Commercial Banking Law took effect in July 1995. The aims of these actions were to strengthen the role of the central bank—the People's Bank of China—and to allow private banks to be established. The People's Bank of China was established in 1948. It issues China's currency and implements the nation's monetary policies. China's oldest bank, founded in 1908, is the Bank of Communications Limited, a commercial enterprise located in Shanghai. China's second oldest bank was established in 1912 as the Bank of China. Since 2004 it has become a shareholding company known as the Bank of China Limited and handles foreign exchange and international financial settlements. The Agricultural Bank of China, founded in 1951, is mainly involved in rural financing and the provision of services to agricultural, industrial, commercial, and transportation enterprises in rural areas. Other major banks include the China Construction Bank; established in 1954 as the People's Construction Bank of China, it has been a state-owned commercial bank since 1994 and maintains some 15,400 business outlets inside and outside China, including six overseas branches and two overseas representative offices. The China Construction Bank was restructured in 2003 into a shareholding bank called the China Construction Bank Corporation, with the state holding the controlling shares. CITIC was founded in 1979 to assist economic and technological cooperation, finance, banking, investment, and trade. The Industrial and Commercial Bank of China was founded in 1984 to handle industrial and commercial credits and international business. The Agricultural Development Bank of China, Export and Import Bank of China, and State Development Bank all were founded in 1994. China's first private commercial national bank, the China Minsheng Banking Corporation, was opened in 1996. Commercial banks are supervised by the China Banking Regulatory Commission, which was established in 2003. In 2005 the commission announced the launching of a new postal savings bank to replace the old system and its more than 36,000 outdated outlets nationwide.

Foreign banks

Since the inception of the "open door policy", a number of foreign banks have been permitted to open their doors in major cities in China. However, these are largely representative branches, with only a few being permitted to carry out branch functions in Shanghai and Shenzhen. Their participation in China's financial system has been limited, but as China starts to borrow more from abroad, their role may become greater in the future.

When first permitted in the mid-1980s, foreign banks were restricted to designated cities and could deal only with transactions by foreign companies in China. After those restrictions were loosened following China's accession to the World Trade Organization in 2001, some foreign banks have been allowed to provide services to local residents and businesses. In 2004 there were some 70 foreign banks with more than 150 branches in China. In 2007 a limited number of foreign banks were allowed to issue debit cards in China (and Bank of East Asia was allowed to issue a credit card). This made banking with a foreign bank more convenient, as money in accounts could be accessed at ATMs like customers of local banks could. In 2009 this number grew to six, but only two of these are not tied to Hong Kong.

Stock exchanges

There are stock exchanges in Beijing, Shanghai (the third largest in the world), and Shenzhen and futures exchanges in Shanghai, Dalian, and Zhengzhou. They are regulated by the China Securities Regulatory Commission.

See also: Stock Exchange Executive Council

Stock market

In 1990 and 1991, China set up stock exchanges in Shanghai and Shenzhen. In the past decade, the Chinese stock market has completed a journey that took many countries over a century to cover; China's stock market today has capital approaching 3,705.6 billion yuan, 1,377 listed companies and 72.16 million investors.

The Chinese stock market has promoted the reform of government-owned corporations and the change of their systems, and enabled a stable transition between the two systems. On the strength of the stock market in the past decade, many large state-owned enterprises have realized system change.

The change also has stimulated medium and small-sized state-owned enterprises to adopt the shareholding system, thus solving the most important issue - the system problem - during the transition from planned to a market economy. As for ordinary citizens, bank deposit is not the only way to put their money, the stock market has become one of the most important channels for investment.

Methods of stock trading are constantly being improved. Today, a network system for securities exchange and account settlement has been formed, with the Shanghai and Shenzhen exchanges as the powerhouse, radiating to all parts of the country. In 2004, China issued 123 kinds of A share, and 23 rights issues, collecting a total of 83.6 billion yuan; and 28 kinds of B and H shares, collecting a total of 67.5 billion yuan.

Development

As China's economy becomes more integrated with the rest of the world its financial system will become more in line with international practices.

China has also learnt from Hong Kong's financial system, with the help of the Hong Kong Monetary Authority.

Trade balance

China had a favorable balance of trade of US$32 billion in 2004 and US$38.7 billion in 2003. These amounts reflect the general course of a favorable trade balance during the previous eight years. In 1996 China's trade balance was US$12.2 billion, peaking at US$43.4 billion in 1998 but declining to US$24.1 billion by 2000 before starting its new increase.

Balance of payments

China's current account balance in 2004 was nearly US$68.7 billion. Added to this total was US$54.9 billion in foreign direct investment (exceeding that invested in the United States). When other investments, assets, and liabilities are brought into the calculation, the overall balance of payments was US$206.1 billion in 2004, compared with US$75.2 billion in 2002 and US$116.5 billion in 2003.

External debt

According to United Nations statistics for 2001, China's external and public, or publicly guaranteed, long-term debt had reached US$91.7 billion. China's debt had grown steadily during the 1990s, peaked at US$112.8 billion in 1997, and then declined annually thereafter. By 2004 China had US$618.5 billion in its international reserve account, 98.6 percent of which was from foreign exchange, not including the Bank of China's foreign exchange holdings.

Foreign aid and foreign investment

China is the recipient of bilateral and multilateral official development assistance and official aid to individual recipients. In 2003 it received US$1.3 billion in such disbursements, or about US$1 per capita. This total was down from the 1999 figures of US$2.4 billion and US$1.90 per capita. Some of this aid comes to China in the form of socioeconomic development assistance through the United Nations (UN) system. China received US$112 million in such UN assistance annually in 2001 and 2002, the largest portion coming from the UN Development Programme (UNDP).

China also obtains foreign capital through foreign loans, foreign direct investment (FDI), and other investment by foreign businesses. Since 1980 foreign businesses from more than 170 countries and regions have invested in Chinese joint-venture enterprises. Most joint-venture activities are located in coastal cities and increasing numbers in inland cities as well. Some 300 of the 500 top transnational companies in the world have invested in China, and foreign investments have become an important capital source for China's economic development. In 1999 FDI totaled US$40.3 billion. Between 1979 and 1999, cumulative FDI totaled US$305.9 billion, US$40.3 billion of which was invested in 1999 alone. In that year, China had approved the establishment of 342,000 foreign-funded enterprises, more than 100,000 of which have gone into operation. Contracted FDI reached nearly US$82.8 billion in 2002, US$115 billion in 2003, US$153.48 in 2004, and US$130.33 billion in the first nine months of 2005.

In 2007, China enacted a new law for corporate income tax which would unify the rates paid by foreign and domestic firms at 25 percent. Domestic firms used to pay 33 percent and foreign-funded firms 15 percent. Analysts say the overall impact on foreign direct investment would be limited due to China's relatively cheap labor and the promise of a huge market.

Currency and foreign exchange control

China's currency is the renminbi (RMB, "people's currency") or yuan. The interbank exchange rate on August 1, 2006, was US$1 = RMB7.98. The RMB is made up of 100 fen or 10 jiao. Coins are issued in denominations of one, two, and five fen; one and five jiao, and one RMB. Banknotes are issued in denominations of one, two, and five jiao; and one, two, five, 10, 50, and 100 RMB.

The Renminbi is issued and controlled solely by the People's Bank of China. RMB exchange rates are decided by the People's Bank of China and issued by the State Administration of Foreign Exchange, the latter exercising the functions and powers of exchange control.

In 1994, China reformed the foreign exchange system, combined the RMB exchange rates, adopted the bank exchange settlement system and set up a unified inter-bank foreign exchange market. On this basis, China included the foreign exchange business of the foreign-invested enterprises in the bank's exchange settlement system in 1996. On December 1, 1996, China formally accepted Article 8 of the Agreement on International Currencies and Funds, and realized RMB convertibility under the current account ahead of schedule. Meanwhile, China has been active in promoting bilateral currency exchange between ASEAN and China, Japan and the Republic of Korea (10+3). At the end of 2004, China's foreign exchange reserves reached US$609.9 billion and its share in the International Monetary Fund has risen from 11th to 8th place. The variety of financial businesses has been increasing steadily, and China has opened an array of new businesses to become integrated into the various aspects of modern international financial business, such as consumer credit, securities investment funds and insurance-linked investments.

Fiscal year

China's fiscal year follows the calendar year (January 1 to December 31).

Insurance

Main article: Insurance companies in China

China's insurance industry started to recover in 1980, after a 20 year standstill. In 1981, the People's Insurance Company of China was transformed from a government department into a specialized company, with branches or sub-branches in every part of China. 1988 witnessed the founding of the Ping An Insurance (Group) Company of China and the Pacific Insurance Company, both mainly active in the coastal areas. In 1996, the People's Insurance Company of China made a big step forward in transforming its administration and operational mode, in setting up a modern enterprise system, and integrating with the international market. The Insurance Law of 1985 and the founding of the China Insurance Regulatory Commission in 1988 provided the legal basis and specific rules for the operation of the insurance market. In 1980, China only had one insurance company; by 2004 there were 62, with a total revenue of premiums of 431.8 billion yuan, of which 100.4 billion were paid as compensation and payment.

See also

- Central Financial Work Commission
- Ministry of Finance of the People's Republic of China
- Financial services in the People's Republic of China
- Foreign exchange reserve of the People's Republic of China
- State Administration of Foreign Exchange
- China Investment Corporation, CITIC
- Panda bond
- Qualified Domestic Institutional Investor
- Hedge fund industry in China
- List of asset management companies of the People's Republic of China
- China Securities Journal
- History of banking in China

People

- K. P. Chen

References

Reference sources

- Gregory C. Chow [1] (2007). *China's Economic Transformation*. Blackwell. ISBN 1405156244
- Cecil R. Dipchand, Zhang Yichun, Ma Mingjia (1994). *The Chinese Financial System*. Greenwood Press. ISBN 0313292825
- Franklin Allen, Jun Qian, Meijun Qian (2007) China's Financial System: Past, Present, and Future [2], in *China's Great Economic Transformation*, edited by Thomas G. Rawski and Loren Brandt. Cambridge University Press. ISBN 0521885574

Further reading

- Twitchett, D., *Financial Administration under the Tang Dynasty* (Cambridge Univ Press, 1970)
- Pitfalls of a State-Dominated Financial System: The Case of China [3] - Genevieve Boyreau-Debray, Shang-Jin Wei

External links

- China Society for Finance and Banking [4]
- Institute of Finance [5] of the People's Bank of China
- China Finance Association [6]
- China Center for Financial Research [7] of Tsinghua University

Chinese currency

> **This article contains Chinese text.** Without proper rendering support, you may see question marks, boxes, or other symbols instead of Chinese characters.

The **Renminbi** (Chinese: 人民币) is the official **currency** of the **People's Republic of China** (PRC). It is the legal tender in mainland China, but not in Hong Kong and Macau. It is abbreviated as RMB, and the units for the Renminbi are the Yuan (元), Jiao (角), and Fen (分): 1 Yuan = 10 Jiao = 100 Fen. Fen have almost disappeared, so the coins in circulation are one yuan, five jiao, and one jiao. Banknotes range from one yuan to one hundred yuan, and vary both in size and color.

Hong Kong and Macau have their own monetary policies and currencies, the Hong Kong dollar and the Macanese pataca, respectively, that may not necessarily be compatible with the renminbi.

Han Dynasty cash coin

Currency of some type has been used in China since the New Stone Age. The Chinese also invented paper money in the 9th century.

Early history

Ancient currencies

Cowry shells are believed to be the earliest form of currency used in Central China, about 3000 to 4500 years ago. In the Chinese writing system, the traditional characters for 'goods' (貨), 'buy/sell' (買/賣), and 'monger' (販), in addition to various other words relating to 'exchange', all contain the radical '貝', which is the pictograph for shell. (Simplification changed 貝 to 贝.) However, the extent of the circulation of shells as currency is still unknown, and barter trade was supposed to dominate in the market. But copies of these shells made out of bone, wood, stone, lead and copper are common enough to suppose a trade system in them was used.

Bronzed shells were found in the Ruins of Yin, the old capital of Shang Dynasty (BC 1500-BC 1046). Bronze became a universal currency in the Zhou Dynasty.

The Chinese seemed to invent the first metal coins before 900 BC, in a tomb near Anyang. At that time, the coin itself was a mock of more earlier used cowry shells, so it was named as Bronze shell.

During the Warring States Period, from the 5th century BC to 221 BC, Chinese money was in the form of bronze objects that were of three main types. The Zhou, the Wei (魏), the Han (韓) and the Qin (秦) all used coins shaped like a spade (*bu*). The Qi (齊) used money in the shape of a knife (*dao*). The Zhao (趙) and the Yan (燕) used knife money before switching over to spade money roughly half way through the Warring States period. The Chu (楚) used money in the forms of "ant nose" coins (*yibi*).

Imperial China

As part of the Unification of China, Qin Shi Huang (Chinese: 秦始皇; pinyin: *Qín Shǐ Huáng*, 260 BC – 210 BC) abolished all other forms of local currency and introduced a national uniform copper coin based on the coins previously used by Qin. These coins were round with a square hole in the middle which remained the common design for most Chinese copper coins until the 20th century. Due to the low value of an individual coin, the Chinese have traditionally strung a nominal thousand copper coins onto a piece of string. However government taxes were levied in both coins and in products such as rolls of silk. Salaries were also paid in both the Qin Dynasty and Han dynasties in "stones" (石, *dàn*) of grain.

During the early Song dynasty (Chinese: 宋, 960–1279), China again reunited the currency system displacing coinages from ten or so independent states. Among pre-Song coins, the northern states tended to prefer copper coins. The southern states tended to use lead or iron coins with Sichuan using its own heavy iron coins which continued to circulate for a short period into the Song dynasty. By 1000, unification was complete and China experienced a rapid period of economic growth. This was reflected in the growth of coining. In 1073, the peak year for minting coins in the Northern Song, the government produced an estimated six million strings containing a thousand copper coins each. The Northern Song is thought to have minted over two hundred million strings of coins which were often exported to Inner Asia, Japan, and South-East Asia, where they often formed the dominant form of coinage. Song merchants rapidly adopted forms of paper currency starting with promissary notes in Sichuan called "flying money" (*feiqian*). These proved so useful the state took over production of this form of paper money with the first state-backed printing in 1024. By the 12th century, various forms of paper money had become the dominant forms of currency in China and were known by a variety of names such as *jiaozi, qianyin, kuaizi,* or *guanzi*.

The Mongol-founded Yuan dynasty (Chinese: 元, 1271–1368) also attempted to use paper currency. Unlike the Song dynasty, they created a unified, national system that was not backed by silver or gold. The currency issued by the Yuan was the world's first fiat currency, known as Chao. The Yuan government attempted to prohibit all transactions in or possession of silver or gold, which had to be turned over to the government. Inflation in 1260 caused the government to replace the existing paper currency with a new paper currency in 1287, but inflation caused by undisciplined printing remained a problem for the Yuan court until the end of the Dynasty.

The early Ming dynasty (Chinese: 明; pinyin: *Míng*, 1368–1644) also attempted to use paper currency in the early re-unification period. This currency also experienced rapid inflation and issues were suspended in 1450 although notes remained in circulation until 1573. It was only in the very last years of the Ming dynasty when Li Zicheng threatened Beijing in 1643 and 1644 that printing took place again. For most of the Ming China had a purely private system of currency for all important transactions. Silver, which flowed in from overseas, began to be used as a currency in the Far South province of Guangdong where it spread to the lower Yangzi region by 1423 when it became legal tender for payment of taxes. Provincial taxes had to be remitted to the capital in silver after 1465, salt producers had to pay in silver from 1475 and corvée exemptions had to be paid in silver from 1485. The Chinese demand for silver was partially met by Spanish imports from the Americas, in particular Potosi Wikipedia:WikiProject Disambiguation/Fixing links in Peru and Mexico, after the Spanish became established at Manila in 1571. However the silver was not minted. It circulated as ingots (known as sycee or *yuanbao*) which weighed a nominal *liang* (about 36 grammes) although purity and weight varied from region to region. The *liang* was often referred to by Europeans by the Malay term *tael*.

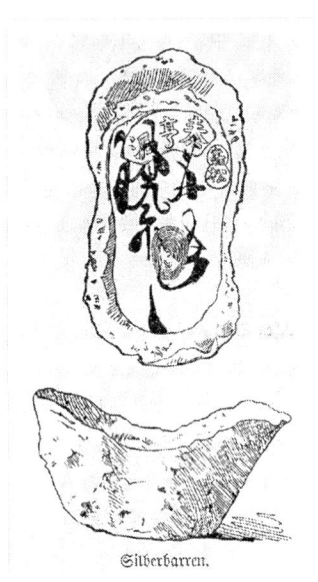

Silver sycee (*yuanbao*) ingots

Late Imperial China maintained both a silver and a copper currency system. The copper system was based on the copper cash (wen). The silver system had several units which by the Qing Dynasty were: 1 tael = 10 mace = 100 candareens = 1000 li (silver cash).

In 1889, the Chinese yuan was introduced at par with the Mexican Peso and was subdivided into 10 jiao (角, not given an English name, cf. *dime*), 100 fen (分, *cents*), and 1000 wen (文, *cash*). The yuan was equivalent to 7 mace and 2 candareens (or 0.72 tael) and, for a time, coins were marked as such in English.

The earliest issues were silver coins produced at the Kwangtung mint in denominations of 5 fen, 1, 2 and 5 jiao and 1 yuan. Other regional mints were opened in the 1890s producing similar coins. Copper coins in denominations of 1, 2, 5, 10 and 20 wen were also issued. The central government began issuing its own coins in the yuan currency system in 1903. Banknotes were issued in yuan denominations from the 1890s by several local and private banks, along with the "Imperial Bank of China" and the "Hu Pu Bank" (later the "Ta-Ch'ing Government Bank"), established by the Imperial government.

Republic of China

Silver coins

The Republic of China was founded after the Xinhai Revolution toppled the Qing Dynasty. The Nanjing Provisional Government urgently needed to issue military currency for use in place of the previous Qing currency. Successively, each province declared independence from the Qing and issued their own military currency. In 1914, the National Currency Ordinance established the Silver Dollar as the national currency of the Republic of China. Although designs changed compared with Imperial era coins, the sizes and metals used in the coinage remained mostly unchanged until the 1930s. The majority of regional mints closed during the 1920s and 1930s, although some continued until 1949. From 1936, the central government issued copper ½, 1 and 2 fen coins, nickel (later cupro-nickel) 5, 10 and 20 fen and ½ yuan coins. Aluminium 1 and 5 fen pieces were issued in 1940.

Unfortunately, the 1920s and 1930s saw the price of silver appreciate in the international market. This led to a massive efflux of silver out of China and the looming prospect of the collapse of the national currency. It became evident that China could not retain the Silver Standard. The situation was exacerbated by the multitude of commercial, provincial and foreign banks issuing currencies all at different values.

Legal tender

In 1935, the Central Government enacted currency reforms to limit currency issuance to four major government controlled banks: the Bank of China, Central Bank of China, Bank of Communications and later the Farmers Bank of China. The circulation of Silver Dollar coins was prohibited, and private ownership of silver was banned. A new currency issued in its place was known as 法幣 (Pinyin: fǎbì) or "Legal Tender".

Customs gold units

Main article: Chinese customs gold unit

Customs Gold Units (關金圓, pinyin: guānjīnyuán) were issued by the Central Bank of China to facilitate payment of duties on imported goods. Unlike the National Currency which suffered from hyperinflation, the CGUs were pegged to the U.S. Dollar at 1 CGU = US$0.40.

Unfortunately, the peg was removed in 1935 and the bank allowed CGUs to be released for general use. Already awash with excessive paper currency, the CGUs only added to rampant hyperinflation.

1945–1948

After the defeat of Japan in 1945, the Central Bank of China issued a separate currency in the northeast to replace those issued by puppet banks. Termed "東北九省流通券" (pinyin:Dōngběi jiǔ shěng liútōngquàn), it was worth approximately 10 times more than fǎbì circulating elsewhere. It was replaced in 1948 by the Gold Yuan. Northeastern Provinces Yuan was an attempt to isolate certain regions of China from the hyperinflation that plagued the fǎbì currency.

Gold Yuan

The onset of World War II saw a sharp devaluation of the fǎbì currency. This was largely due to unrestrained issuance of the currency to fund the war effort. After the defeat of Japan and the return of the Kuomintang Central Government, a further reform was instituted in August 1948 in response to hyperinflation. The Gold Yuan Certificate replaced the fǎbì at the rate of 1 Gold Yuan = 3 million Yuan fǎbì = US$0.25. The Gold Yuan was nominally set at 0.22217g of gold. However, the currency was never actually backed by gold and hyperinflation continued.

1949–2000

Finally, in 1949, the Kuomintang again announced a reform with the introduction of the Silver Yuan Certificate, returning China to the Silver Standard. The Silver Yuan would be exchanged at 1 Silver Yuan = 100 million Gold Yuan and was backed by Silver Dollars minted by the Central Mint of China.

This currency was short-lived, as the Communist Party of China soon gained control of the Mainland provinces. It was replaced by currency issued by the People's Bank of China which was less prone to inflation.

After the retreat of the Kuomintang to Taiwan, the Silver Yuan remained the de jure legal currency of account of the Republic of China. This was despite the fact that only Taiwan Dollars issued by the Bank of Taiwan were circulating in areas controlled by the ROC. After a currency reform in 1949 created the New Taiwan Dollar, the statutory exchange rate was set at 1 Silver Yuan = NT$3.

An amendment was passed in 2000 to make the New Taiwan Dollar the official legal currency of the Republic of China.

Taiwan Dollar

The Bank of Taiwan was originally established by the Japanese in 1899 whilst Taiwan was under Japanese administration. The Bank issued Taiwanese Yen which was pegged to the Japanese Yen. After the retrocession of Taiwan to the Republic of China, the new Bank of Taiwan was allowed to continue issuing its own currency. Called "Taiwan Dollar", it replaced the Taiwanese Yen at par. This was an attempt by the Kuomintang to prevent hyperinflation affecting Fǎbì from affecting Taiwan.

Chinese currency

However, mismanagement by the Governor-General Chen Yi meant that the Taiwan Dollar also suffered depreciation. It was replaced by the New Taiwan Dollar in 1949 at the rate of 40,000 to 1.

Japanese Occupation Money

The Japanese Imperial Government issued currency through several means during their occupation of China.

Manchuria

At the time of invasion of China's northeast in 1931, multiple currencies were circulating. These included local provincial issues, the Kuomintang fabi and Yen currencies issued by the Bank of Chosen and the Bank of Taiwan.

After the puppet state of Manchukuo was created, the Japanese founded the Central Bank of Manchou on July 1, 1932 in Changchun (長春), then known as Hsinking (新京). While the bank provided commercial functions, it also acted as a central bank and issuer of currency. The Manchukuo yuan was initially set at 1 Manchukuo yuan = 23.91g silver, but became pegged to the Japanese Yen at 1:1 in 1935 after Japan left the gold standard. The currency lasted until the end of World War II. It was replaced by the Northeastern Provinces Yuan issued by the Central Bank of China.

Inner Mongolia

Prior to Japanese occupation, the predominant bank of China's northern provinces (including Suiyuan, Chahar and Shanxi) was the Charhar Commercial Bank. When the Japanese invaded, the bank evacuated the area taking all of its capital and all unissued currency. The Japanese military government quickly established the Channan Commercial Bank to replace its note issuing functions.

With the formation of Mengchiang puppet state, the authorities established the Bank of Mengchiang which amalgamated the Channan Commercial Bank with three other smaller regional banks. The Bank of Mengchiang issued Mengchiang Yuan from 1937 which was pegged to the Japanese Military Yen and Japanese Yen at par.

Coin issued in 1938 by the Bank of Mengchiang

Collaborationist Governments

The Japanese managed to establish two collaborationist regimes during their occupation in China. In the north, the "Provisional Government of China" (中華民國臨時政府) based in Beijing established the Federal Reserve Bank of China (中國聯合準備銀行, pinyin: Zhōngguó liánhé zhǔnbèi yínháng). The FRB issued notes in 1938 at par with Kuomintang fabi. Although initially equivalent, the Japanese banned the use of Nationalist currency in 1939 and set arbitrary exchange rates in favour of the FRB Yuan. The FRB Yuan was replaced by Kuomintang fabi in 1945 at 1 FRB Yuan = 0.2 fabi.

The Wang Jingwei government in Nanjing established the collaborationist Nanjing Reformed Government (南京維新政府) in 1938. This was later reorganised into the Nanjing National Government (南京國民政府) in 1940. They established the Central Reserve Bank of China (中央儲備銀行, pinyin: Zhōngyāng chúbèi yínháng) which began issuing CRB Yuan in 1941. Although initially set at par with the Nationalist fabi, it also was arbitrarily changed to equal 0.18 Japanese Military Yen. In 1945, it was also replaced by the Nationalist fabi at 1 CRB Yuan = 0.005 fabi.

Japanese Military Yen

The Japanese Military Yen was distributed in many regions throughout East Asia under Japanese occupation. Initially, these were issued as payment to soldiers. The intention was the pay out an infinite amount of Military Yen which could not be converted into Japanese Yen and therefore could not cause inflation in Japan. However, the destructive effects on local East Asian economies was not a major concern.

The currency became legal tender in China commencing in 1937. It was later replaced by issues from puppet banks. However, the currency remained in force in Hong Kong between 1941 and 1945. Initially set at HK$2 = JMY1, the Hong Kong Dollar was largely preferred by locals and hoarded away. In order to address this, the Japanese government made possession of Hong Kong Dollar illegal in 1943 and required a conversion to JMY at 4 to 1.

When the British returned to Hong Kong in 1945, Japanese Military Yen was changed back into Hong Kong Dollars at 100 JMY to HK$1.

People's Republic of China

Renminbi

Main article: Renminbi

The Communist Party of China gained control of large areas of the northeast of China during 1948 and 1949. Although several regional banks were established, they were united in December 1948 as the People's Bank of China. Established in Shijiazhuang, the new bank took over currency issuance in areas controlled by the Communist Party.

After the promulgation of the People's Republic of China, there was a brief period where 100,000 Gold Yuan could be exchanged for 1 Yuan Renminbi.

Renminbi notes were issued in 12 denominations: 1, 5, 10, 20, 50, 100, 200, 500, 1000, 5000, 10000, and 50000 yuan. These denominations were subdivided into 62 styles. After adjusting the currency value with ratio 1:10000 in March 1955, the second edition of Renminbi were issued in 12 denominations, including 1 fen, 2 fen, 5 fen, 1 jiao, 2 jiao, 5 jiao, 1 yuan, 2 yuan, 3 yuan, 5 yuan and 10 yuan.

RMB200 note issued in 1949

The People's Republic of China began issuing aluminum coins in December 1957, in denominations of 1, 2 and 5 fen. From 1961, China outsourced the printing of 3, 5 and 10 yuan notes to the Soviet Union.

The fifth and latest editions of the currency of the People's Republic of China have been produced since 1 October 1999. Notes have been produced in 8 denominations: old types of 1 fen, 2 fen and 5 fen, as well as new issues depicting Mao Zedong: 5 yuan, 10 yuan, 20 yuan, 50 yuan and 100 yuan. In 2004, a 1 yuan note depicting Mao Zedong first came into production. Since 1999, coins have been produced in denominations of 1 fen, 2 fen, 5 fen, 1 jiao, 5 jiao and 1 yuan.

Foreign Exchange Certificates

The Bank of China on the Mainland was chartered as the main foreign trade and exchange bank. Foreign visitors to China were required to conduct transactions with Foreign Exchange Certificates issued by the Bank of China between 1979 and 1994. These have been abolished, and all transactions now occur in Renminbi.

See also

- Ancient Chinese coinage
- Chinese Silver Panda
- Economic history of China

References

Chinese

English	Hanzi
Dai Jianbing (1993). Modern Chinese Paper Money. China Financial Publishing House, Beijing.	戴建兵：《中国近代纸币》，中国金融出版社1993年版。
Dai Jianbing (1994). Modern Chinese Commercial Bank Paper Money. China Financial Publishing House, Beijing.	戴建兵：《中國近代商業銀行纸币》，中国金融出版社1994年版。

English

- Chang, H.: The Silver Dollars and Taels of China. Hong Kong, 1981 (158 pp. illus.). Including Subsidiary Notes on "The Silver Dollars and Taels of China" Hongkong, 1982 (40 pp. illus.).
- Cribb, Joe: A Catalogue of Sycee in the British Museum. Chinese Silver Currency Ingots c. 1750–1933. British Museum Press, London, 1992.
- Dong Wenchao: An Overview of China's Gold & Silver Coins of Past Ages – the Gold and Silver Coins and Medals of Modern China. Beijing 1992,
- Kann, Edward: Illustrated Catalog of Chinese Coins. Second edition. Mint Productions, Inc., New York, 1966 (476 pp. and 224 plates).
- Lu, W.H. (editor): Paper Money Catalogue of the People's Republic of China (1948–1998). Paper Money Catalogue of Macau (1907–1998). International Stamp and Coin Sdn. Bhd., Kuala Lumpur, n.d. (50 plus 32 pp., colour illus.).
- Peng Xinwei: A Monetary History of China (Zhongguo Huobi Shi). Translated by Edward H. Kaplan. Two volumes. Western Washington University, Bellingham, 1993.
- Shanghai Museum: Chinese Coin Gallery. Shanghai, n.d. (1990s). In Chinese and English.
- Shanghai Museum: Chinese Numismatic Gallery. Shanghai, n.d. (1990s). In Chinese and English (44pp., colour illus.).
- Smith, Ward D. and Matravers, Brian: Chinese Bank Notes. Shirjeh Publications, Menlo Park, California, 1970.
- Ting Fu-Pao: A Catalog of Ancient Chinese Coins (Including Japan, Forra & Annan). Taipei, n.d. (no pagination, illus.).

- White, Byron R. and White, Marjorie: A Comprehensive Finding List of Chinese Cash 618 AD to 1912 AD. Together with Lochhart's Listing of the Chinese Dynasties. Bai Publications, USA, n.p., 1976. (no pagination).

French

- Thierry, François: Monnaies d´extrême Orient, I Chine. Administration des Monnaies et Médailles. Les Collections Monétaires. Paris, 1986.

German

- Staack, Herbert: Die Lochmünzen Chinas. Published by the author, Berlin, 1988.
- Schlösser, Richard: Chinas Münzen. Erläutert an der Sammlung im Missions-Museum des Franziskanerklosters zu Dorsten in Westfalen. Franziskus-Druckerei, Werl (Westfalen), 1935 (114 pp. and 20 plates).
- Patalas, Wilhelm: Chinesische Münzen. Von ihrem Ursprung bis 1912. Ein Bestimmungsbuch. Klinkhardt & Biermann, Braunschweig, 1965 (156 pp, illus.).

Spanish

- Cossio, José L.: Monedas Antiguas de China. Publicaciones de la Sociedad Numismática de México, Mexico City, 1963. (16 pp. and 53 plates).

Romanized Russian

- Bykow, Alexeji Andrevich.: Monety Kitaja. Leningrad, 1969 (78 pp. and 23 plates).

Central Financial Work Commission

The **Central Financial Work Commission** (CFWC, *Zhongyang jinrong gongzuo weiyuanhui*) was created in 1998 to supervise the Chinese financial system on behalf of the Chinese Communist Party (CCP) and to prevent deviations on the part of CCP-appointed managers. It was proposed by the staff of the Central Finance and Economics Leading Group (CFELG) and pursued by Zhu Rongji with the support of Jiang Zemin and Li Peng. The CFCW had political supervision and personnel authority over the People's Bank of China and state financial regulatory bodies, as well as over China's most important national firms.

The Central Financial Work Commission consisted of several core departments: the Organization Department, the Financial Discipline Inspection Work Commission and the Department of Supervisory Board Work. It had about 200 officials and was ranked above ministerial level. Its operations were supervised by Executive Deputy Secretary Yan Haiwang, and it regularly reported directly to its head, CFCW Secretary Wen Jiabao, who concurrently served as a member of the Politburo and as vice-premier in charge of work on finance. Wen was CFCW Secretary from 1998 until the organization's demise in 2002. Some have interpreted this to be evidence of the fact that Wen was being groomed and tested for the position of premier, since he clearly lacked the experience to run effective financial policy. The CFCW facilitated comprehensive personnel reshuffles during its existence, particularly in 1999 and 2000.

The CFWC was abolished at the 16th Party Congress in late 2002, and most of its functions were transferred to state regulatory bodies. Sebastian Heilmann argues that the CFCW was created as part of a strategy to stop the breakdown of the hierarchies in the Chinese financial industry and to restore central policy decisiveness in the aftermath of the Asian financial crisis. While this strategy was successful in establishing centralized supervision and homogenizing financial regulation, it failed to produce market-driven incentive structures for financial executives and clashed with nascent forms of corporate governance emerging in China. According to Heilmann, the dissolution of the CFCW constituted a major redefinition of Party control in economic regulation.

See also

- Economy of the People's Republic of China

China's Industry and Labor Conditions

Industry of China

Main article: Economy of the People's Republic of China

Industry produced 53.7 percent of China's gross domestic product (GDP) in 2005. Industry (including mining, manufacturing, construction, and power) contributed 52.9 percent of GDP in 2008 and occupied 2.5 percent of the workforce. The manufacturing sector produced 44.1 percent of GDP in 2004 and accounted for 11.3 percent of total employment in 2006. China is the world's leading manufacturer of chemical fertilizers, cement, and steel. Prior to 1978, most output was produced by state-owned enterprises. As a result of the economic reforms that followed, there was a significant increase in production by enterprises sponsored by local governments, especially townships and villages, and, increasingly, by private entrepreneurs and foreign investors, but by 1990 the state sector accounted for about 70 percent of output. By 2002 the share in gross industrial output by state-owned and state-holding industries had decreased with the state-run enterprises themselves accounting for 46 percent of China's industrial output.

As part of US$586 billion economic stimulus package of November 2008, the government plans to further subsidize in particular high-tech and service sector industries. [1]

History

Main article: Industrial history of China

Industry and construction account for about 48% of China's GDP. China ranks second worldwide in industrial output. It is expected to rank first sometime in 2011. Major industries include mining and ore processing; iron and steel; aluminum; coal; machinery; armaments; textiles and apparel; petroleum; cement; chemical; fertilizers; food processing; automobiles and other transportation equipment including rail cars and locomotives, ships, and aircraft; consumer products including footwear, toys, and electronics; telecommunications and information technology. China has become a preferred destination for the relocation of global manufacturing facilities. Its strength as an export platform has contributed to incomes and employment in China. The state-owned sector still accounts for about 40% of GDP. In recent years, authorities have been giving greater attention to the management of state assets — both in the financial market as well as among state-owned-enterprises — and progress has been noteworthy.

Since the founding of the People's Republic, industrial development has been given considerable attention. Among the various industrial branches the machine-building and metallurgical industries have received the highest priority. These two areas alone now account for about 20-30 percent of the total gross value of industrial output. In these, as in most other areas of industry, however, innovation has generally suffered at the hands of a system that has rewarded increases in gross output rather than improvements in variety, sophistication and quality. China, therefore, still imports significant quantities of specialized steels. Overall industrial output has grown at an average rate of more than 10 percent per year, having surpassed all other sectors in economic growth and degree of modernization. Some heavy industries and products deemed to be of national strategic importance remain state-owned, but an increasing proportion of lighter and consumer-oriented manufacturing firms are privately held or are private-state joint ventures.

Structure

Since the 1950s, the trend away from the agricultural sector toward industrialisation has been dramatic, and is a result of both policy changes and free market mechanisms. During the 1950s and 1960s, heavy industry received most attention and consequently grew twice as rapidly as agriculture. After the reforms of 1978, more attention to the agricultural sector as well as a move away from heavy industry toward light resulted in agricultural output almost doubling with only marginal increases for industry.

Before 1978, state-owned and collectively-owned enterprises represented 77.6 percent and 22.4 percent respectively of China's exclusively public-ownership economy. The policy of reform and opening-up has given extensive scope to the common development of various economic sectors. Individual and private industrial enterprises and enterprises have mushroomed with investment from outside mainland China.

Domestically, modernisation and economic growth has been the focus of the reformist policies introduced by Deng Xiaoping, and in attempting to achieve this, the leadership has implemented the Four Modernizations Program that lays special emphasis on the fields of agriculture, industry, education, science and technology, and defence.

In the countryside, the "responsibility system" has been implemented and basically represents a return to family farming. Under this system, families lease land for a period of up to thirty years, and must agree to supply the state an agreed quota of grain or industrial crops at a fixed low cost in return. The remaining surplus can either be sold to the state or on the free market. As a result, peasants have been increasing their agricultural output in response to these incentives.

Together with the responsibility system, there have also been a number of reforms relating to rural businesses — especially in the spheres of commerce and manufacturing. The increase in personal income bought about through the responsibility system has led to a burgeoning of small-scale enterprises that remain completely in private hands.

Reform of state-owned enterprises has always been the key link of China's economic restructuring. The Chinese government has made various attempts to solve the problem of chronic extensive losses in this sector and by now almost every state-owned enterprise has adopted the company system. After being transformed into joint stock companies, the economic benefit of the state-owned enterprises increased steadily and their overall strength and quality were remarkably enhanced, gaining continuously in their control, influence and lead in the whole national economy.

The role of free market forces has also been instrumental in altering China's sectoral make-up. After 1979, the forces of supply and demand meant that consumers could play a greater role in determining which crops would be planted. This had the effect of making more profitable the planting of such crops as fruit, vegetables and tea. As a consequence, however, traditional grain crops have suffered, as farmers prefer to plant the more profitable cash crops.

Increases in light industrial production and more profitable crops bought about by the loosening of market controls had not always been enough to satisfy consumer demand, which in turn lead to inflation. Rather than increased demand being met with increased supply, the manufacturing sector and economic infrastructure were still too underdeveloped to supply a population of over one billion people with the commodities they wanted or needed. Instead, a 'dual track' pricing system aose which had promoted arbitrage between official and free-market prices for the same commodities.

Inflation and the unavailability of consumer goods had made some commodities too expensive for ordinary Chinese workers, as well as resulting in a general decline in living standards. Another factor arising from inflation in China had been corruption among the higher echelons of the CCP. Managers of factories in regulated industries — usually high-level Party cadres — have been selling factory produce on the free market at grossly inflated prices. Inflation and corruption had become so embedded in the system by 1988, that the leadership was forced to take some drastic economic measures.

In response to the general economic malaise, Li Peng - Prime Minister — adopted several austerity measures in the middle of 1988. The primary goal of these measures was to reduce economic growth and included such measures as limiting joint ventures, curtailing capital investment, tightening fiscal and monetary controls, reimposing centralised control on local construction projects and cuts in capital investment.

China's eighth Five Year Plan - 1991 to 1995 - reflected the goals of slowing the economy down to a manageable level after the excesses of the late 1980s. The growth rate of GNP was planned to average 6% per annum, and government investment to be drawn away from national construction programs towards agriculture, transportation and communications.

However, the national economy also showed similar signs of stagnation. Although eighteen months of austerity measures had lowered inflation to 2.1%, after eighteen months of rising unemployment, stagnation of industrial output and a breakdown of the Chinese financial system because of debt defaults, the government was forced to loosen the economic screws in the mid-1990s.

Increased investment into capital construction programs and Township and Village Enterprises (TVEs) was the government's solution to reviving the economy. However, by mid-1991 signs re-emerged that the economy was about to overheat once again. Rises in industrial production within TVEs of 32% for the first half of 1991, refusal to heed calls for curbs on investment capital construction in the provinces as well as the re-emergence of double-digit inflation. The rapid growth of early 1991 indicated that the government was still going to have to struggle further with enforcing its economic policies.

The national economy had been characterised by a large share of industry — standing at 61.2% of total GDP in 1990 - with a smaller share of 24.4% devoted to agriculture and a much smaller service sector constituting only 14.4% of GDP. Such a constitution of GDP was a reflection of the Soviet influence of a planned economy since the 1950s. The dominance of the industrial sector in the PRC's GDP constitution has not always been the case however, and it has been largely through governmental intervention that this evolution took place.

In 2004, of the industrial added value created by all state-owned industrial enterprises and non-state industrial enterprises with annual turnover exceeding five million yuan, state-owned and state stock-holding enterprises accounted for 42.4 percent, collectively-owned enterprises 5.3 percent, the rest taken up by other non-public enterprises, including enterprises with investment from outside mainland China, and individual and private enterprises. The result is a dynamic juxtaposition of diversified economic elements.

In 2004, of Chinese enterprises ranking in the world's top 500, 14 enterprises of China's mainland were all state-owned. Of China's own top 500, 74 percent (370) were state-owned and state stock-holding enterprises, with assets of 27, 370 billion yuan and realizing profit of 266.3 billion yuan, representing 96.96 percent and 84.09 percent respectively of the top 500 corresponding values. Small and medium-sized enterprises and non-public enterprises have become China's main job creators. Private enterprises alone provided 50 percent of employment of the entire society.

Industrial output

China has achieved a rapid increase in the gross value of industrial output (used before China switched to GNP accounting in 1986), which, according to official Chinese statistics, rose by 13.3% annually between 1950 and 1979. The greatest sustained surge in growth occurred during the first decade, with the rate averaging 22% annually during 1949–60. During 1961–74, the yearly growth rate fell to about 6%, partly as a result of the disruptions brought on by the collapse of the Great Leap Forward (which accompanied the withdrawal of Soviet technicians in mid-1960) and of work stoppages and transportation disruptions during the Cultural Revolution. Growth averaged 10% from 1970 to 1980 and 10.1% from 1979 to 1985. Major policy reforms of 1984 further accelerated the pace of industrial growth, which reached 20.8% by 1988. After a brief retrenchment period in 1989–90 as government policies prioritized inflation control over other concerns, expansion of the country's industrial sector resumed apace, exceeding 20% in 1992 and 18% in 1994. Industrial output was officially up 13.4% in

1995, with state enterprises contributing the majority.

While approximately 50% of total industrial output still derives from the state-owned factories, a notable feature of China's recent industrial history has been the dynamic growth of the collectively owned rural township and village enterprise as well as private and foreign joint-venture sectors. Also apparent has been the spatial unevenness of recent industrial development, with growth concentrated mainly in Shanghai, the traditional hub of China's industrial activity, and, increasingly, a number of new economic centers along the southern coast. The coastal provinces of Jiangsu, Guangdong, Shandong, Shanghai and Zhejiang provinces together account for close to 33% of the country's total industrial output and most of its merchandise exports. One key factor in this industrial geography has been the government's establishment of several Special Economic Zones in Guangdong, Fujian and Hainan provinces, and its designation of over 14 "open coastal cities" where foreign investment in export-oriented industries was actively encouraged during the 1980s.

China's cotton textile industry is the largest in the world, producing yarn, cloth, woolen piece goods, knitting wool, silk, jute bags, and synthetic fibers. Labor-intensive light industries played a prominent role in the industrial boom of the late 1980s and early 1990s, accounting for 49% of total industrial output, but heavy industry and high technology took over in the late 1990s. In addition to garments and textiles, output from light industry includes footwear, toys, food processing, and consumer electronics. Heavy industries include iron and steel, coal, machine building, armaments, petroleum, cement, chemical fertilizers, and autos. High technology industries produce high-speed computers, 600 types of semiconductors, specialized electronic measuring instruments, and telecommunications equipment.

Since 1961, industry has been providing agriculture with farm machines, chemical fertilizers, insecticides, means of transportation, power, building materials, and other essential commodities. Handicraft cooperatives also have been busy making hand-operated or animal-drawn implements. Production of a variety of industrial goods has expanded, increasingly in order to supply the country's own expanding industrial base. In addition to fertilizers, the chemicals industry produces calcium carbide, ethylene, and plastics. Since 1963, great emphasis has been placed on the manufacture of transportation equipment, and China now produces varied lines of passenger cars, trucks, buses, and bicycles. In 1995, output included 1,452,697 motor vehicles (more than double the 1991 figure). Output for 2009 was over 13.7 million units. The industry underwent a major overhaul in the late 1990s in order to stimulate efficiency and production. Large numbers of joint ventures with foreign firms helped introduce new technology and management to the industry.

Machinery manufacturing

China's machinery manufacturing industry can provide complete sets of large advanced equipment, including large gas turbines, large pump storage groups, and nuclear power sets, ultra-high voltage direct-current transmission and transformer equipment, complete sets of large metallurgical, fertilizer and petro-chemical equipment, urban light rail transport equipment, and new papermaking and textile machinery. Machinery and transportation equipment have been the mainstay products of Chinese exports, as China's leading export sector for successive 11 years from 1996 to 2006. In 2006, the export value of machinery and transportation equipments reached 425 billion US dollars, 28.3 percent more than 2005..

Energy industry

See also: Energy policy of China

Thermal, hydro and nuclear power industries are the fastest growing of all industrial sectors. At the end of 2009, the installed capacity of generators totaled 874 million kW, and the total generated electricity came to 3.2 trillion kwh, ranking second in the world.

Power grid construction has entered its fastest ever development; main power grids now cover all the cities and most rural areas, with 501-kv grids beginning to replace 220-kv grids for inter-province and inter-region transmission and exchange operations. An international advanced control automation system with computers as the mainstay has been universally adopted, and has proved practical. Now China's power industry has entered a new era featuring large generating units, large power plants, large power grids, ultra-high voltage and automation.

Starting in the 1980s, China has invested hugely into creating a number of large-scale modern coal mines, contributing to the gradual increase of coal output, maintained at more than one billion tons annually since 1989. China now has the ability to design, construct, equip, and administer 10-million-ton opencast coalmines and large and medium-sized mining areas. China's coal washing and dressing technologies and abilities have constantly improved and coal liquefaction and underground gasification are being introduced.

Petroleum and natural gas are important energy resources. For eight years running from 1997 to 2004, annual crude oil output exceeded 160 million tons, ranking fifth in the world. Oil industry development has accelerated the growth of local economies and related industries, such as machinery manufacturing, iron and steel industries, transport and communications. In 1996, China's natural gas output surpassed 20 billion cu m, a figure that has increased steadily over the following years, reaching 41.49 billion cu m in 2004.

In 2004, China's nuclear-power-generated electricity topped 50 billion kwh, setting a record high. By 2020, China will build 36-million-kW nuclear power facilities, in addition to the 8.7-million-kW nuclear power generation capacity already in use and under construction.

To relieve the shortage of energy supplies that fetters China's economic growth, China is developing new energy resources, such as wind, solar, geothermal, and tidal power. Its abundant wind energy resources give China the potential for mass-produced wind power. Between 2001 and 2005, the government invested 1.5 billion yuan in the wind power industry. Some 200,000 small wind generators already play an important power generation role in agricultural and pastoral areas and according to government targets the national installed capacity of wind generators is to increase greatly. It is expected to add 18GW to the installed base of 20 GW by 2010. Given northern China's rich wind energy resources, its wind power industry has attracted domestic and overseas investment and Asia's largest wind power station, with an investment of 10 billion yuan and a capacity of one million kW, will be completed in Inner Mongolia before 2008. Meanwhile, in western China, with a radiation flux of three thousand kwh per day, solar energy has been widely utilized. Asia's largest demonstration base for solar heating and cooling technologies in Yuzhong County, Gansu Province, has become the training center of applied solar technologies for developing countries.

Automobile

Main article: Automobile industry in China

An example of an emerging heavy industry is automobile manufacture, which has soared during the reform period. In 1975 only 139,800 automobiles were produced annually, but by 1985 production had reached 443,377, then jumped to nearly 1.1 million by 1992 and increased fairly evenly each year up until 2001, when it reached 2.3 million. In 2002 production rose to nearly 3.3 million and then jumped again the next year to 4.4 million. Domestic sales have kept pace with production. After respectable annual increases in the mid- and late 1990s, sales soared in 18 the early 2000s, reaching 3 million automobiles sold in 2003. With some governmental controls in place, sales dipped to 2.4 million sold in 2004.

Sales automobiles and vans reached 13 million in 2010. So successful has China's automotive industry been that it began exporting car parts in 1999. China began to plan major moves into the automobile and components export business starting in 2005. A new Honda factory in Guangzhou was being built in 2004 solely for the export market and was expected to ship 30,000 passenger vehicles to Europe in 2005. By 2004, 12 major foreign automotive manufacturers had joint-venture plants in China. They produced a wide range of automobiles, minivans, sport utility vehicles, buses, and trucks. In 2003 China exported US$4.7 billion worth of vehicles and components, an increase of 34.4 percent over 2002. By 2004 China had become the world's fourth largest automotive vehicle manufacturer.

Steel

Concomitant with automotive production and other steel-consuming industries, China has been rapidly increasing its steel production. Iron ore production kept pace with steel production in the early 1990s but was soon outpaced by imported iron ore and other metals in the early 2000s. Steel production, an estimated 140 million tons in 2000, rose to more than 420 million tons by 2007.

Before the first five-year plan (1953–57), China had only one major steel center— Anshan, in the northeast—and several minor ones. All these produced 1.93 million tons of pig iron and 1.35 million tons of steel in 1952. By 1995, China was producing 92,970 million tons of crude steel and 101,700 million tons of pig iron. China had one trillion tons of confirmed coal reserves and an estimated five trillion tons of coal reserves and 48.7 billion tons of iron ore in 2000. Anshan continues to be the hub of the industry, but other huge steel complexes have been constructed at Baotou, Benxi (about 50 km east of Anshan), Taiyuan, Wuhan, and Ma'anshan (near Nanjing).

See also

- **Industries of China**

External links

- China Industry Association Network [2]
- China Enterprise Confederation & China Enterprise Directors Association [3]
- Chinese Industry & Commerce [4] An Annotated Directory of Internet Resources
- China Information Industry Net [5]
- China Business Information Center [6]

Labor relations in the People's Republic of China

As the Economy of the People's Republic of China has rapidly developed issues of labor relations have developed.

Background

One of the hallmarks of China's socialist economy was its promise of employment to all able and willing to work and job-security with virtually lifelong tenure. Reformers targeted the labor market as unproductive because industries were frequently overstaffed to fulfill socialist goals and job-security reduced workers' incentive to work. This socialist policy was pejoratively called the iron rice bowl.

"Help wanted" ads in Wuhan

In 1979–1980, the state reformed factories by giving wage increases to workers, which was immediately offset by sharply rising inflation rates of 6%–7%. In other words, although they were given more pay, their money was worth less and they could buy less, which meant they were poorer. The state remedied this problem, in part, by distributing wage subsidies.

The reforms also dismantled the iron rice bowl, which meant it witnessed a rise in unemployment in the economy. In 1979, immediately after the iron rice bowl was dismantled, there were 20 million unemployed people. Official Chinese statistics reveal that 4.2% of the total urban workforce was unemployed in 2004, although other estimates have reached 10%. As part of its newly developing social security legislation, China has an unemployment insurance system. At the end of 2003, more than 103.7 million people were participating in the plan, and 7.4 million laid-off employees had received benefits.

A 10-percent sample tabulation of census questionnaires from the 1982 census provided needed statistical data on China's working population and allowed the first reliable estimates of the labor force's size and characteristics. The quality of the data was considered to be quite high, although a 40-million-person discrepancy existed between the 10-percent sample and the regular employment statistics. This discrepancy can be explained by the combination of inaccurate employment statistics and varying methods of calculation and scope of coverage. The estimated mid-1982 labor force was 546 million, or approximately 54 percent of the total population. Males accounted for slightly more than half of the estimated labor force, and the labor force participation rates for persons age fifteen years and older were among the highest in the world.

The 10-percent sample showed that approximately three-fourths of the labor force worked in the agricultural sector. According to the National Bureau of Statistics, in the mid-1980s more than 120 million people worked in the nonagricultural sector. The sample revealed that men occupied the great majority of leadership positions. The average worker was about thirty years old, and three out of every four workers were under forty-five years of age. The working population had a low education level. Less than 40 percent of the labor force had more than a primary school education, and 30 percent were illiterate or semiliterate.

In mid-1982 the overall unemployment rate was estimated to be about 5 percent. Of the approximately 25 million unemployed, 12 million were men and 13 million were women. The unemployment rate was highest in the northeast and lowest in the south. The unemployment rates were higher than those of East Asian, Southeast Asian, and Pacific island countries for which data were available but were lower than the rates found in North America and Europe. Virtually all of the unemployed persons in cities and towns were under twenty years of age.

By the 1990s and 2000s, agriculture has remained the largest employer, though its proportion of the workforce has steadily declined; between 1991 and 2001 it dropped from about 60% to 40% of the total. The manufacturing labor force has also become smaller at a slower rate, partially because of reforms implemented at many of the state-run enterprises. Such reforms and other factors have increased unemployment and underemployment in both urban and rural areas. Women have been a major labor presence in China since the People's Republic was established. Some 40–45 percent of all women over age 15 are employed.

China's estimated employed labor force in 2005 totaled 791.4 million persons, about 60% of the total population. During 2003, 49% of the labor force worked in agriculture, forestry, and fishing; 22% in mining, manufacturing, energy, and construction industries; and 29% in the services sector and other categories. In 2004 some 25 million persons were employed by 743,000 private enterprises. Urban wages rose rapidly from 2004 to 2007, at a rate of 13 to 19% per year with average wages near $200/month in 2007.

All-China Federation of Trade Unions

The All-China Federation of Trade Unions (ACFTU) was established in 1925 to represent the interests of national and local trade unions and trade union councils. The ACFTU reported a membership of 130 million, out of an estimated 248 million urban workers, at the end of 2002. Chinese trade unions are organized on a broad industrial basis. Membership is open to those who rely on wages for the whole or a large part of their income, a qualification that excludes most agricultural workers. In theory, membership is not compulsory, but in view of the unions' role in the distribution of social benefits, the economic pressure to join is great. The lowest unit is the enterprise union committee. Individual trade unions also operate at the provincial level, and there are trade union councils that coordinate all union activities within a particular area and operate at county, municipal, and provincial levels. At the top of the movement is the ACFTU, which discharges its functions through a number of regional federations.

In theory the appropriate trade union organizations have been consulted on the level of wages as well as on wage differentials, but in practice their role in these and similar matters has been insignificant. They have not engaged in collective bargaining, as their principal duties have included assisting the party and promoting production. In fulfilling these tasks, they have had a role in enforcing labor discipline. From the point of view of the membership, the most important activities have concerned the social and welfare services. Thus, the unions have looked after industrial safety, organized social and cultural activities, and, provided services such as clinics, rest and holiday homes, hostels, libraries, and clubs. They also administer old-age pensions, workers' insurance, disability benefits, and other welfare schemes. More recently, however, reforms of the social security system have involved moving the responsibility for pensions and other welfare to the provinces.

Labor laws

Main articles: China Employment Law and Labor Contract Law of the People's Republic of China

In China there exist labor laws which, if fully enforced, would greatly alleviate common abuses such as not paying workers. In 2006, a new labor law was proposed and submitted for public comment. Enacted in 2008, the Labor Contract Law of the People's Republic of China permits collective bargaining in a form analogous to that standard in Western economies, although the only legal unions would continue to be those affiliated with the All-China Federation of Trade Unions, the Communist Party's official union organization. The new law has support from labor activists, but was opposed by some foreign corporations, including the American Chamber of Commerce and the European Chamber of Commerce. There is some expectation that the law would be enforced. In 2010 a substantial increase in labor related cases brought to court in 2008 was reported.

Foreign companies

An ongoing effort to organize Chinese operations of foreign companies succeeded in 2006 at Wal-Mart. The campaign is projected to include Eastman Kodak, Dell and other companies. It was reported in 2008 that problems with sweatshops persist. By Fall, 2008 it was apparent that union organizing efforts were widespread with emphasis on foreign corporations.

Honda strikes and other events in 2010

Main article: 2010 Chinese labour unrest

Honda

In May, 2010 a strike was permitted to proceed against a Honda transmission and parts plant employing 1,900 in Foshan. The strike, which began on May 17, 2010, has resulted in suspension of operations at 4 Honda assembly plants. The main issue appears to be money with a substantial raise being demanded. Wages at the plant currently average $150 a month, a rate somewhat low for the area. The workers involved are mostly young high school and vocational school graduates with no apparent political agenda. A 24% wage increase was offered by Honda which for many workers would be an increase of about 366 renminbi ($54) a month. News reports on June 5, 2010 reported settlement of the strike with a pay raise of about 34% and other benefits giving workers at the plant a wage of about 300 dollars a month. A second strike, this time at an exhaust-systems plant, also in Foshan, followed. And a third, at a Honda lock plant in Zhongshan, where workers demanded the right to form an independent union. The strike at the Zhongshan was broken in a few days by a combination of concessions and hiring replacement workers.

Foxconn

On June 1, 2010 it was announced by Foxconn Technology Group, a major manufacturer of electronic products for export, that they would increase wages by 30%. For example, a worker previously paid 900 renminbi ($131.77) will be paid 1,200 renminbi effective immediately. Foxconn had been plagued by worker shortages and a number of worker suicides. A few days later a further increase was announced raising wages of employees who have worked for the company for three months to $294 a month. It is believed by economic experts such as Andy Xie that there is ample scope for increased wages in China due to its superior infrastructure as compared to competing low wage alternatives.

Toyota

On June 18, 2010 there were news reports of strikes at two Toyota parts plants in Tianjin, both operated by a Chinese subsidiary Toyoda Gosei. On June 22, 2010 it was reported that a Toyota assembly plant had been closed due to a strike at a supplier.

Minimum wage increases and other events

Effective July 1, 2010 the minimum wage in Beijing was raised 20% to 960 renminbi ($140) a month. In Shenzhen the minimum wage will be increased to 1,100 renminbi, about $161 a month in July. In June, 2010 there were reports of several other incidents including one in which a government controlled ACFTU union was reported to be negotiating regarding wages with Kentucky Fried Chicken. On June 10, 2010 strikes were reported in 5 additional cities.

A copy-cat strike at a former state-owned, now privatized, textile factory in Pingdingshan, the Pingdingshan Cotton Textile Co., where workers with 20 years service toil for little more than $100 a month was reported on June 8, 2010 by *The Toronto Star*. According to the *Star* information about such strikes is not being publicized inside China as information about those involving foreign or Taiwanese owned factories is.

During the initial Honda strikes the media in China was permitted to report on them, but as strikes spread reporting was suppressed.

See also: Social welfare in China

See also

- China Labour Bulletin
- Hukou system

External links and further reading

- "Dismantling Factories in a Dreamweaver Nation" [1] analysis by Andy Xie Caing Online 06.07.2010
- "China's Shift From Cheap Labor Hard on All" [2] Associated Press article by Elaine Kurtenback in *Time* May. 31, 2010
- "Changes in China Could Raise Prices Worldwide" [3] News analysis by David Barboza in *The New York Times* June 7, 2010
- "After Suicides, Scrutiny of China's Grim Factories" [4] news analysis by David Barboza in *The New York Times* June 6, 2010
- "In China, Unlikely Labor Leader Just Wanted a Middle-Class Life" [5] article by David Barboza in *The New York Times* June 13, 2010

- "In China, Labor Movement Enabled by Technology" [6] article by David Barboza and Keith Bradsher in *The New York Times* June 16, 2010
- "A Night at the Electronics Factory" [7] article by David Barboza in *The New York Times* June 18, 2010
- "China's long march to high wages" [8] article by Michael Sheridan in *The Sunday Times*, *The London Times* June 13, 2010
- "As China Aids Labor, Unrest Is Still Rising [9] article by Edward Wong in *The New York Times* June 20, 2010
- China Labour Bulletin [10]
- Text of the Labor Contract Law of the People's Republic of China [11] includes supplementary materials

Article Sources and Contributors

People's Republic of China *Source*: http://en.wikipedia.org/?oldid=390031619 *Contributors*: Ohconfucius

Government of the People's Republic of China *Source*: http://en.wikipedia.org/?oldid=389699682 *Contributors*:

Constitution of the People's Republic of China *Source*: http://en.wikipedia.org/?oldid=389502706 *Contributors*: 1 anonymous edits

National People's Congress *Source*: http://en.wikipedia.org/?oldid=381484861 *Contributors*: Shenhemu

President of the People's Republic of China *Source*: http://en.wikipedia.org/?oldid=388198833 *Contributors*:

State Council of the People's Republic of China *Source*: http://en.wikipedia.org/?oldid=390308578 *Contributors*:

Central Military Commission (People's Republic of China) *Source*: http://en.wikipedia.org/?oldid=387907860 *Contributors*:

Supreme People's Court of the People's Republic of China *Source*: http://en.wikipedia.org/?oldid=379702681 *Contributors*: Tabletop

Economic history of China (pre-1911) *Source*: http://en.wikipedia.org/?oldid=388677480 *Contributors*: GrahamHardy

Economic history of modern China *Source*: http://en.wikipedia.org/?oldid=390089221 *Contributors*: 1 anonymous edits

Economic history of the People's Republic of China *Source*: http://en.wikipedia.org/?oldid=390441104 *Contributors*: 155ws

Economy of the People's Republic of China *Source*: http://en.wikipedia.org/?oldid=390302187 *Contributors*:

Great Leap Forward *Source*: http://en.wikipedia.org/?oldid=390287261 *Contributors*: C.J. Griffin

Chinese economic reform *Source*: http://en.wikipedia.org/?oldid=390168419 *Contributors*: Nev1

Grasping the large, letting go of the small *Source*: http://en.wikipedia.org/?oldid=323476093 *Contributors*: Joseph Solis in Australia

China Western Development *Source*: http://en.wikipedia.org/?oldid=386824677 *Contributors*: Clee7903

Northeast Area Revitalization Plan *Source*: http://en.wikipedia.org/?oldid=390510360 *Contributors*: Joseph Solis in Australia

Rise of Central China Plan *Source*: http://en.wikipedia.org/?oldid=379424435 *Contributors*: Hibernian

Third Front (China) *Source*: http://en.wikipedia.org/?oldid=381602117 *Contributors*: Everyking

Go Out policy *Source*: http://en.wikipedia.org/?oldid=375302426 *Contributors*: Joseph Solis in Australia

Chinese financial system *Source*: http://en.wikipedia.org/?oldid=390601807 *Contributors*: Beardfrun

Chinese currency *Source*: http://en.wikipedia.org/?oldid=383120219 *Contributors*:

Central Financial Work Commission *Source*: http://en.wikipedia.org/?oldid=313204864 *Contributors*:

Industry of China *Source*: http://en.wikipedia.org/?oldid=385694443 *Contributors*: Vrenator

Labor relations in the People's Republic of China *Source*: http://en.wikipedia.org/?oldid=385197900 *Contributors*: Fred Bauder

Image Sources, Licenses and Contributors

File:Zhongwen.svg *Source*: http://bibliocm.bibliolabs.com/mwAnon/index.php?title=File:Zhongwen.svg *License*: Public Domain *Contributors*: AnonMoos, Asoer, Hämbörger, King of Hearts, Kjoonlee, Rjanag, 6 anonymous edits

File:Flag of the People's Republic of China.svg *Source*: http://bibliocm.bibliolabs.com/mwAnon/index.php?title=File:Flag_of_the_People's_Republic_of_China.svg *License*: Public Domain *Contributors*: User:Denelson83, User:SKopp, User:Shizhao, User:Zscout370

File:National Emblem of the People's Republic of China.svg *Source*: http://bibliocm.bibliolabs.com/mwAnon/index.php?title=File:National_Emblem_of_the_People's_Republic_of_China.svg *License*: Public Domain *Contributors*: 澳门特別行政区立法会 / Assembleia Legislativa da Região Administrativa Especial de Macau / Legislative Assembly of the Macau Special Administrative Region

File:People's Republic of China (orthographic projection).svg *Source*: http://bibliocm.bibliolabs.com/mwAnon/index.php?title=File:People's_Republic_of_China_(orthographic_projection).svg *License*: unknown *Contributors*: -

File:PRCFounding.jpg *Source*: http://bibliocm.bibliolabs.com/mwAnon/index.php?title=File:PRCFounding.jpg *License*: Public Domain *Contributors*: Hou Bo

File:State organs of the People's Republic of China.svg *Source*: http://bibliocm.bibliolabs.com/mwAnon/index.php?title=File:State_organs_of_the_People's_Republic_of_China.svg *License*: unknown *Contributors*: User:CPHK

File:Tiananmen Square Visit.jpg *Source*: http://bibliocm.bibliolabs.com/mwAnon/index.php?title=File:Tiananmen_Square_Visit.jpg *License*: Creative Commons Attribution 2.0 *Contributors*: FlickrLickr, FlickreviewR, Gryffindor, Mamebacks, Olivier2

File:Hu Jintao Bush.jpg *Source*: http://bibliocm.bibliolabs.com/mwAnon/index.php?title=File:Hu_Jintao_Bush.jpg *License*: unknown *Contributors*: -

File:PRC Province Population2.svg *Source*: http://bibliocm.bibliolabs.com/mwAnon/index.php?title=File:PRC_Province_Population2.svg *License*: Creative Commons Attribution-Sharealike 3.0 *Contributors*: User:Arna11420

file:Longji terrace - 03.JPG *Source*: http://bibliocm.bibliolabs.com/mwAnon/index.php?title=File:Longji_terrace_-_03.JPG *License*: unknown *Contributors*: -

file:Everest North Face toward Base Camp Tibet Luca Galuzzi 2006 edit 1.jpg *Source*: http://bibliocm.bibliolabs.com/mwAnon/index.php?title=File:Everest_North_Face_toward_Base_Camp_Tibet_Luca_Galuzzi_2006_edit_1.jpg *License*: unknown *Contributors*: -

file:Sanya Sun Photo by Dale Preston.jpg *Source*: http://bibliocm.bibliolabs.com/mwAnon/index.php?title=File:Sanya_Sun_Photo_by_Dale_Preston.jpg *License*: unknown *Contributors*: Ppntori, Ö

File:Panda Cub from Wolong, Sichuan, China.JPG *Source*: http://bibliocm.bibliolabs.com/mwAnon/index.php?title=File:Panda_Cub_from_Wolong,_Sichuan,_China.JPG *License*: Public Domain *Contributors*: Original uploader was Sheilalau at en.wikipedia

File:J-10a zhas.png *Source*: http://bibliocm.bibliolabs.com/mwAnon/index.php?title=File:J-10a_zhas.png *License*: Creative Commons Attribution-Sharealike 3.0 *Contributors*: User:Retxham

File:Shanghai Stock Exchange Building.jpg *Source*: http://bibliocm.bibliolabs.com/mwAnon/index.php?title=File:Shanghai_Stock_Exchange_Building.jpg *License*: unknown *Contributors*: -

File:DengXiaoping.jpg *Source*: http://bibliocm.bibliolabs.com/mwAnon/index.php?title=File:DengXiaoping.jpg *License*: Public Domain *Contributors*: White House photo

Image:Country foreign exchange reserves minus external debt.png *Source*: http://bibliocm.bibliolabs.com/mwAnon/index.php?title=File:Country_foreign_exchange_reserves_minus_external_debt.png *License*: Creative Commons Attribution-Sharealike 3.0 *Contributors*: User:Peace01234

File:Shanghai - Nanjing Road.jpeg *Source*: http://bibliocm.bibliolabs.com/mwAnon/index.php?title=File:Shanghai_-_Nanjing_Road.jpeg *License*: GNU Free Documentation License *Contributors*: Kevyn, Lateiner, Mats214, Olivier2, P.B., Twthmoses, Zolo

Image:China Xichang Satellite Center - Tianlian I-01 Launch.jpg *Source*: http://bibliocm.bibliolabs.com/mwAnon/index.php?title=File:China_Xichang_Satellite_Center_-_Tianlian_I-01_Launch.jpg *License*: Public Domain *Contributors*: User:AAxanderr

File:Central Jingshi Expressway9.jpg *Source*: http://bibliocm.bibliolabs.com/mwAnon/index.php?title=File:Central_Jingshi_Expressway9.jpg *License*: GNU Free Documentation License *Contributors*: Original uploader was Naus at en.wikipedia

File:200908 China Railways CRH5 409.JPG *Source*: http://bibliocm.bibliolabs.com/mwAnon/index.php?title=File:200908_China_Railways_CRH5_409.JPG *License*: Creative Commons Attribution-Sharealike 3.0 *Contributors*: User:颐园新居

File:PRC Population Density.svg *Source*: http://bibliocm.bibliolabs.com/mwAnon/index.php?title=File:PRC_Population_Density.svg *License*: Public Domain *Contributors*: Bambuway (talk). Original uploader was Bambuway at en.wikipedia

File:Shanghai-pudong night.jpg *Source*: http://bibliocm.bibliolabs.com/mwAnon/index.php?title=File:Shanghai-pudong_night.jpg *License*: unknown *Contributors*: -

Image:Hong_Kong_Skyline_Restitch_-_Dec_2007.jpg *Source*: http://bibliocm.bibliolabs.com/mwAnon/index.php?title=File:Hong_Kong_Skyline_Restitch_-_Dec_2007.jpg *License*: Creative Commons Attribution 3.0 *Contributors*: User:Diliff

File:Guangzhou dusk 11-5-2008.png *Source*: http://bibliocm.bibliolabs.com/mwAnon/index.php?title=File:Guangzhou_dusk_11-5-2008.png *License*: unknown *Contributors*: -

File:Shenzhen night street.JPG *Source*: http://bibliocm.bibliolabs.com/mwAnon/index.php?title=File:Shenzhen_night_street.JPG *License*: unknown *Contributors*: -

File:Shenyang Skyline.png *Source*: http://bibliocm.bibliolabs.com/mwAnon/index.php?title=File:Shenyang_Skyline.png *License*: Creative Commons Attribution-Sharealike 3.0 *Contributors*: User:ASDFGHJ

File:Beijingcbd1.jpg *Source*: http://bibliocm.bibliolabs.com/mwAnon/index.php?title=File:Beijingcbd1.jpg *License*: unknown *Contributors*: -

File:Wuhan Skyline.jpg *Source*: http://bibliocm.bibliolabs.com/mwAnon/index.php?title=File:Wuhan_Skyline.jpg *License*: Creative Commons Attribution-Sharealike 3.0 *Contributors*: User:ASDFGHJ

File:Tianjin Skyline 2009.jpg *Source*: http://bibliocm.bibliolabs.com/mwAnon/index.php?title=File:Tianjin_Skyline_2009.jpg *License*: Creative Commons Attribution-Sharealike 3.0 *Contributors*: User:ASDFGHJ

Image Sources, Licenses and Contributors

File:Chongqing 2008.png *Source*: http://bibliocm.bibliolabs.com/mwAnon/index.php?title=File:Chongqing_2008.png *License*: Creative Commons Attribution-Sharealike 3.0 *Contributors*: User:ASDFGHJ

File:ChinaDemography.svg *Source*: http://bibliocm.bibliolabs.com/mwAnon/index.php?title=File:ChinaDemography.svg *License*: Creative Commons Attribution 3.0 *Contributors*: User:Demmo, User:Quilokos

File:Tsinghua Observatory.jpg *Source*: http://bibliocm.bibliolabs.com/mwAnon/index.php?title=File:Tsinghua_Observatory.jpg *License*: unknown *Contributors*: -

Image:Wind power plants in Xinjiang, China.jpg *Source*: http://bibliocm.bibliolabs.com/mwAnon/index.php?title=File:Wind_power_plants_in_Xinjiang,_China.jpg *License*: Creative Commons Attribution-Sharealike 2.0 *Contributors*: 林 慕尧 / Chris Lim from East Coast (东海岸), Singapore (新加坡)

File:Huxisanxiaotu.jpg *Source*: http://bibliocm.bibliolabs.com/mwAnon/index.php?title=File:Huxisanxiaotu.jpg *License*: unknown *Contributors*: Dominic Z., HéctorTabaré, Miuki, PericlesofAthens, 2 anonymous edits

Image:CircularMound.jpg *Source*: http://bibliocm.bibliolabs.com/mwAnon/index.php?title=File:CircularMound.jpg *License*: Creative Commons Attribution-Sharealike 2.5 *Contributors*: Ian and Wendy Sewell

File:Saint Sophia Cathedral Harbin.JPG *Source*: http://bibliocm.bibliolabs.com/mwAnon/index.php?title=File:Saint_Sophia_Cathedral_Harbin.JPG *License*: unknown *Contributors*: -

File:Chinese meal.jpg *Source*: http://bibliocm.bibliolabs.com/mwAnon/index.php?title=File:Chinese_meal.jpg *License*: Creative Commons Attribution-Sharealike 2.5 *Contributors*: Conscious, Donut, Giorgiomonteforti, Ogre, 2 anonymous edits

file:Pekin przedstawienie tradycjnego teatru chinskiego 7.JPG *Source*: http://bibliocm.bibliolabs.com/mwAnon/index.php?title=File:Pekin_przedstawienie_tradycjnego_teatru_chinskiego_7.JPG *License*: Creative Commons Attribution-Sharealike 3.0 *Contributors*: user:Kwz

File:Wangfujingbasketball.jpg *Source*: http://bibliocm.bibliolabs.com/mwAnon/index.php?title=File:Wangfujingbasketball.jpg *License*: unknown *Contributors*: -

Image:PD-icon.svg *Source*: http://bibliocm.bibliolabs.com/mwAnon/index.php?title=File:PD-icon.svg *License*: Public Domain *Contributors*: User:Duesentrieb, User:Rfl

Image:National Emblem of the People's Republic of China.svg *Source*: http://bibliocm.bibliolabs.com/mwAnon/index.php?title=File:National_Emblem_of_the_People's_Republic_of_China.svg *License*: Public Domain *Contributors*: 澳門特別行政區立法會 / Assembleia Legislativa da Região Administrativa Especial de Macau / Legislative Assembly of the Macau Special Administrative Region

Image:2008 NPC Seat Composition.png *Source*: http://bibliocm.bibliolabs.com/mwAnon/index.php?title=File:2008_NPC_Seat_Composition.png *License*: GNU Free Documentation License *Contributors*: ASDFGH (talk). Original uploader was ASDFGH at en.wikipedia

Image:GreatHall auditorium.jpg *Source*: http://bibliocm.bibliolabs.com/mwAnon/index.php?title=File:GreatHall_auditorium.jpg *License*: GNU Free Documentation License *Contributors*: Original uploader was AcidBomber at en.wikipedia

File:State_organs_of_the_People's_Republic_of_China.svg *Source*: http://bibliocm.bibliolabs.com/mwAnon/index.php?title=File:State_organs_of_the_People's_Republic_of_China.svg *License*: unknown *Contributors*: User:CPHK

file:National Emblem of the People's Republic of China.svg *Source*: http://bibliocm.bibliolabs.com/mwAnon/index.php?title=File:National_Emblem_of_the_People's_Republic_of_China.svg *License*: Public Domain *Contributors*: 澳門特別行政區立法會 / Assembleia Legislativa da Região Administrativa Especial de Macau / Legislative Assembly of the Macau Special Administrative Region

File:Supreme peoples court china.jpeg *Source*: http://bibliocm.bibliolabs.com/mwAnon/index.php?title=File:Supreme_peoples_court_china.jpeg *License*: unknown *Contributors*: -

File:Golden canteen with dragon, Ming Dynasty.jpg *Source*: http://bibliocm.bibliolabs.com/mwAnon/index.php?title=File:Golden_canteen_with_dragon,_Ming_Dynasty.jpg *License*: unknown *Contributors*: -

File:Yan State sword coins.JPG *Source*: http://bibliocm.bibliolabs.com/mwAnon/index.php?title=File:Yan_State_sword_coins.JPG *License*: Creative Commons Attribution-Sharealike 3.0 *Contributors*: User:BrokenSphere

File:Woven silk, Western Han Dynasty.jpg *Source*: http://bibliocm.bibliolabs.com/mwAnon/index.php?title=File:Woven_silk,_Western_Han_Dynasty.jpg *License*: unknown *Contributors*: Chinese artist

File:Pottery dog 1.JPG *Source*: http://bibliocm.bibliolabs.com/mwAnon/index.php?title=File:Pottery_dog_1.JPG *License*: GNU Free Documentation License *Contributors*: Gary Lee Todd

File:S-114 W Han wuzhu, Han Wudi, 140-87, 25 5mm.jpg *Source*: http://bibliocm.bibliolabs.com/mwAnon/index.php?title=File:S-114_W_Han_wuzhu,_Han_Wudi,_140-87,_25_5mm.jpg *License*: unknown *Contributors*: -

Image:Chinese Boddhisattva statue.jpg *Source*: http://bibliocm.bibliolabs.com/mwAnon/index.php?title=File:Chinese_Boddhisattva_statue.jpg *License*: Creative Commons Attribution-Sharealike 2.0 *Contributors*: AnRo0002, Fordmadoxfraud, G.dallorto, Geofrog, Howcheng, Jat, Johnbod, Paddy, PericlesofAthens, Quadell, Wst

File:Tang sancai camel with persian merchant.JPG *Source*: http://bibliocm.bibliolabs.com/mwAnon/index.php?title=File:Tang_sancai_camel_with_persian_merchant.JPG *License*: Creative Commons Attribution 2.0 *Contributors*: User:Rosemania

Image:Chou Fang 004.jpg *Source*: http://bibliocm.bibliolabs.com/mwAnon/index.php?title=File:Chou_Fang_004.jpg *License*: Public Domain *Contributors*: Diwas, Jonathan Groß, PericlesofAthens, Zolo

File:China coin1.JPG *Source*: http://bibliocm.bibliolabs.com/mwAnon/index.php?title=File:China_coin1.JPG *License*: unknown *Contributors*: -

File:Jiao zi.jpg *Source*: http://bibliocm.bibliolabs.com/mwAnon/index.php?title=File:Jiao_zi.jpg *License*: Public Domain *Contributors*: Infrogmation, King of Hearts, Lawrencekhoo, Ran, Shizhao, 3 anonymous edits

File:Yuan Dynasty - waterwheels and smelting.png *Source*: http://bibliocm.bibliolabs.com/mwAnon/index.php?title=File:Yuan_Dynasty_-_waterwheels_and_smelting.png *License*: Public Domain *Contributors*: Wang Zhen

Image:Hongwu1.jpg *Source*: http://bibliocm.bibliolabs.com/mwAnon/index.php?title=File:Hongwu1.jpg *License*: Public Domain *Contributors*: User Hardouin on en.wikipedia

File:Yellow dragon jar.JPG *Source*: http://bibliocm.bibliolabs.com/mwAnon/index.php?title=File:Yellow_dragon_jar.JPG *License*: unknown *Contributors*: -

Image:Ch'iu Ying 001.jpg *Source*: http://bibliocm.bibliolabs.com/mwAnon/index.php?title=File:Ch'iu_Ying_001.jpg *License*: Public Domain *Contributors*: Bohème, EDUCA33E, Jann, PericlesofAthens, 1 anonymous edits

File:Pine, Plum and Cranes.jpg *Source*: http://bibliocm.bibliolabs.com/mwAnon/index.php?title=File:Pine,_Plum_and_Cranes.jpg *License*: unknown *Contributors*: Shen Quan

Image Sources, Licenses and Contributors

File:Foochow arsenal in Mawei.jpg *Source*: http://bibliocm.bibliolabs.com/mwAnon/index.php?title=File:Foochow_arsenal_in_Mawei.jpg *License*: unknown *Contributors*: -

File:Shanghai Pudong Skyline.jpg *Source*: http://bibliocm.bibliolabs.com/mwAnon/index.php?title=File:Shanghai_Pudong_Skyline.jpg *License*: unknown *Contributors*: User:Dynastie des Tang on en: wiki

File:10 Custom Gold Units 1930.JPG *Source*: http://bibliocm.bibliolabs.com/mwAnon/index.php?title=File:10_Custom_Gold_Units_1930.JPG *License*: Public Domain *Contributors*: Pavle Jeric author of scan, Central Bank of China creators of original bill

File:Fushun Coal Mine.jpg *Source*: http://bibliocm.bibliolabs.com/mwAnon/index.php?title=File:Fushun_Coal_Mine.jpg *License*: Public Domain *Contributors*: Original publisher was South Manchuria Railway Co. (南叩洲鉄道株式会社). The image was photographed by from the publication.

File:Chinese stamp in 1950.jpg *Source*: http://bibliocm.bibliolabs.com/mwAnon/index.php?title=File:Chinese_stamp_in_1950.jpg *License*: Public Domain *Contributors*: AnonMoos, Berrucomons, Butko, Javierme, Leonid Dzhepko, Man vyi, Mariluna, Mbz1, Michael Romanov, Mywood, Nanae, Origamiemensch, Shizhao, Takabeg, Ww2censor, Нирваньчик, Сдобников А., 3 anonymous edits

Image:INDUSTRIAL AND COMMERCIAL BANK OF CHINA.jpg *Source*: http://bibliocm.bibliolabs.com/mwAnon/index.php?title=File:INDUSTRIAL_AND_COMMERCIAL_BANK_OF_CHINA.jpg *License*: Public Domain *Contributors*: GeorgHH, Haingh, J o, Vmenkov, Waterfox, 陈少举

Image:Prc1952-2005gdp.gif *Source*: http://bibliocm.bibliolabs.com/mwAnon/index.php?title=File:Prc1952-2005gdp.gif *License*: unknown *Contributors*: Original uploader was Intsokzen at en.wikipedia

Image:Gdp accumulated change.png *Source*: http://bibliocm.bibliolabs.com/mwAnon/index.php?title=File:Gdp_accumulated_change.png *License*: GNU Free Documentation License *Contributors*: Bombastus, Lokum, MaCRoEco, Timeshifter

File:Shanghaiviewpic1.jpg *Source*: http://bibliocm.bibliolabs.com/mwAnon/index.php?title=File:Shanghaiviewpic1.jpg *License*: Creative Commons Attribution 2.0 *Contributors*: dawvon

File:Prc1952-2005gdp.gif *Source*: http://bibliocm.bibliolabs.com/mwAnon/index.php?title=File:Prc1952-2005gdp.gif *License*: unknown *Contributors*: Original uploader was Intsokzen at en.wikipedia

File:Gdp accumulated change.png *Source*: http://bibliocm.bibliolabs.com/mwAnon/index.php?title=File:Gdp_accumulated_change.png *License*: GNU Free Documentation License *Contributors*: Bombastus, Lokum, MaCRoEco, Timeshifter

Image:Zhongguo jingji bankuai.png *Source*: http://bibliocm.bibliolabs.com/mwAnon/index.php?title=File:Zhongguo_jingji_bankuai.png *License*: GNU Free Documentation License *Contributors*: Ran, Shibo77

File:INDUSTRIAL AND COMMERCIAL BANK OF CHINA.jpg *Source*: http://bibliocm.bibliolabs.com/mwAnon/index.php?title=File:INDUSTRIAL_AND_COMMERCIAL_BANK_OF_CHINA.jpg *License*: Public Domain *Contributors*: GeorgHH, Haingh, J o, Vmenkov, Waterfox, 陈少举

File:Shanghaistockexchange.jpg *Source*: http://bibliocm.bibliolabs.com/mwAnon/index.php?title=File:Shanghaistockexchange.jpg *License*: Creative Commons Attribution-Sharealike 2.0 Germany *Contributors*: Original uploader was Heurik at de.wikipedia (Original text : Manuel Pajer)

File:Jiangxia-peanuts-9707.jpg *Source*: http://bibliocm.bibliolabs.com/mwAnon/index.php?title=File:Jiangxia-peanuts-9707.jpg *License*: Creative Commons Attribution-Sharealike 2.5 *Contributors*: User:Vmenkov

File:China-wheat-prod.png *Source*: http://bibliocm.bibliolabs.com/mwAnon/index.php?title=File:China-wheat-prod.png *License*: Creative Commons Attribution 2.0 *Contributors*: HenkvD, Juiced lemon, Mdd, Timeshifter, Valérie75

File:Daye-pond-system-fishermen-0078-rotated.jpg *Source*: http://bibliocm.bibliolabs.com/mwAnon/index.php?title=File:Daye-pond-system-fishermen-0078-rotated.jpg *License*: Creative Commons Attribution-Sharealike 2.5 *Contributors*: User:Vmenkov

File:China fuels 1983.jpg *Source*: http://bibliocm.bibliolabs.com/mwAnon/index.php?title=File:China_fuels_1983.jpg *License*: Public Domain *Contributors*: Ran, Sfan00 IMG, Tetris L, Zolo

File:China-Today oil reserves and demand-en.svg *Source*: http://bibliocm.bibliolabs.com/mwAnon/index.php?title=File:China-Today_oil_reserves_and_demand-en.svg *License*: unknown *Contributors*: User:Ksiom, User:Yug

File:Shanghaid02.jpg *Source*: http://bibliocm.bibliolabs.com/mwAnon/index.php?title=File:Shanghaid02.jpg *License*: Creative Commons Attribution-Sharealike 2.5 *Contributors*: Deadstar, Donut

File:Current Account Balance 2006.png *Source*: http://bibliocm.bibliolabs.com/mwAnon/index.php?title=File:Current_Account_Balance_2006.png *License*: Public Domain *Contributors*: Alexander Emilfaro

File:2006Chinese exports.PNG *Source*: http://bibliocm.bibliolabs.com/mwAnon/index.php?title=File:2006Chinese_exports.PNG *License*: Public Domain *Contributors*: Original uploader was Anwar saadat at en.wikipedia

File:Jawaharlal Nehru Trust Port.jpg *Source*: http://bibliocm.bibliolabs.com/mwAnon/index.php?title=File:Jawaharlal_Nehru_Trust_Port.jpg *License*: Creative Commons Attribution 3.0 *Contributors*: Jaxer (talk) Original uploader was Jaxer at en.wikipedia

File:Floridasoftshellturtle-cropped.jpg *Source*: http://bibliocm.bibliolabs.com/mwAnon/index.php?title=File:Floridasoftshellturtle-cropped.jpg *License*: GNU Free Documentation License *Contributors*: User:Johnskate17

File:E7210-NN-kitaj-auto.jpg *Source*: http://bibliocm.bibliolabs.com/mwAnon/index.php?title=File:E7210-NN-kitaj-auto.jpg *License*: Creative Commons Attribution-Sharealike 2.5 *Contributors*: User:Vmenkov

Image:Flag of the People's Republic of China.svg *Source*: http://bibliocm.bibliolabs.com/mwAnon/index.php?title=File:Flag_of_the_People's_Republic_of_China.svg *License*: Public Domain *Contributors*: User:Denelson83, User:SKopp, User:Shizhao, User:Zscout370

File:Great Leap forward poster.jpg *Source*: http://bibliocm.bibliolabs.com/mwAnon/index.php?title=File:Great_Leap_forward_poster.jpg *License*: Public Domain *Contributors*: Arilang1234, Cantons-de-l'Est, KTo288, Mbdortmund, Rockfang, Stout256, 1 anonymous edits

Image:20031125123522.jpg *Source*: http://bibliocm.bibliolabs.com/mwAnon/index.php?title=File:20031125123522.jpg *License*: GNU Free Documentation License *Contributors*: User Wikipedia on zh.wikipedia

Image:China-wheat-prod.png *Source*: http://bibliocm.bibliolabs.com/mwAnon/index.php?title=File:China-wheat-prod.png *License*: Creative Commons Attribution 2.0 *Contributors*: HenkvD, Juiced lemon, Mdd, Timeshifter, Valérie75

Image:2006Chinese exports.PNG *Source*: http://bibliocm.bibliolabs.com/mwAnon/index.php?title=File:2006Chinese_exports.PNG *License*: Public Domain *Contributors*: Original uploader was Anwar saadat at en.wikipedia

Image Sources, Licenses and Contributors

Image:Shanghaistockexchange.jpg *Source*: http://bibliocm.bibliolabs.com/mwAnon/index.php?title=File:Shanghaistockexchange.jpg *License*: Creative Commons Attribution-Sharealike 2.0 Germany *Contributors*: Original uploader was Heurik at de.wikipedia (Original text : Manuel Pajer)

Image:Gini Coefficient World CIA Report 2009.png *Source*: http://bibliocm.bibliolabs.com/mwAnon/index.php?title=File:Gini_Coefficient_World_CIA_Report_2009.png *License*: Public Domain *Contributors*: User:Hysohan

File:china india gdp.jpg *Source*: http://bibliocm.bibliolabs.com/mwAnon/index.php?title=File:China_india_gdp.jpg *License*: unknown *Contributors*: -

File:2007-10-11-BJFS.JPG *Source*: http://bibliocm.bibliolabs.com/mwAnon/index.php?title=File:2007-10-11-BJFS.JPG *License*: Creative Commons Attribution-Sharealike 3.0 *Contributors*: User:CobbleCC

Image:Hancoin1large.jpg *Source*: http://bibliocm.bibliolabs.com/mwAnon/index.php?title=File:Hancoin1large.jpg *License*: Public Domain *Contributors*: User Randy Benzie on en.wikipedia

File:ChinesischeSilberbarren.jpg *Source*: http://bibliocm.bibliolabs.com/mwAnon/index.php?title=File:ChinesischeSilberbarren.jpg *License*: GNU Free Documentation License *Contributors*: Original uploader was Zhou Yi at de.wikipedia

File:MENG CHIANG BANK 5 CHIAO 1938.jpg *Source*: http://bibliocm.bibliolabs.com/mwAnon/index.php?title=File:MENG_CHIANG_BANK_5_CHIAO_1938.jpg *License*: Public Domain *Contributors*: User:Nickpo

File:Renminbi1ban 200yuan.jpg *Source*: http://bibliocm.bibliolabs.com/mwAnon/index.php?title=File:Renminbi1ban_200yuan.jpg *License*: Public Domain *Contributors*: Hawyih

File:VM 4645 Wuchang - workers wanted.jpg *Source*: http://bibliocm.bibliolabs.com/mwAnon/index.php?title=File:VM_4645_Wuchang_-_workers_wanted.jpg *License*: Creative Commons Attribution-Sharealike 3.0 *Contributors*: User:Vmenkov

The cover image herein is used under a Creative Commons License and may be reused or reproduced under that same license.

http://farm4.static.flickr.com/3161/3033615378_6389cc510c_o.jpg

CPSIA information can be obtained at www.ICGtesting.com
Printed in the USA
LVOW100821021111

253136LV00004B/23/P

9 781240 936922